POLITICS AND THE IMAGINATION

POLITICS AND THE IMAGINATION

Raymond Geuss

PRINCETON UNIVERSITY PRESS   PRINCETON AND OXFORD

Published by Princeton University Press, 41 William Street,
Princeton, New Jersey 08540

In the United Kingdom: Princeton University Press, 6 Oxford Street,
Woodstock, Oxfordshire OX20 1TW

Library of Congress Cataloging-in-Publication Data

Geuss, Raymond.
  Politics and the imagination / Raymond Geuss.
      p. cm.
  Includes bibliographical references and index.
  ISBN 978-0-691-14227-2 (hardcover : alk. paper) —
  ISBN 978-0-691-14228-9 (pbk. : alk. paper)
  1. Political science—Philosophy. 2. Imagination (Philosophy) I. Title.
  JA71.G47 2010
  320.01—dc22

                                                2009017105

British Library Cataloging-in-Publication Data is available

This book has been composed in Sabon

Printed on acid-free paper. ∞

press.princeton.edu

Printed in the United States of America

10 9 8 7 6 5 4 3 2 1

Contents

Preface _____

It has sometimes been claimed that the oldest continuous fragment of Western philosophical thought is a brief remark attributed by a commentator on the works of Aristotle, Simplicius, to the sixth-century Ionian philosopher Anaximander:

[λέγει ὁ Ἀναξίμανδρος] ἐξ ὧν δὲ ἡ γένεσίς ἐστι τοῖς οὖσι, καὶ τὴν φθορὰν εἰς ταῦτα γίνεσθαι κατὰ τὸ χρεών διδόναι γὰρ αὐτὰ δίκην καὶ τίσιν ἀλλήλοις τῆς ἀδικίας κατὰ τὴν τοῦ χρόνου τάξιν.[1]

Almost nothing about the text or interpretation of any part of this archaic statement is uncontroversial, and any translation of it must be highly speculative, but the approximate sense seems to be:

[Anaximander says that] from whatever it is that things have their origin, of necessity they must also have their destruction into that, for they must give justice and make amends to each other for their injustice according to the order of time.

Whatever the exact details of the metaphysical views which find expression in this fragment, in *one* respect its basic meaning is clear enough. It is a slightly spruced-up and intellectualized—and characteristically gloomy—Hellenic version of a piece of enduring peasant wisdom: men will reap what they sow; what goes around, comes around. A kind of order which is both moral and "natural" prevails in the world, and this order will eventually, but necessarily—κατὰ τὸ χρεών—reestablish itself. Any apparent violations of this order will show themselves in the longer run to be mere momentary aberrations. The gloomy gloss on this thought consists in the tacit assertion that being-something—*being anything at all*—is already an injustice that deserves, and will incur, punishment. Even to be in existence at all makes something culpable.[2] If one ignores for a moment the pessimistic twist,[3] one can see why the rest of this piece

---

[1] Hermann Diels and Walther Kranz (Weidman, 1951), Fragment 1, p. 89. For further analysis of this fragment see Friedrich Nietzsche, "Die Philosophie im tragischen Zeitalter," in *Kritische Studienausgabe*, ed. Giorgio Colli and Mazzino Montinari (de Gruyter, 1967) vol. 1, pp. 817–22, or the highly speculative Heidegger, "Der Spruch des Anaximandros," in *Holzwege* (Klostermann, 1950), pp. 296–344.

[2] As Mephistopheles puts it in *Faust* (line 1339f): "denn alles was entsteht / ist wert daß es zugrunde geht" ["Everything that comes into being / deserves to perish"].

[3] One can trace a development here from this form of metaphysical pessimism to a political version of the same thing in 1938. See also Brecht, "An die Nachgeborenen" (1938):

of peasant wisdom is still so deeply entrenched even in modern and purportedly enlightened ways of thinking and why the view expressed is so difficult to eradicate: it is too comforting to lose. Wrongdoers may seem invincible now, but eventually they will pay. So powerful is the human imagination that people can take some comfort in this thought, even if they know they will no longer themselves be around to view the reestablishment of the "natural order," the triumph of "justice," etc. Much ingenuity over two and a half millennia has been devoted to finding a way of putting this belief in a form which hides its essentially mythological structure and makes it seem like a sober and cognitively well-grounded assessment of the world.

At some point in the past, this story acquired an imaginative competitor. Instead of deriving solace from the idea that everything will always "really" remain the same, so that violations of "natural justice" will right themselves and all will be as it was, people begin to think of doing something themselves to improve the future, and they begin to derive consolation from the fact that no matter how difficult things seem now to be, they can imagine that things will get better, or at any rate they could get better if everyone pulled together in the right direction. It isn't the thought of the basic invariability of the world that gives solace, but the fantasy of its plasticity, of a potentially infinite process of change and improvement, of the unlimited transformation of the world into something more perfect and more to our taste. How much of reality can, however, be changed?

To jump ahead from the sixth-century BC to the beginning of the twenty-first century, we see that we still have no settled attitude on the limits of the malleability of reality. In 2002 a reporter interviewed a high-ranking but unnamed aide to U.S. president George W. Bush. Let us call this aide "Anonymos." Anonymos is reported to have said that journalists were part of the "reality-based community . . . people who believe that decisions emerge from your judicious study of discernible reality. . . . That's not the way the world works anymore. . . . We're [i.e., the United States] an empire now, and when we act, we create our own reality. And while you're studying that reality—judiciously, as you will—

Man sagt mir: Iß und trink du! Sei froh, daß du hast!
Aber wie kann ich essen und trinken, wenn
Ich dem Hungernden entreiße, was ich esse, und
Mein Glas Wasser dem Verdurstenden fehlt?
Und doch esse und trinke ich.

This poem does not yet express a fully developed ecological consciousness, because in 1938 hunger and thirst were "merely" a political problem of distribution, and not a problem of absolute depletion. Finally to ecology: see George Monbiot, "Is the Pope Gay?" in *Bring on the Apocalypse* (Grove Atlantic, 2008), p. 17.

we'll act again, creating other realities, which you can study too, and that's how things will sort out. We're history's actors. . . . and you, all of you, will be left to just study what we do."[4]

This statement draws attention to a sufficient number of extremely important features of all human politics to merit some further consideration. As the young Heidegger noted, human beings are always "ahead of themselves";[5] our lives are constituted by uncompleted projects, and anyone with *no* concernful tasks outstanding, anyone with *no* unfinished business in the world, would not be alive at all. *Vixit*. My relation to my own future, and our relation to our future, is always "open" and to some extent "ungrounded."[6] I don't have conclusive reasons for the projects I have—they are neither fully explicable nor fully "justifiable" by my antecedent beliefs and desires—nor are any of my projects fully under my own power, but rather they are always at the mercy of external circumstances and events over which I have little control. To act is in an important sense always to create something new, an object, a change in an existing situation, a new reality. Politicians, in particular, are supposed to deal with emergencies as they arise and to ward off threats to those aspects of the status quo that are particularly valued, but they are also sometimes supposed to change the way things are, to create new facts. Margaret Thatcher saw this very clearly when she embarked on her policy of rejecting "consensus politics" in favor of trying to bring into existence new brute realities with which all other politicians would have to learn to deal, one way or the other, and Anonymos put some similar important points in a salutarily provocative way. Any organized attempt at improvement of our situation will include some at least minimal exercise of the imagination, in that it will require agents to think of ways in which their environment or modes of acting could be different from what they now are. What is provocative about Anonymos's statement is not the claim about creating new facts, but the suggestion that the government of the United States was so limitlessly powerful it could successfully conjure a completely new reality into existence *without regard* to antecedent conditions. This, of course, is the point at which Heidegger,[7] and most of the rest of us, I trust, would part company from Anonymos.

This collection puts together essays I have written during the past few years that deal with several issues concerning the nature of the imagination and its role in politics. These issues include such questions as: What

---

[4] Ron Suskind, "Faith, Certainty, and the Presidency of George W. Bush," in *New York Times Magazine*, 17 October 2004.

[5] Heidegger, *Sein und Zeit* (Niemeyer, 1963), §§31–32, 41, 68a.

[6] Ibid., §58.

[7] Ibid., §§29, 31, 38.

is the relation between these two forms of the imagination distinguished above, the Anaximandrean and the form exhibited in the remarks by Anonymos? How and to what extent is it possible to free oneself or take one's distance imaginatively from the beliefs, values, and attitudes of one's surroundings? To what extent is such distancing necessary for radical social criticism?

Most of the beliefs, attitudes, desires, and values we hold, after all, we have acquired in social contexts in response to individual and institutional forces and pressures of various kinds. There is every reason to believe that I (and we) share the illusions of our epoch as much as the men of the Roman republic or medieval nuns or sixteenth-century Calvinist preachers shared those of their respective times and places. If the Cartesian project of setting aside everything we know and value, and starting *ab nihilo* to build up our views about the world on a certain and incontrovertible base that owes nothing to social conventions, is unworkable, to what extent is it possible for us to free ourselves from our own illusions and work our way to a realistic, or at least a more realistic, worldview? Effective engagement in the political sphere requires not merely that we see how things really stand, but also that we understand, and perhaps even to some extent sympathize with, the way in which others see them, even if they are deluded, and we know that they are deluded. How is it possible to be realistic without getting caught up in the web of powerful fantasies which our society spins around us? How can one get the appropriate imaginative distance from one's own society, its practices, norms, and conceptions? What is the "appropriate" distance? "Appropriate" in what sense; for what? What are the possibilities, and what the limits of criticism?

Different forms of politics are associated with different forms of the imagination. I want to pursue two distinct lines of argument which, if correctly understood, complement each other. First, I wish to argue for the importance of the imagination in all forms of politics. This means rejecting a set of common assumptions that are often, albeit usually tacitly, made, namely that there is some natural affinity between conventional, business-as-usual politics, and a hardheaded realism that altogether eschews imaginative constructs, and responds in an instrumentally rational way to the facts of the situation alone. Conservative *Realpolitik* is then contrasted with utopian speculation, the pursuit of fantasies, the politics of beautiful illusions; in these the imagination is thought to run wild. Contrary to this, I want to argue that even the deepest kind of political conformism and any defense of the status quo require acts of imagining of some kind, albeit a particular kind of productive imagination.[8] At the

---

[8] See Mona Chollet, *Rêves de droite* (Zones, 2008).

same time, and this is my second point, I want to argue that the distance I am able to put between myself and my social world with its associated beliefs, intellectual habits, and attitudes is a crucial variable in determining how much I can see, how much I can understand, and whether I can occupy a position from which radical social criticism is possible.

The first three essays in this collection deal with politics in the narrow sense, and the reader may be struck by the way in which some of the pieces circle again and again around the analysis of Tony Blair's decision to participate in the invasion of Iraq in 2003. Monumental folly, of course, might be thought to be inherently fascinating, but there is also a specific epistemic reason for recurrence to this particular issue. The easiest way to present this epistemic issue clearly is through a brief autobiographical excursus: I and every knowledgeable person I knew thought we were able to see very clearly before the fact that the invasion was a recipe for human and political disaster and a potentially self-destructive policy for the UK to pursue, so why wasn't Blair able to see this? However, even to ask the question in *this way* means one has not come very far. The tradition of philosophy that descends from Hegel to the early Frankfurt School holds that philosophical thinking, including philosophically informed political thinking, must be reflexive.[9] Whatever questions I might put about claims my interlocutor makes, I must *also* put the very same questions to myself with exactly the same or even greater rigor. In the heat of the moment it is very tempting to look for one's opponents' failure of imagination, that is, for a diagnosis of *Blair's* problem, but to do this is to see only half the story. Equally important, and perhaps more important for me and those who thought as I did, was to reflect on what problem *I* had that prevented me from being able easily to imagine that a politician could see projects like the invasion as merely one among other possible, unobjectionable options for action, rather than as nothing but a clear disaster waiting to happen. My initial state of puzzlement about the rationale of the invasion had been a result of my own lack of imagination. Given my own values, I found it difficult to imagine that anarchy or a state of low-level civil war in Iraq would be a price a politician would be willing to pay—or rather, to allow the people of Iraq to pay—in order that he could cut a bold figure on the stage of world politics, and so I entirely failed to comprehend the calculations that led to and accompanied the implementation of the policy. This was simply naïve on my part, a result of my own very limited conception of what could possibly count as a "positive" outcome of political action and a possible motivational set.

---

[9] See T. W. Adorno, *Der Positivismusstreit in der deutschen Soziologie* (Luchterhand, 1969), pp. 7–102. See also R. Geuss, *The Idea of a Critical Theory* (Cambridge University Press, 1981), pp. 55–95.

The second essay in particular was written in the autumn of 2004 and is focused on discussing what might seem to be a highly particular political configuration. With the departure from the world stage of Blair and Bush and the advent of the world economic crisis it might seem to be at best of merely antiquarian interest. I decided to include it in this collection because the central conception and thesis still seem to me correct, and easily visible through the mist produced by the mass of slightly antiquated details.

The fourth and fifth essays in this collection address some issues about the way in which in general we are encouraged to imagine modern societies: basically as systems of (potentially) mandatorily imposed rules. These essays discuss the historically specific character of this particular mode of conception and the limits of its usefulness, and they try to suggest some other ways of thinking about societies as a whole.

Essays 6 and 7 discuss cultural imagination with particular reference to the question of how we impose relevant shapes on events and objects that stand at a distance from us in space and time. How important is the avoidance of anachronism in studying history? To what extent can we get a reasoned overview of the whole variety of human cultures through collections of objects? Essays 8 through 12 deal with some of the various ways in which imaginative distance finds expression internally in cultural artifacts. To what extent does a cultural object identify itself or cause us to identify ourselves with its, or our, given world? One might think of the possible responses to this question as lying on a spectrum that stretches from extreme alienation—Fritz Heidegger's Baroque-Catholic Ash Wednesday discourses *in contemptum mundi*, and Paul Celan's anarcho-communist poems[10]—at one end point to comfortable and homely bourgeois conformism at the other end. One might fear that too abstract and radical a form of critique, such as (Fritz) Heidegger's religiously based criticism of *everything* sublunary, or too accepting an attitude, as in Celan, leaves everything as it is, and so is as politically disarming as one that tries merely to bring good order into our existing world.

The reflections in these essays came to stand increasingly under the influence of my growing conviction that the present political, social, and economic situation of our world is desperate. The combination of already intolerable overpopulation and effectively irreversible pollution and degradation of the environment poses problems which may have no "solution," at any rate no "solution" that is even minimally acceptable for the

---

[10] See also "Poetry and Knowledge," in *Outside Ethics* (Princeton University Press, 2005), pp. 184–206, and Peter Szondi, *Celan-Studien* (Suhrkamp, 1972), pp. 113–25.

human species. If complexly organized social life survives at all, political agencies will have the task of exercising much of the discipline needed to force people in the West to adopt the drastic reductions in their absolute level of consumption that will be necessary, and of preventing populations in the rest of the world from even developing the aspiration to attain current Western levels of affluence. If there is a solution at all, and that is a very big "if," it certainly will not lie in any scheme that permits the continuation of unbridled human productivity or the so-called "free market," or that assigns to individual humans any significant discretion about how they will act in those of their encounters that have any bearing on other humans or the environment. Some thoughts may remain free, but nothing much else will be, certainly not any form of human action. In this new world "freedom," that pampered pet idea of the bourgeois world, will have to yield pride of place to concepts like austerity, control (and self-control), commitment, discipline (and self-discipline), and authority.[11] It will, then, make a big difference whether we are dragged forward to face this reality *à contre-coeur* or whether we can find a way of imaginatively stylizing the transition so that we associate it with at least some positive values.[12]

If any of the above prognosis is at all correct, it is going to have a very significant effect on the structure of our emotional lives and on the form our imagination takes. In this context the work of Nietzsche seems to me to acquire considerable importance. He foresaw with surprising clarity the end of the era of "freedom," and his historical analyses are devoted to helping us to see how we could learn to take a certain pleasure in restraint. We could learn that because, in a past that is still vividly accessible to us in memory, we did submit *nolens volens* to very considerable forms of compulsion, we did learn to practice some limited forms of self-control, and some of us even came to take pleasure in forms of asceticism. Of course, the forms of appropriate discipline will not necessarily be the same as those which flourished in the past, but whatever shape they take is unlikely to be completely painless.

---

[11] See Jacques Attali, *Une brève histoire de l'avenir* (Fayard, 2007) for some similar general thoughts, although I do not agree with all of Attali's specific analyses and proposals.

[12] The end of the era of "freedom" does not mean there will be no place whatever in social life for freedom or a concept of "freedom." Central organizing principles of this kind don't usually just disappear. At the beginning of book 3 of *Die fröhliche Wissenschaft* (Nietzsche, *Kritische Studienausgabe*, ed. Colli and Montinari, vol. 3, p. 467, §108) Nietzsche speaks of the way in which God's "shadow" lingered on in the world long after he died. Just as "honor," which in the seventeenth century was an extremely robust concept, gradually became more and more etiolated, its use more restricted and marginalized, and it came to be subject to numerous, and perhaps increasingly far-fetched, reinterpretations.

Acknowledgments

SOME OF THE ESSAYS in this collection have previously appeared in print in one form or another; they have the following provenance.

Essays 4, 7, and 12 are previously unpublished.

Essay 1 appeared as "Was ist ein politisches Urteil?," in *Deutsche Zeitschrift für Philosophie*, vol. 3, 2007. This is my English version of the German original.

Essay 2 was originally written in the autumn of 2004, and was published in *Theoria: A Journal of Social and Political Theory* in December 2005. I have added three or four paragraphs to that text to take account of some recent developments, but it is otherwise unchanged.

Essay 3 appeared in a significantly shortened version (less than half the length of the text printed here) in *Journal of the Royal Society of Art* in September 2008.

Essay 5 was a commission from the marvelous editor of the journal *Mittelweg 36*, Martin Bauer, for which I am very grateful. I wrote the essay in German, and it appeared in *Mittelweg 36* in the December 2005/January 2006 issue. The English translation printed here was made by Dr. Keith Tribe, whom I wish to thank for his careful efforts. This translation has previously appeared in *Journal of the History of European Ideas* in 2007.

Essay 6, also originally written in German, was published as "Kultur als Vorbild und als Schranke" in *Nietzsche—Philosoph der Kultur(en)?* ed. Andreas Sommers (de Gruyter, 2008). I produced this English version for *Arion*, where it was published in summer 2008.

Essay 8 was originally published in *boundary 2*, vol. 33, no. 3, fall 2006.

Essay 9 is an expansion of a review of the book by Hans Dieter Zimmermann, *Martin und Fritz Heidegger. Philosophie und Fastnacht* (Beck, 2005), which was published in *Journal of the History of European Ideas* in 2006.

Essay 10 has its origin in a talk I gave at Princeton in the autumn of 2007 at a memorial service for Richard Rorty. The full text on which that talk was based was published in *Arion* in winter 2008; this version is a slight expansion of that text.

Essay 11 appeared in *Wagner Moments* (Amadeus Press, 2007), edited by J. K. Holman.

I am particularly grateful to Manuel Dries, John Dunn, Zeev Emmerich, Fabian Freyenhagen, Istvan Hont, Richard Raatzsche, Jörg Schaub, and Christian Skirke for discussions of the material in these essays. I am, however, most indebted to Hilary Gaskin for having repeatedly cast her impeccable editorial eye over these pieces and given me the benefit of her excellent judgment. Ian Malcolm of Princeton University Press has been a model of support and good sense.

POLITICS AND THE IMAGINATION

I

Political Judgment in Its Historical Context

IN HIS RECENTLY PUBLISHED memoirs[1] the former British ambassador to the United States, Sir Christopher Meyer, describes a dinner party which he attended in Washington in early February 2001. George W. Bush had just been elected—or at any rate, inaugurated as—president of the United States, and the members of his new administration were awaiting the first visit of the British prime minister Tony Blair.[2] Present at the dinner were several close advisers of the new U.S. president, figures strongly associated with the Republican Right, so-called "neoconservatives" such as Richard Perle and David Frum. The conversation quickly moved to Britain's recent decision at the meeting of the Council of Europe in Nice to support closer European defense cooperation. These "neoconservatives" thought that Blair had fallen victim to a French plot to harm the United States by introducing a new, independent military force in Europe, which could in principle compete with NATO. Sir Christopher, however, tried to convince them that the projected new form of defense cooperation represented no more than an increase in Europe's ability to discharge subaltern functions *within* a NATO that would continue to be dominated by Washington. The new arrangements, correctly understood, were therefore not only no threat to the United States; they were in Washington's own best long-term interest. Sir Christopher then continues:

> I found it an uphill struggle to place our initiative in the context which Blair had intended.
>
> I withstood a full frontal assault from all concerned against our alleged sell-out to the French . . . . [One of the neoconservatives present] argued that now we were allowing ourselves to be corrupted by political correctness and socialist Europe. We were, he said, drifting away from our traditional transatlantic loyalties—look at the threat to fox-hunting, for Pete's sake!

[1] Christopher Meyer, *DC Confidential* (Weidenfeld and Nichols, 2005), pp. 171–74.
[2] This event probably seemed more momentous to Sir Christopher than it did to the members of the new Republican administration in the United States. In fairness, Sir Christopher seems never to have been under any illusions about the asymmetrical nature of the relation between the political elites of the United States and those of its major client state.

Some of this was barking mad. But lurking in there was a serious point. How could even Tony Blair, the most gifted performer of his generation in the circus of British politics, ride the American and the European horses at the same time, without falling between two saddles?

The real answer was: with difficulty. At [this] dinner I fell back on the holy mantra of British foreign policy. There was no choice to be made between Britain's European and Atlantic vocations. If we were strong and influential in Europe, this would strengthen our hand in the US. If we were close to the US, this would redound to our benefit in Europe.

"No, no!" the cry went up around the table, in an unconscious echo of General De Gaulle, "Britain must choose." To this audience of Manicheans I sounded feeble and temporising, a typical product of the Foreign Office.[3]

This anecdote seems to me to present an archetypical instance of a "political" disagreement. One of the first features of it that strikes me is that it has a certain specific historical density. Sir Christopher in 2005 tells the story of a group of people who encountered each other in Washington in February 2001. At this meeting in 2001 each group presented, and tried to argue for, a radically different interpretation of a series of decisions which already at that time lay in the past, namely the decisions made at the meeting of the European Council in Nice in December 2000 about European defense. Each of the two different interpretations contains, as an integral part of itself, a divergent projection about what future we can expect to result from the events in Nice. Sir Christopher thinks it will strengthen Washington's ability to project its military power around the world; his neoconservative interlocutors deny this strenuously. This disagreement takes place within the framework of a set of values shared by both of the two participants to the discussion, namely the assumption that it is a good thing for the United States to be able to project its power as widely and effectively as possible. This, of course, is an assumption with which it would also be possible to disagree. It seems natural for us to say that the disagreement between Sir Christopher and the neoconservatives mirrors or results from differences in the respective "political judgments" each of the two parties make about the project of closer European cooperation on defense.

If one wants to understand what was going on in Sir Christopher's anecdote, one must keep in mind that most of the individuals engaged in this discussion had specific institutional roles which in some cases might give their words extra weight, but which would also require them to be especially circumspect in expressing themselves, and which might even require them on occasion to "represent" in public an institutional position about

[3] Meyer, *DC Confidential*, p. 174.

which they actually had some private doubts. In his memoirs Sir Christopher is admirably clear about the distinction between his role as a diplomat and thus a member of the Civil Service, and his own private views. He is equally clear about the distinction between either of these and particular policy decisions of the current UK government. Thus, in saying that the UK did not need to choose between an Atlantic and a European "vocation" he was, as he explicitly says above, voicing the institutional opinion of the British diplomatic corps. When he writes in the passage cited above that this policy was difficult to pursue successfully, I think we can assume that he is speaking in his private capacity, and I think we can be rather sure that Sir Christopher never said to his U.S. interlocutors even in private conversation that, to use his own pungent formulation, Mr. Blair's project was to ride them as one of the horses in a two-horse circus act.

The political judgment expressed in a directive to the members of a highly centralized Leninist cadre party has a very different standing and meaning from the manifesto of a contemporary British political party. The abstraction of (mere) opinions or beliefs from their wider context may be highly useful, or even necessary, for certain purposes, but any kind of adequate understanding of political judgments will require reference back to that original full matrix of individual and institutional action. Even when the abstraction is perfectly justified, as it is for most normal cases, one will never know when extracting the judgment from its wider action context and formulating it as a "mere" belief will distort it, and in what way it will distort it.

The decision at the conference in Nice was a political act, a choice made by agents empowered to represent recognized states about a future set of courses of collective action, but the later disagreement between Sir Christopher and the neoconservatives about the retrospective interpretation of that original decision was also a political controversy and not a seminar discussion. I think it is a great failing of much contemporary political philosophy that it tends to focus too exclusively on discussion and also tries to construe discussion on the model of a highly idealized conception of what purely rational or scientific discussion is. Forming and holding opinions and engaging in discussion of those opinions are, of course, important parts of human life, but (a) opinion formation and discussion are not all there is to politics, and (b) even the formation and evaluation of opinions is comprehensible only in one or another of a number of different wider historical and institutional contexts; most of these contexts will be in one way or another action-orienting. Genuine understanding of any real or envisaged course of action, however, requires one to understand the concrete constellation of power within which it is located.

So in the rest of this paper I would like to try to elaborate an intentionally rather overdrawn distinction between a political disagreement and a certain ideal-typical account of academic discussion. I will exaggerate slightly in order to bring out some features of the political which philosophers sometimes lose sight of. I wish to emphasize that I am *not* trying to assert any general distinction here between politics and science, but rather between politics and a certain set of philosophical claims that have been made about the nature of rational human discussion.

The political philosophers from whose untender embraces I would like to save politics focus their attention on deliberation resulting in a political judgment, where the process of deliberation is construed as a kind of discussion, the model for which is an idealized version of a Socratic dialogue. This idealized model is characterized by the following eight elements:

1. A judgment is essentially an opinion (or belief), that is, the affirmation or negation in thought of some proposition ("Tabitha has four paws"; "Thou shalt not kill").
2. The content of an opinion is always expressed in language.
3. An opinion is always in the final analysis the opinion of an individual.
4. Those who express opinions in discussion must expect these to be subjected to scrutiny to determine whether or not they are correct or true; this means that the whole apparatus of evaluating truth claims that has been an obsession of Western philosophy since its origins can be activated in the discussion.
5. Opinions can be investigated atomistically, that it, one can abstract them—without remainder and without falsifying them—from the context of actions and other opinions in which they are usually embedded, and treat each one in isolation.
6. Participants in the discussion are anonymous; they do not speak *as* bearers of any social roles or offices or with any special authority, but always as naked individuals. The opinions discussed are treated ahistorically, as if it were irrelevant what the person who holds the opinion might have said or done in the past.
7. "Ethical judgments" formulate a particular "moral ought" which prescribes once and for all how each individual should act and trumps all other practical considerations.
8. Political philosophy is a part of applied ethics; that is, in discussion ethical judgments are clarified and justified, and they are then applied in the political sphere.

As I said the above is an ideal type, that is, a constructed paradigm which is taken to have importance because it gives understanding both of cases that conform to it and of cases that deviate. It is not intended as a description of any reality. Nevertheless, this paradigm seems to me to provide such a distorted view of anything that could reasonably be called "politics," that it is not a useful starting point for any kind of illuminating analysis. Roughly speaking, each of the eight theses is either false or so misleading that it might as well be false. Traditional philosophy was utterly fixated on the search for a single fundamental concept the analysis of which would allow one to decipher a whole area of human experience, and for a very wide range of human activities philosophers thought they had discovered an Archimedean point in the concept of a "belief" or an "opinion." I would like to suggest that this traditional approach might in some ways stand in the way of a proper understanding of politics. In contrast to the traditional views, I would like to propose two theses. First, if one thinks it necessary to isolate a single political concept that was purportedly more central than others, one would be well advised to take as basic not "belief" or "opinion" but "action" or the "context of action." Political judgments are not made individually one by one, but always stand as parts of larger sets of beliefs and judgments, and a political judgment is always embedded in a context of *action*.[4] A political judgment

---

[4] It has often been noted that the term "political judgment" is ambiguous in English as between:

a) an act of judging made either by a person or a group about what courses of collective action are desirable.

For instance, the members of my university faculty can discuss our curriculum and conclude our discussion by judging that we ought to reduce the number of examinations we require of our undergraduates. This is an action we take at a particular time, i.e., on a particular day in a particular meeting, and it is an action which may turn out to have been a good idea or not.

b) a linguistic entity expressing an act of judging.

For instance, "The Faculty Board has decided to reduce the number of examinations" or simply "The number of examinations will be reduced."

c) the general capacity to make judgments.
d) the ability to make *good* judgments.

I wish to suggest that it is a mistake simply to collapse (a) and (b) because I can make a kind of very rudimentary action-guiding judgment without it being the case that I would endorse a specific linguistically formulated proposition. *A fortiori* I can make a judgment without being consciously guided by a particular linguistically formulated proposition. There are, I wish to contend, two correlative mistakes here. One is to overintellectualize human action, to assume that in order to act I (or we) must have a specific belief or set of beliefs in mind which guide us. Certainly, we are familiar with a phenomenon which we find it natural to describe by attributing to it a proto-judgment, that is, by saying: the cat is treating you as a friend/enemy. This should be taken to indicate to us a certain dimension of very primitive human possibilities, ways of judging that are in some sense prior to linguistic formulation. The other correlative mistake is to overlook the role of language in constituting most human is itself specifically directed at focusing, guiding and orienting future action; expressing, or even entertaining, such a judgment is performing an action.[5] Second, "context of action" would not be a concept that could serve as an essential definition of politics in the traditional sense in which philosophers have sought such a definition. At best, "context of action" is an open concept with indeterminate contours, and boundaries that can expand and contract depending on a variety of other factors.

It is by no means an unimportant feature of politics that it is a kind of interaction between concrete individuals and groups that have different powers and abilities. These individuals and groups act, try to preempt, counter, or control the actions of others and discuss the rationale for and the actual consequences of pursuing a variety of possible and actual courses of action, appealing to general principles and shared assumptions, blustering, threatening, cajoling and arguing to assert themselves and to further particular policies and orientations toward the world. The people engaged in the discussion are also not anonymous or abstract tokens of universal rationality, but persons who have individual histories, and track records of previously held opinions, actions, and associations that are to some degree known to the others.[6] Particularly in the case of politicians

---

situations, especially those which display any kind of complexity or sophistication. Thus, at the end of World War II the Allies decided to grant to the Kingdom of Italy, as it then was, the status of "non-allied co-belligerent" in the war against Hitler. The cat may judge that you are a friend without entertaining an appropriate linguistically formulated belief, but it is hard to see how anyone could make any particular judgment about the advisability of granting or withholding the status of "non-allied co-belligerent" without having something like human language. This, in turn, does not mean one must have a *specific* linguistic item "non-allied co-belligerent" in order to grant or withhold this status—in fact in English we do not have a *single word* for that—but it does mean we must have a sufficiently rich stock of appropriate general words to express what we mean. In short, from the fact that *some* linguistic expression is necessary for more sophisticated forms of human interaction to be possible, one must not draw the conclusion that human behavior can in some sense be reduced to beliefs/language. It is important to recognize both that action and language are connected and that there is a potential looseness of fit between the two. We can have collective hostility to you—to have this enmity it is perhaps necessary that we have *some* linguistic means at our disposal; but it is not the case either that we absolutely must use *this* particular language, or that in order to act in a particular way, we need exactly to have had some particular, antecedently formulated, linguistically shaped belief in mind to guide us. There is a residual gap or space between language and action, an indeterminateness, which nothing can overcome.

[5] See John Dewey, *The Late Works, 1925–1953*, vol. 4: *1929: The Quest for Certainty*, in *John Dewey*, ed. Jo An Boydston (Southern Illinois University Press, 1988), and *Human Nature and Conduct* (Random House, 1930).

[6] This is obviously directed at the views held by John Rawls and by Jürgen Habermas, who in one way or another believe one can orient oneself in the world of politics by analyzing what would be the object of consensus in an idealized discussion conducted by agents who are deprived of any knowledge of their own empirical singularity or of the contingent historical situation.

who are known magnitudes the possibility of recalling their past actions, the positions they took, and the arguments they used can throw a surprisingly long shadow on a present discussion. This means that agents involved in the interaction will need to think about the consistency of their commitments over time, and about reasons they could publicly give for having changed their views (when they have done so)—reasons that do not do them too much discredit. Thus, everyone present at the Washington dinner party Sir Christopher describes will have known that Richard Perle had been a staunch opponent of any form of arms control agreement with the Soviet Union during the Cold War, and was closely associated in the 1990s with a group called "The Project for the New American Century."[7] This group elaborated a plan for U.S. domination of the world by making use of the uncontested military superiority of the United States over any possible constellation of conventional enemies that was one result of the collapse of the Soviet Union. One of the central planks of the program put forward by the Project for the New American Century was the proposal to "discourage" allies, for example the United Kingdom, from acquiring the military capacity to operate independently of the United States. If Richard Perle one day presented himself as an apostle of peace and advocate of genuinely universal disarmament, this deviation from his earlier position would at the very least require him to have some articulable reasons ready to explain why he had changed his mind, or how his new position could be made compatible with the one with which he is so strongly associated. That would not be impossible, but it would be an extra rhetorical task he would have to discharge that might put him at a slight disadvantage in certain discussions. In general participants in a political discussion have internalized at least some minimal historical knowledge about the other participants to such an extent that the past is an essential integral component of the present situation, and one cannot understand what is taking place without knowledge of this historical dimension.

When Richard Perle says to Sir Christopher Meyer that Britain "must" choose, he is not merely floating for disinterested consideration a speculative hypothesis about historical or contextual necessity, in the way in which a biologist might say that all living things must eventually die. Rather, particularly in view of Richard Perle's position as a professional politician and his past, which strongly suggests that he is a bit of a bully, in saying that Britain must choose Perle is most probably trying to influence Sir Christopher's attitude, that is, trying to bring it about that Britain *does* choose. Even *saying* this makes it harder for Britain not

[7] On Richard Perle and the neoconservatives, see also James Mann, *The Rise of the Vulcans* (Viking Penguin 2004), and Stefan Halper and Jonathan Clarke, *America Alone* (Cambridge University Press, 2004).

to choose, and given Perle's connections he is, and is known to be, in a position to make it even harder if he wishes. Western philosophers have historically focused on the analysis of beliefs or opinions, have construed these on the model of detached vision, and have discussed obsessively the conditions under which such beliefs could be considered to represent the existing world correctly. It is not false to think of a political judgment as a belief, but this is an abstraction, an artificial isolation of one element or component or aspect from a wider nexus of actions and action-related attitudes, habits, and institutional arrangements, within which alone the judgment (finally) makes sense.

In addition, although to express the view that "Britain must choose" might look like a simple prediction, it can also be seen as a kind of threat. What Britain "must" do is connected to what it "can" do, and what it politically "can" do is not anything picked out by logical or physical necessity, but by what it can reasonably be expected to be able to do without having to pay an exorbitantly high price. The neoconservatives in the Bush administration, however, who wish Britain to choose, are also in a position to impose a price that would make failure to choose unreasonable. In saying that Britain must choose, Richard Perle is perhaps reminding British diplomats of this, signaling his intention to exact this price if necessary and seeking thereby to bring it about that they choose. Although in very many political contexts stating what looks to be a prediction is actually changing the situation, this does not mean that no prediction is possible in such cases, merely that it must be approached with more care than one needs to use in more straightforward cases of prediction.

It is however by no means the case that attempts to engage in self-fulfilling prophecies will necessarily succeed; an interventive prediction may even backfire, so that what is intended as a self-fulfilling prophecy ends up undermining itself. Diplomats, politicians, and national populations can be highly counter-suggestible, and precisely putting this pressure on Britain may convince a majority of the population that it is best not to allow oneself to be bullied: if choose we must, let it be the EU, where at least we have an institutionally secured set of powers to participate in decision-making. Whether this reaction of defiance can be maintained or not depends on a number of different factors. In particular it depends on the answers to two questions:

a. What means of coercion does the extortionist actually have at his disposal? What could he in principle do to us?
b. What is the likelihood that the extortionist will actually apply the sanctions he threatens us with?

To the start with the first question, it should be noted that in many cases the effectiveness of a threat depends to some extent on the attitude and reaction of the person threatened. The blackmailer's threat to disclose the contents of some of my correspondence loses its force if I become indifferent to the publication of the correspondence. States, of course, have at their disposal means of extreme coercion the effectiveness of which cannot be blunted simply by a change in our attitudes, but it seems fair to assume that in February 2001 Perle did not seriously envisage a series of direct military actions, or even indirect acts of subversion against Great Britain, and, in fact if he had been known concretely to have envisaged any such thing that in itself would have changed the situation drastically. Short of military intervention or subversion, however, it would seem that the U.S. government has three possible instruments to hand. First, it can impose various kinds of economic and commercial sanctions, try to destabilize the currency, etc.; second, it can refuse to supply Britain with advanced military equipment of various kinds; and third, it can try to isolate us diplomatically and politically. Economic sanctions might be very painful, but their effectiveness would depend partly on how much we were willing to stand. It is at least arguable that we need the most advanced military systems only if we wish to operate as junior partners in joint operations with the United States, so if we were willing to give up some pretensions to Great Power status, we could easily dispense with them. Finally, the idea that the United States would be in a position to isolate the UK politically was a bit of a joke even in 2001. After all, Blair's reasons for supporting the invasion of Iraq seem partly to have been his need to cut a vivid figure on the international stage and accumulate enough influence with the United States to use its power to fuel his religious fantasies about a never-ending war against Evil. Sources close to Blair, however, have occasionally hinted that another important part of his motivation was his fear that if Britain didn't join the United States, Washington would be so isolated politically that the U.S. government would not be able to control its own paranoia and would run amok. So a threat to isolate Britain was not to be taken terribly seriously. On closer inspection, then, none of the three instruments then seems utterly irresistible if the UK could keep its nerve.

As far as the second of the two questions is concerned, Perle probably assumes, as General de Gaulle did, that if really forced to choose, there is no question but that Britain would choose a basically Atlantic orientation whatever the damage to our relation with Europe. It is part of Perle's calculation to pretend that he would prefer Britain to be with the European Union rather than a neutral between Washington and the EU, but that pretense is a bluff.

Sir Christopher, as an experienced diplomat, sees through most of what Perle is up to without much difficulty precisely because he does not take the content of what he asserts in isolation and at face value as a set of propositions to be evaluated for their truth or falsity. Rather he sees them as specific actions in a particular context, and he can interpret them correctly as attempts to influence British foreign policy in a particular way *because* he knows Perle's own history, and that of the groups with which he is most closely associated, and thus he can locate Perle rather exactly in the landscape of contemporary American politics. Meyer, for his part, is trying to bring it about that Perle sees the world in a certain way, in particular that Perle comes to assume that what is politically important is the context Blair intended. Why, though, should Perle and Co. be at all interested in the context Blair *intended*? His policies might well have harmed U.S. interests (as interpreted by Perle) without intending to do so, and Perle might believe that Blair ought to have been able to see that this would be the case. Is politics about intentions or real results? Doesn't the answer to this question depend on a still further context?

Saying that "Britain must choose" is performing an action which in the context also articulates the attitude of a particular group, the neo-conservatives. This context is partly constituted by a series of historical and institutional facts which one must take account of if one wishes to understand the statement. If one wishes, one can isolate the pure content of this political judgment and formulate it, as it were, as an abstract prediction. This might be a perfectly reasonable and useful thing to do for some purposes, and unobjectionable as long as one remembers that one is artificially extracting the content from a wider context in which it is actually embedded, and as long as one does not forget that what parts of the context are relevant will depend on the particular purpose at hand. This, however, it seems to me, is sufficient to undermine the traditional conception which I outlined above, in which politics is understood on the model of a quasi-academic discussion.

There are two rather different things the term "political judgment" can mean. First of all, it can refer to a judgment made about a certain domain of the world. Just as a chemical judgment refers to chemical processes, and a biological judgment to the properties of biological systems, a "political judgment" could be construed as a judgment *about* politics, that is about affairs of state, relations of power, the way in which collective human action is coordinated, or however else one wanted to specify the domain of "politics," say as opposed to whatever one wanted to oppose it to. Second, one could speak of a political judgment as a judgment not about a certain domain, but rather as a judgment about almost any domain whatever that as a judgment has a certain character. To say that a judgment "has a political character," however, means that someone can *look at it* in a certain way, namely as an action with implications for further instances or forms of collective human action. So Truman's conversation with Stalin at the Potsdam Conference about the successful testing of the first atomic bomb was a conversation *about* a particular topic, namely a certain experiment with explosive radioactive materials, but it was clearly also a conversation that had a political character, since the point of it was to intimidate Stalin. A historian's description of the Potsdam Conference will contain any number of political judgments in the first sense, but since it is possible to see these judgments, like the judgments Sir Christopher and Richard Perle express in retrospectively interpreting the meeting of the Council of Europe in Nice, under the aspect of their relation to the possibilities of collective human action, they can also be considered "political judgments" in the second sense. There is, to be completely explicit about this, no reason why an external observer might not wish to look for a political aspect even of actions which are considered by those who perform them to be "unpolitical," just as there is no reason in principle why I should be disbarred from judging the way the man behind the counter in the post office weighs my letter "from an aesthetic point of view," even though he has no nonutilitarian intentions. To be sure, if we do this—if we look at the postal worker as if he were a mime or performance artist of some kind—we might not come much closer to an understanding of what he is doing, at any event in *one* sense of "understanding." "Understanding" itself, however, is not usually an end in itself, but a means to something else, usually to some kind of action.

As I have tried to emphasize, political judgments do not generally occur as isolated individual statements, but rather as part of sets of beliefs and judgments that are interconnected with forms of individual and institutional action. These sets are Janus-faced, exhibiting two aspects. One aspect makes them look a bit like predictions; the other makes them look like value judgments. They are in fact both at the same time, and regardless of the fact that it might be "in principle" or "logically" or "analytically" possible to distinguish them, in fact these two aspects are so interconnected that in actual political practice it is essential to see them together. In addition, the prediction-aspect and the evaluation-aspect of systems of political judgment are not like the usual models we have and use of either simple prediction or simple evaluation. I have mentioned one important way in which they diverge from our standard models of prediction, namely that they are what some philosophers call "reflexive," that is, they can have a potentially self-fulfilling or for that matter self-undermining property. I would now like to say something about political judgments in their evaluative aspect.

The usual model that is used for classing or grading is one in which I have a set of fixed standards and apply them to candidates for evaluation. The example that is often given is grading eggs or apples.[8] We assume that

---

[8] See J. O. Urmson, "On Grading," in *Mind*, vol. 59 (1950), pp. 145–69. This (pre-Wittgensteinean) analysis is still useful as an account of our everyday assumptions.

there are firm and fixed criteria or standards for designating something a "Grade A" apple: it has a certain size, color, perhaps a certain degree of ripeness and freshness, it must lack certain disfigurations, etc. The standards will be established relative to a certain fixed human purpose. Grade A apples will be those that have properties which make them especially highly suited to those human purposes. These criteria will themselves not be absolutely precise, and their application to individual cases will rarely be beyond reasonable disagreement,[9] but one of the usual assumptions we make when discussing this kind of grading is that the process of deciding on the criteria to be used, and the process of classifying individual instances, are separate and distinct. The reason for this is that the whole point of grading things like apples, eggs, timber, or undergraduates is to introduce predictability into life. Grading is supposed to allow us to know what we are getting. When the grader is classifying, he or she *accepts* and applies pre-given criteria; a grader does not change the goalposts while the game is going on. If this happened, it would defeat the whole point of grading. That, at any rate, is the conception implicit in the usual model.

Simple classification or grading of the kind described above, however, is exactly what does *not* characteristically happen in politics. In politics simple grading plays an extremely important but distinctly subordinate role. We collect and use statistics on crime, employment, productivity, health, but we also constantly question the way the statistics are put together. More generally, political action takes place in an arena in which the standards for evaluating what is "success," what is a good idea, what is a desirable outcome, are themselves always changing and always in principle up for renegotiation. Thus, on 1 May 2003 George W. Bush announced that the war in Iraq had ended in "victory" for U.S. forces, and very clearly presented this as a vindication of his policy of invasion in the interests of "regime change." In conventional terms this was clearly a Grade A military "victory": the field army of the enemy was decisively defeated and dispersed, the command structure utterly dissolved, and the national territory occupied. Even the further goal of "regime change" was attained. Whatever one might think of the political situation in Iraq after 1 May 2003, the Baathist Party was clearly no longer in control of the apparatus of state power. Is it so obvious, however, that this automatically counts as a political success?

The prospects of a stable democracy in Iraq do not look very rosy, but then one would have to be extraordinarily naïve to think that this was an important part of the motivation for the invasion anyway. If the point

---

[9] If Wittgenstein is right, this is a philosophical, not a practical point. Even apparently fixed everyday "evaluation" is in fact indeterminate, so our everyday *view* of it is incorrect. In politics the real situation is revealed for all to see.

really was to prevent the establishment of any political agency in the Middle East that was independent of the United States, then a democratic Iraq would be a potential danger anyway, because it might at some point be tempted to steer an independent course. So the complete destruction of the country as a viable society capable of setting its own goals and acting on them effectively would be to that extent a success, although one the perception of which would have to be managed carefully given the claims made to justify the war. On the other hand, the price paid for the military victory was the weakening of the UN, the diplomatic isolation of the United States, a split in NATO, the generation of thousands of new recruits to a political agenda hostile to the United States,[10] and a significant drain on the U.S. economy because major allies refused to do what they had done in the First Gulf War, namely foot the entire bill for the war. Is it clear that "regime change" in this sense will be the realization of a good or will contribute to "the good life"? Whose good life? Is it clear that it has furthered broad U.S. interests or the wider interests of the populations in Europe, the Middle East, and the rest of the world? Was Richard Perle really giving good advice when he counseled invasion? Political success is always subject to reevaluation in the light of changing circumstances and changing overall conceptions of "the good life." There is no reason to think that discussions of what constitutes a good life will ever, certainly not within any finite period of time, end in the kind of normatively binding consensus some philosophers have expected.[11] One thing that seems to have happened in the case of the Second Gulf War is that as a result of action large numbers of people changed the concrete understanding of what would count as "success" that they antecedently had had. This is not an unusual outcome.[12]

Is there, then, nothing but shifting processes of political judgment that comprise changing predictions and infinitely contestable evaluations? Surely, though, one might argue, there are limits to the malleability of concepts like "success," a "good outcome," a "desirable result." At any

---

[10] Of course, the *main* self-declared political aim of Al-Qaeda is an end to the stationing of U.S. troops in Saudi Arabia. See *Messages to the World: The Statements of Osama bin Laden*, ed. Bruce Lawrence (Verso, 2005), or *What Does Al-Qaeda Want?* ed. Robert O. Marlin IV (North Atlantic Books, 2004); see also Farhad Khosrokhavar, *Quand Al-Qaïda parle* (Grasset, 2006).

[11] Again this is directed primarily against Rawls and Habermas.

[12] One of the most deeply illuminating discussions of the differences between everyday grading and the more complex forms of interaction between classing, acting, and changing the standards of classing is that to be found in Hegel, particularly in his discussion of the difference between "*Verstand*" and "*Vernunft*." See *Enzyklopädie der philosophischen Wissenschaften*, in *Werke in zwanzig Bänden*, ed. Eva Moldenhauer and Karl Markus Michel (Suhrkamp, 1970), vol. 8, pp. 1–168, or the briefer treatment in *Phänomenologie des Geistes*, vol. 3 of the same collection, pp. 68–81.

rate, life itself, biological survival, sets certain limits to what any of us can construe as a "good life." The phenomenon of martyrdom familiar in the West since antiquity, and the use of coordinated suicide bombing attacks since World War II, means that not even the human desire for self-preservation can be taken unquestionedly as the basis for political valuation.[13] For as long as humans are capable of a moral and social, and not a merely biological, understanding of "the good life," martyrdom, voluntary self-immolation, and suicide attack will remain as human possibilities. This continued openness of "success" (or "the good life") to reevaluation is not, I think, merely a local property of democratic politics, although it is a feature of politics in general that comes most vividly to the surface in democracies. Evaluation in politics will not always be simple, and is almost never definitive. To be sure, if you let yourself be killed as a martyr or kill yourself as a suicide bomber, you close the context for yourself by this action, but what your action means for those of us who survive, and how we will judge it, is still an open question *for us*, which we will try to answer, if we find it pressing enough, by the usual series of complicated acts of interpretation.

Ever since, at the latest, Thucydides, πρόνοια, the ability correctly to foresee what was likely to happen, has been valued as one of the most important virtues of the politician. This includes not merely the ability to predict or foresee what will happen but also to foresee what *will seem good*, both to oneself and more importantly to "effective" others, that is, to those whose views about what is good or satisfactory count politically.[14] When the war has been lost catastrophically, which policy will have more appeal, one based on a call for *revanche*, or on a call for lasting peace at almost any price? The combination of an ability to foresee or predict and an ability to evaluate is not the only important political capacity *tout court*. Obviously, other important traits are persistence, discipline, resourcefulness, the ability to persuade and organize others, etc.; but I would like specifically to mention a further, particularly important cognitive-practical ability. There is a distinct ability of practical imagination, inventiveness, or creativity, of coming up with new possibilities, or seeing new possibilities or constructiveness, which is very important in politics.[15]

---

[13] See *Making Sense of Suicide Missions*, ed. Diego Gambetta (Oxford University Press, 2005), esp. the chapters by Hopgood (pp. 43–76) and Gambetta (pp. 259–99).

[14] I mean "effective" here in the sense in which economists speak of "effective demand."

[15] I'm suggesting here a parallel to the distinction sometimes made by aestheticians between the "genius" who is able to produce works of art that deviate in a both original and interesting way, and the critic or person of taste who is capable of judging works. Kant's discussion of taste and genius in *Kritik der Urteilskraft* is the obvious classic treatment.

I mean by this, for instance, the sort of ability exhibited by those who organized the attacks on the Pentagon in Washington and the World Trade Center in New York. Someone had to have the utterly ingenious idea of construing civilian passenger aircraft as missiles with suicide hijackers as pilots who would fly them so as to destroy large buildings. More important, however, than this exercise of technical imagination was the kind of *political* imagination that seems to have been at work. We don't know much, or at any rate I don't know much, about the actual planning of these attacks, but to the extent to which one can infer back from the actual results of what was a very well-organized operation to the intentions of those who planned it, it seems likely that the planners knew they were about to inflict a deep narcissistic wound on the American psyche, which the population would neither comprehend nor be able to tolerate. The form that reflection took after the attacks—the frantic attempt to answer the question "Why do '*they*' hate '*us*'?" —was sufficiently incoherent to indicate that a deep nerve had been touched. It would not have been difficult, then, to expect the Bush regime to embark on a course of internal repression and foreign military adventure so wild, destructive, and dangerous that international public opinion would shift decisively against the United States, which is what has happened. So far—as of November 2006—this strategy, if in fact it was a strategy and not a mere series of accidents, has been working like a well-engineered Swiss watch. Viewed from the outside, the plan also seems to exhibit great subtlety in utilizing American blind spots—the gross ignorance on the part of the population about the rest of the world and their extremely limited ability to see themselves and their actions as others see them—to subvert U.S. military power and cause it to discharge itself in politically self-destructive ways. To come up with this kind of plan requires not merely political judgment, but inventiveness of a high order. The kind of imaginativeness I have in mind might or might not be well grounded, that is, the plan might or might not work; one might or might not approve of the results. An agent may well be capable of coming up with a variety of new suggestions none of which is any good. That is, as I would express it, someone may have political imagination without political judgment. And of course, people may well have both political imagination and judgment without also having a moral sense, or at any rate without exercising that sense.[16]

---

[16] One might say that there are three "genuine" dimensions of politics:

a) inventiveness—finding new things that work
b) prediction, foresight
c) trying actively to change people's conception of the good

One of the most interesting aspects of the events of the 11th of September 2001 has always seemed to me to be the fact that the attacks were carried out wordlessly as far as the international media were concerned. There was no reading out of a set of demands in front of television cameras, no explanations, no public political announcements of any kind, no group immediately fell all over itself to try to lay claim to this tremendous coup. Through their actions themselves the perpetrators expressed a rather clear political judgment about a civilization based on militarism and economic exploitation *without saying a word*.

---

and (at least) one very prominent but debased dimension:

  d) spin doctoring—trying to cause people to think that outcomes are good by certain accepted standards, which are not, or trying to confuse people about the standards being used.

II

The Politics of Managing Decline

THE LAST TWENTY YEARS have seen very significant changes in the pattern of economic activity around the world, including major increases in the manufacturing capacity of various countries in Asia. In addition, the collapse of the Soviet Union initiated a process of political restructuring in Europe which has not perhaps yet reached its final stage. For citizens of the European Union it might seem timely to think again about what attitudes we wish to adopt toward some of the new political constellations that seem to be emerging in the world. For those of us who live in the UK, two important facts have loomed particularly large on the international landscape for a long time. The first has been NATO, and more generally the close military and political cooperation with the United States. Despite the tensions that one would expect in any military alliance, continued participation in NATO has not ever been sufficiently seriously questioned in mainstream politics for there to have been a realistic prospect of British withdrawal from the organization. The second fact has been the success of European integration and the highly problematic relation most British politicians and parties have had to this phenomenon. If the point of NATO was really to "keep the Russians out, the Americans in, and the Germans down," then it would seem that history itself has rendered the first and last of these tasks now superfluous, and so the desirability of the second night be thought to be ripe for scrutiny.

Recently some commentators have begun remarking on various ways in which the United States and Europe seem to be moving further and further apart politically, socially, and culturally. Along some dimensions the facts of this contrast are clear, although, of course, the interpretation of their significance is difficult and controversial. Thus there does not seem to be any reasonable doubt but that the United States is a significantly more violent and more inegalitarian society than any in Europe, and that it is characterized by a much higher level of religious belief and participation than any of the larger Western European societies. The United States has a proportionally much higher prison population, a strikingly high level of child poverty, and no National Health Service. The death penalty, banned in all EU countries, is in force in a number of American states, and is applied overwhelmingly to members of racial and ethnic minorities; needless to say, virtually all those who are actually executed are poor. Statistics about violent crimes, the state of public health, levels of participation in religious rituals, and, in particular, about any aspect of the economy may all have to be taken with a grain of salt as indicators of underlying features of a society, for reasons with which we are all familiar, but it would be rash to assume they had no significance.

These differences between the EU countries and the United States are real enough, but they are not in themselves decisive. Necessity makes strange bedfellows (Churchill and Stalin in 1943). The question is whether there is a sufficiently pressing and visible necessity operating in the world now, and, if so, in what direction it will direct whose steps. The former British prime minister Tony Blair, with his characteristic flair for flamboyant speech, made it a habit during his last few years in office of conjuring up a world full of extreme and unprecedented danger and appealing to the other members of the EU to cooperate actively with Washington as a means of working toward peace in a perilous world. Unfortunately Blair seriously misdiagnosed the source of the main danger confronting the contemporary world.

"Dangers" can arise from various factors: from the personal idiosyncrasies, the psychological weakness, the hunger for power or the malice of those in positions of power, from miscalculations, from the conjunction of accidents, or from a variety of other adventitious causes. There are, however, also dangers that are rooted in *structural* features of situations and do not depend very much on the personalities, or the good or evil intentions of the particular political leaders who happen to be in power at any moment. For structural reasons having to do with its internal constitution and with its position in the wider world, the United States is an extremely dangerous political agent. After all, at the moment the country possesses large and technologically very advanced military forces, which have at their disposal highly developed, if crude, destructive capacities; yet the country is experiencing a slow, but manifestly irreversible, relative economic decline. Its population is frustrated, resentful, deeply ignorant of the wider world, and subject to recurrent and intense bouts of collective paranoia. This combination does not constitute a very stable basis for contributing constructively to world peace. One of the main ways, in particular, in which the United States represents a particular menace is that at the moment it has come to be in Washington's short-term interest to make the world a place in which the quick recourse to military action, and the constant threat of violence, is accepted as part of normal practice in international relations. The use of military power presents itself as an increasingly attractive option primarily because the United States is becoming weaker and weaker economically and politically, and force is one of the few means American politicians can deploy that offer any hope whatever of allowing them to advance or protect what they think are their vital interests.

It is not surprising that agents in what they perceive to be difficult situations will be tempted to use whatever effective means they happen to have at hand to attain their ends. If the situation is pressing enough, they may feel they must act, and if they do act they are unlikely to use means they know to be ineffectual. This is as true of governments in their dealings with other countries as it is of individuals or corporations in their dealings with each other. The tools a government has at its disposal will be varied: an agricultural surplus that can be distributed to needy clients, a large air force and navy that can be used to intimidate or intervene, or the influence that results from control over international economic and political institutions, or of various forms of advanced technology. What is perhaps more significant, the governments of large and powerful countries don't merely adopt specific measures to attain specific ends, but they can through their general pattern of policy and action influence the general international political environment. Astute governments, that is, try not merely to intervene at particular moments in particular circumstances with the means that happen to be at their disposal, they also try actively to shape the world in general to make it the kind of place in which the instruments they have—their own particular strengths—will be as much in demand and as effective as possible. States, that is, not unreasonably try to create a climate in international affairs which will be maximally amenable to influence by the use of their own available instruments. Militarily weak states with large and efficient manufacturing sectors support free trade and the resolution of conflict by negotiation. A militarily powerful but politically, diplomatically, and economically weak country will be tempted to opt for militarization of existing disputes, including clandestine militarization. Finally, it is in some ways a clearly admirable feature of modern Western societies that they have forms of government that are at least minimally responsive to popular pressure; they cannot, therefore, be completely indifferent to the death of large numbers of their citizens, including their military personnel. If the domestic population will not tolerate even a moderately high level of casualties among its own armed forces, but insists on an immediate show of success, this will put any government under pressure to adopt whatever measures promise quick, apparently decisive results, even if they are indiscriminately devastating in the short term, and highly counterproductive in the long run.

The sources of the political frustration large parts of the U.S. population now feel are probably complex, but one element in the mixture is likely to be the discrepancy between the illusory image of national power propagated by a variety of their institutions and the nagging perception of actual failure. If the military machine is the most advanced in the world, why is it incapable of controlling a small Third World country like Iraq? If the economy is strong and the national way of life uniquely satisfying and attractive, why the diplomatic isolation, the dependence on foreign creditors to finance public debt, and the high levels of poverty, inequality, and violence?

For a brief moment after the attacks on the Pentagon and the World Trade Center in 2001, it seemed as if the shock of these events might bring about a general process of reflection by Americans on the place of the United States in the wider world. Unfortunately, the form this reflection eventually took was self-defeating. One normal way of going about determining why someone did something is to ask the person in question. The question why Al-Qaeda bombed the Pentagon and the World Trade Center has a relatively clear answer: "They say they did it because of U.S. support for the corrupt Saudi monarchy and the garrisoning of American troops in Saudi Arabia." One might then expect people to start asking why U.S. troops should be in Saudi Arabia anyway, why exactly control of this region is so important, and finally, how much real power the United States has and how it can be best deployed. Instead public discussion almost immediately began to focus on elaborating various fantasies about Islamic fundamentalism, "their" hatred of "our" values, freedom, and way of life, etc. The creation of imaginary hate figures may give some immediate psychic satisfaction, but in the long run it only spreads and increases confusion and aggression. Troops can in principle be withdrawn from Saudi Arabia, policy toward the Saudi monarchy can change, but how can one deal in a satisfactory way with inherently spectral "Islamic terror"? It no doubt suits some political circles in the United States that the population continue to be fearful, mystified, and frustrated, the better to gain their acquiescence in various further military operations, but it is hard to believe that this kind of emotional and cognitive derangement of the population contributes to increasing U.S. political power.

If power means ability effectively to attain desired outcomes—rather than mere ability to wreak havoc—then American power is now very limited indeed. Under the circumstances, one could understand the explanation the Blair government occasionally gave (in private) about its policy of unquestioning loyalty to Washington, even if one thought it misguided: it was an attempt to calm down the Bush administration and steady its hand. After all, the United States is now facing an extremely difficult transition from a period in which it was the economically buoyant leader, invested with great political authority, of a broad and ultimately successful coalition against the Soviet Union, to the much weaker position it now occupies. What is more, if present economic and political trends continue, it can look forward to an even more modest future. There is every reason to believe that the deterioration of the economic position of North America relative to China and the East Asian region will continue. This is not to suggest that there is any reason to expect imminent collapse of the U.S. economy, or even an absolute decline in economic activity, but in the competitive world of international politics "power" is *relational,* that is, it is *relative* vigor and weight that is most important, and the period of clear and overwhelming American economic predominance of the kind Washington enjoyed in the '60s, and the afterglow of which lasted until the '90s, does seem now gone for good. The visible superior prosperity of American society to all others played an absolutely crucial legitimatory role in large areas of domestic U.S. politics, and was a central component of the sense of self of large portions of the population. The assumption that steadily increasing economic well-being is assured by the maintenance of a relatively unfettered capitalist system and by a system of international "free trade" was deeply ingrained. During the period (1940–70) in which the United States had by far the largest, most efficient, and most productive industrial plant in the world, it was possible for Americans to believe in good faith that "free trade" would be both good for everyone in the world, and *especially* good for the United States. Once it becomes clear that increases in international free trade now will bring about the shift of most jobs to Asia, an important ideological pillar of social and political stability is removed, with results that are difficult to predict in detail, but which, if they take any of the forms it is most reasonable to expect them to take, do not bode well for the consistent, effective exercise of peaceful power in the international domain.

The loss of power is most emphatically not a mere result of economic decline. The demise of the Warsaw Pact also means that NATO members who might previously have believed they had no choice but to accept virtually anything Washington saw fit to demand, now find they have political alternatives, including, for instance the creation of stronger bilateral ties between the EU and China. Attempts to play up a "Terrorist Threat" to replace the "Soviet Threat" are unlikely to be successful in Europe for at least two reasons. First, Western Europe was in a straightforward geographical sense the front line against the Warsaw Pact, whereas Islamic terrorism is directed in the first instance against the United States, and against European countries only to the extent that they are allies of Washington. Second, conventional military power of the kind the United States still has in abundance was a reasonable defense against possible attack by the Soviet Union and its allies in the 1950s in Europe. "Terrorism," however, is a completely different kind of threat. It is not self-evidently absurd to deny outright that "terrorism" is a serious threat to Europe. After all, we have lived with the IRA, ETA, and other groups for decades, and even at their worst "(Islamic) terrorists" have up to now never succeeded in killing as many people per year as die in traffic accidents, or are murdered by their spouses. Still, even if one grants the more fevered claims about the extent of the danger, conventional military power is helpless against the forms of terrorism now being practiced and envisaged. Simply recall the inability of the state of Israel to use its absolute military superiority to halt Palestinian attacks against its citizens and territory, or the complete irrelevance of any of the usual forms of military action as a defense against attacks like those carried out against the Pentagon and the World Trade Center. To Western European countries an alliance with Washington seems now no longer an obvious great asset, as it was in 1950, but rather, increasingly, a peculiar decision voluntarily to put oneself in harm's way in order to further the interests of a foreign power. Bombs go off in Madrid, London, and a resort in Bali frequented by Australian tourists, but not in other places that fully share "our values and way of life" such as Toronto, Oslo, or Vienna, because Spain, Australia, and Britain were belligerent members of the "coalition of the willing" against Iraq. One can see major European states slowly drawing the consequences from this changed state of affairs. To the extent to which political power and influence has a moral and diplomatic component, the actions of the Bush administration during the early years of the twenty-first century, including its evident contempt for the United Nations and indifference to the fate of Iraqi civilians, have effectively destroyed any stock of good will there might have been toward the United States among Western European populations. For the United States to maintain a peaceful mode of cooperation with the wider world in the face of such diminution of its own power, standing, and perspectives does require very strong nerves, and since even a seriously diminished United States will remain for the near future a large presence on the international stage as an economic agent and a very large presence as a military force, it behooves all of us to welcome any initiatives that might help America accommodate as peacefully as possible to an international order in which it has less power.

The main international problem is not, as many European commentators would have it,[1] that the United States represents a *"hyperpuissance"* with which it is no longer possible to deal on terms of rough equality, but rather that the United States is in fact now far too weak to play the role it attributes to itself, and which many European countries were happy to allow it to play in the past. It has succeeded in projecting a *semblance* of power, both to its own population and to the rest of the world, which no longer corresponds to reality. Repeated, ruthless, highly visible use of de-

---

[1] See, for instance, Hubert Védrine, *Face à l'hyperpuissance: Textes et discours 1995–2003* (Fayard, 2003).

structive force in the international arena against weaker opponents (e.g., the Taliban in Afghanistan) who can be plausibly presented to have been resoundingly defeated, plus a full-scale ideological offensive about the irresistible nature of U.S. power (lots of speeches, books, films), may shore up *perceptions* for a while, but will not change the underlying reality of the situation. An image of power, to the extent to which it is accepted by others, is not nothing; it can have a temporary intimidating effect. It is not, however, a viable basis for continuing international stability.

The general structure I am describing is not specific to the politics of the so-called neoconservatives, the U.S. Republican Party, or the political Right, although it perhaps presented itself in an especially vivid and unapologetic form in the persons of Rumsfeld, Wolfowitz, Rice, and their close associates. Rather it is a shared orientation of U.S. policy based on a perception of the world, and of self, that is common across the political spectrum. After all, it was Madeleine Albright, minister for foreign affairs ("Secretary of State") for one of the most liberal Democratic regimes the United States is likely to have for a long time to come, who called the United States "the indispensable country." That was true in the period between 1945 and 1975, but not now. That the views of many influential segments of the British political class do not track the world correctly in this respect is a serious problem for everyone affected by the decisions the UK political establishment makes.

To return to Blair's proposal of steadying Bush's hand by increasing accommodation, this could have had a positive outcome only if someone in the British government had been willing to tell Bush some unpleasant truths about the world, and also only if someone had been capable of doing this in a way that had some chance of changing U.S. policy. In fact, Bush gave no indication of being willing to listen to views that challenge his preconceptions, and Blair seems to have shared, and to continue to share, the neoliberal economic doctrine and the illusions of continuing American power and authority that are a major part of the problem. The positive alignment Blair proposed would be more likely in the long run to hinder than to further the adjustment of the United States to a reality it must find painful.

One might think that recent events show that it is sufficient for Europe, as the very loose association of independent states which it now is, simply to refuse to take part in military adventures that do not concern it. After all, of the three largest European countries only the UK actively participated in the invasion of Iraq. Countries like Spain and Hungary which, contrary to the will of the majority of their populations, had originally joined the coalition have now, after new elections, withdrawn their troops. Even in the UK the war was highly unpopular and the decision to go to war was a very close run thing indeed. Only now in retrospect is it becoming clear just how much manipulation of information, corruption, and deceit was required to attain even the minimal amount of consensus that existed among the politicians who took Britain into the war; had any one of a number of relatively small accidental factors been different, Britain would have stood aside, too, like most of its major European allies. What was possible then will remain possible in the foreseeable future; sovereign states can always, finally, opt out.

I think this view is too optimistic. The invasion of Iraq was by any standards an "optional" war of aggression, the disastrous consequences of which were widely foreseen and predicted. To refuse to join the invasion was a decision that it was, therefore, in principle very easy to make, which makes it all the more striking that Blair's advocacy of the invasion was able to prevail. To understand why he was able to succeed requires reference to the details of British political history, the accidental constellation of forces in Parliament at the time of the invasion, and the specific way the parliamentary system worked. Basically, a very large number of members of the opposition Conservative Party simply could not resist the attractions of a neocolonial war against Arabs, and the governing Labour Party was, for various reasons, afraid of the domestic consequences of deposing Tony Blair, who had given them their first electoral successes in over a decade. I suspect, however, that part of the reason for the large scale acquiescence by Parliament in a war many of the members must have known was inexpedient was the residual hold which that Churchillian invention, the "special relationship" between the United States and the UK, continues to exercise on the imagination of the politically most active classes of this country. Blair's policy of trying to moderate the excesses of the Bush administration "from within the "special relationship" led directly to the present state of affairs in Iraq. If this is supposed to be success, one does wonder what failure would look like.

The pursuit of the mirage of "special relationship" has done damage to successive generations of British politicians. To ordinary Americans the very idea that British politicians could have some special influence on U.S. foreign policy for any reason whatsoever is preposterous. Some politicians in Washington are, of course, only too happy to receive unsolicited pledges of loyalty and to reciprocate with warm words, but one would be hard put to point to a single instance during the past few decades in which American foreign policy changed on any point that was of importance to Washington as a result of British advocacy of one course of action rather than another. Blair's influence in the period before the invasion of Iraq seems to have amounted to an antecedent unconditional promise to go to war alongside the United States no matter what, combined with an expression of preference that this be done under UN auspices. Since this preference happened to coincide with the view being vigorously and independently pressed by the U.S. State Department and also by various senior figures in previous Republican administrations (including Henry Kissinger and Bush Senior), it was able to have some weight. The basic decision to go to war, however, was treated as a foregone conclusion, an issue on which only the members of the U.S. administration had any effective say. It should perhaps also be noted, though, that it is at least as undesirable for the United States to have the virtually automatic support of the British government for any initiative it undertakes as it is for the UK to be locked into courses of action over which it has no actual control. One price we paid for the unquestioning endorsement our government gave to the policies of the current U.S. government was a drastic loss of influence in the main larger political agency in which we do have a significant independent voice, the EU; another was the bombings in London in July 2005.

There was never any military threat to the UK from Iraq. We thus had a choice, even if we chose not to exercise it but simply to follow Washington's lead. If, however, the U.S. administration continues to militarize international relations, we might well find ourselves in a situation in which we no longer have the luxury of reflection and even limited choice, but are forced to respond with military action to genuine threats or even material damage. An aggressive American foreign policy coupled with even a small amount of diplomatic ineptness, miscalculation, or insouciance could, even without any specific malign intent, bring about a large-scale military conflict that would not be optional for any of us. One clear result of the invasion of Iraq has been to make it much more likely that any state interested in preserving its independence will try to acquire nuclear weapons. After all, the lesson which the war in Iraq taught any astute observer was that nonnuclear states, like Iraq, are at risk in a way in which equally obnoxious states that possess nuclear weapons, like North Korea, are not. Any nuclear conflict in the Middle East, even if we were initially not at all involved in bringing it about, would confront us with forced choices none of which would be pleasant to contemplate.

One of the few bright spots in this gloomy prospect is the emergence of China. China is now a major industrial power, and represents a huge market. It has a strong interest in the acquisition of advanced technology, in the training of the next generation of its engineers and technicians to the highest possible standard, and in the stability of international institutions that would give form to a genuinely polycentric world. There has already been a significant increase in the last few years in the number of Chinese postgraduate students in the UK as a response, apparently, to the increasing restrictions placed on them in the United States. Strong bilateral economic and educational ties between the EU and China would have as their natural concomitant a diplomatic rapprochement.

A further reason to think that greater political cooperation between the EU and China is possible is that China over the last decade or so has been one of the least internationally aggressive of the major powers. China's recent economic development has been meteoric; it clearly has an interest in a stable, peaceful international order within which that development can continue in an uninterrupted way. The remarks I made at the beginning of this essay about the propensity of governments to try to transform the world so that their peculiar strengths have maximal purchase applies here too. China, with its huge, disciplined, culturally self-confident and increasingly well-educated population and its expanding, ultra-modern infrastructure, doesn't need war, but can afford to sit back and wait until the "natural" operation of the neoliberal international economy diverts to it an increasing share of the world's wealth.

I'm not suggesting that China will come to be the singular *"hegemon"* of a new world order. Rather, my proposal is that the pattern of a world organized into one, or two, *hegemones* surrounded by a cloud of clients is one which, whatever might have been its analytic virtues in the past, is no longer a good reflection of reality. The position of *hegemon* that the United States and the Soviet Union respectively could play in their two spheres in the 1950s, and that for a brief period in the 1990s Washington thought it could monopolize—if not *omnium consensu*, at any rate *nemine obstante*—is one that is no longer accessible to anyone. If British politicians in the 1950s learned from Suez that we were too small and weak to be capable of waging war against the wishes of the United States, they also overgeneralized the lesson, internalizing the glance over their shoulder toward the Potomac in a way that was, even in the second half of the twentieth century, excessive, and is now completely unwarranted by the structure of the contemporary world, stultifying for the national imagination, and crippling for British foreign policy. Changes in the world mean that in 2006 we had more freedom of maneuver than we might have expected in 1956. To be sure, making use of that freedom requires negotiating our way through a complex political field in which we cannot be sure always of getting our own way, but then what else would one expect?

One can see the beginning of what might be possible in the convergence between France, Germany, Russia, and China in the Security Council debate on the so-called "second" resolution on Iraq. No individual country or coalition of countries can at the moment prevent Washington from undertaking any military action it wishes to initiate, but the refusal of the Security Council to endorse the war against Iraq had the effect of imposing the cost of the invasion and occupation directly on U.S. and British taxpayers. The prospect of having to pay *ourselves* for further optional military interventions like the one in Iraq should certainly have a dampening effect on British enthusiasm for them. Given that the U.S. economy is now largely dependent on investment from China, Japan, and Saudi Arabia, and in particular on massive Chinese purchase of U.S. state bonds, similar considerations might seem to apply. Will China continue to have an unlimited appetite for supporting the maintenance of a foreign military apparatus that might be used against its interests? The shift of even a small part of Chinese investment from the United States to the EU, if managed deftly so as to avoid a financial collapse, could contribute significantly to bringing about a more equitable, stable, pluri-centric international order based on more realistic assessment of the world as it now is.

Those who would claim that there are limits on the possibility of closer relations between China and the EU because of differences in "values" are, of course, completely right. There are limits, and we should be aware of them. Equally, however, one must point out that a country which maintains a system of extra-judicial prison camps like that at Guantanamo Bay, which in many of its constituent states continues to apply capital punishment—overwhelmingly to members of racial minorities—which refuses to join the International Court or sign the Kyoto Protocols, which tolerates extensive private ownership of firearms and seems unashamed of lacking any systematic form of national health care or medical insurance, and whose population shows a statistically high rate of deep attachment to religious beliefs and observances—to name only a few especially striking features—is *also* a country whose value system is at variance with that of the EU, and with which *unconditional* cooperation is inappropriate. There is no need to idealize either the United States or China, and no obvious reason why Europe could not deal with both Washington and Beijing (and Moscow, Delhi, and Tokyo, for that matter) as befits its *own* interests, in the light of its own political and moral values and its own judgment about what would be best for the world as a whole, and within the limits of what is possible, given the great differences that exist between these large and diverse political entities.

The major question that will face all of us during the next decade, then, is the way in which inevitable U.S. decline will be managed. Will the outcome be apocalyptic? A nuclear exchange with China? Merely "very violent," like the French withdrawal in Algeria in the 1960s? Or relatively peaceful? To say that Washington has a prima facie short-term interest in making the world a more dangerous place is not to say that it will necessarily act on that interest. Whether or not the temptation can be resisted depends on a variety of factors, many of them not under anyone's control. Europe, however, may be in a position to make a significant contribution to world peace by making it absolutely clear that it will refuse to enlist as a foot soldier in defense of parochial American economic and political interests. Maximal explicitness on this point is imperative to prevent a miscalculation by the U.S. government. Stronger ties with East Asia will give this stance added weight.

The course set by the Bush administration (and supported by the Labour government) clearly points to the grim possibility of a future comprised of a never-ending series of intensifying, ill-conceived military interventions and ripostes. If Blair and his successor succeed in convincing people that there was no connection between the London bombings and the invasion of Iraq, and in focusing attention exclusively on the "evil ideology" of Islamic fundamentalism, the UK is doomed to a cycle of violence and repression both at home and abroad, from which it will be extremely difficult to exit. It is not at all clear that there is anything effective that can be done to prevent Europe from being drawn into the maelstrom Bush and Blair created. If, however, there is a way forward at all, it seems to pass through Brussels.

There are, it would seem, a number of concrete steps that can be taken. The first is to free ourselves from certain illusions that have their roots in correct perceptions of what is now the past, but are no longer well grounded: Europe today has no serious external enemies against which it needs conventional military protection beyond what it can easily provide for itself. NATO as originally conceived has become pointless. In addition, the United States of 2004 is not the United States of 1944, or 1964, but a political entity which is in every respect (except in its a highly limited kind of high-tech military power) a much weaker international agent. We in Europe must accept this new situation, and make the appropriate arrangements in our politics. Condoleezza Rice promised to "punish" France for its opposition to the invasion of Iraq. Did this take place? If it did, how is it that I did not notice? What use exactly would "smart bombs" be to the United States in any *realistic* attempt to "punish" France?

Another concrete step that could be taken is to foster further European integration, including a more active British role in helping to animate common institutions, and in particular a closer ideological integration of the new member-states of Eastern Europe into the project of creating an EU capable of taking an independent political stand in the world. This EU project has received two severe, but not fatal, blows during the past decade. The first was Blair's support for the invasion of Iraq, which split the Union seriously, and the second was the vote against the "constitution" in France and the Netherlands. There is no reason to believe that the rejection of the constitution, which looms as such a large political fact at the moment, will have any long-term effects. Most of those who voted "no" have made it sufficiently clear that they were not voting against European integration, but against a very heavy-handed attempt to impose by means of a highly flawed document a particular political structure on Europe which they thought was undemocratic, economically inadvisable, and ill-thought-out. The superficial high drama of "constitution-making" ought not to obscure the fact that it is historically extremely unusual for any kind of lasting political structure to arise through a single foundational act. This should not be a point that requires lengthy elaboration in a country like the UK, which has never had a written constitution. The architects of the Common Market had deep skepticism about the political value of high-flown documents announced with a great flourish, and put their trust instead in a long, slow process of small, almost imperceptible steps, each one in itself locally uncontroversial, that would gradually bring about a dense network of interdependence and an increasing convergence of interests and perceptions among the European peoples. There is no reason to think that this process has suffered a setback; no sizeable sector of the Dutch or French population wishes to withdraw from the EU. In the long, and even in the medium, term the economic and political advantages of European integration are as evident as they ever were, and the forces that would move us in this direction are as strong as ever.

The main problem in the EU at the moment is, frankly, still Britain, whose recent foreign policy decisions have made the worst Gaullist nightmares seem benign. De Gaulle feared that in case of conflict, Britain would always opt for its own national interest against the collective interests of the Continent. The war in Iraq has shown that the two major British political parties are fully capable of breaking EU solidarity, in order to do something that is manifestly contrary to the UK's own clear national self-interest, all for the sake of maintaining the illusion of a "special relationship" with the United States. Fortunately for us, although not for the population of Iraq, the invasion was such a clear catastrophe that it is less likely that a British government will commit itself to that particular kind of folly anytime in the near future, but it would be worthwhile for the sake of our own future to try actively to break with the bad habits of the past as much as possible and enter fully into the project of deeper political integration in Europe. The European Union could clearly survive complete British withdrawal, and although that would be an own-goal for the UK, it would at least have the advantage of simplifying the task of reconstructing the EU as a coherent, weighty political presence on the world stage. In the larger scheme of things the goal of European integration is probably more important than the specific question of whether or not the UK remains a member of the Union, although it would be best not to have to chose.

One final concrete step we can take is to encourage the EU to intensify the process of cultivating strong economic and diplomatic ties with China in the interest of collaboration on the long-term goal of demilitarizing international politics.

[handwritten margin note: Weber: Not good or evil but "freedom"]

Realism in politics does not mean trying to engage in the utterly incoherent task of thinking about practical politics while abstaining completely from making value judgments. It is a value judgment of a kind to think that a world in which the use of extreme military force is routine is, other things being equal, less good than one in which the use of force is uncommon. Realism does mean that one does not think about politics merely in terms of moral categories like "evil" or vague aspirational concepts like "freedom," but that one starts, as Max Weber taught us, from action and its consequences. Who has what power to act in what way, who has a motive to act in what way, and what will be the consequences of adopting one, rather than another, course of action? Realism is not compatible with basing one's foreign policy on unconditional subservience to a *hegemon* who no longer has the power to protect us, and whose illusions endanger us all.

III

Moralism and Realpolitik

PHILOSOPHERS ARE AT a serious disadvantage when it comes to understanding politics, and it is a disadvantage that results from the very pe-
culiarity of their special vocation and training. From almost the very
beginning of its existence as a distinct activity, Western philosophy has
been committed to certain principles of at least minimal self-awareness,
clarity, coherence, and consistency of thought, speech, valuation, and
action. Socrates, who notoriously took no part in city politics beyond
what was strictly required of him by his obligations as a citizen, also
started philosophy down the path of exhortation to *individuals* as the
focus of the philosopher's attention.[1] The irreducible core of the message
traditional philosophers had for the peoples of the world for the past
two thousand years was a maxim with three parts: "(First), *You there,*
think about what you are saying and doing, (second) don't contradict
yourself, and (third) act on the results of these reflections." Philosophers,
to be sure, did not in general think of themselves as preachers of a new
religion, and so they didn't think their basic maxim was a revelation
handed down from on high. It was not a freestanding imperative imposed on recalcitrant, struggling humanity from the outside, but was in
some way rooted in human nature, or reality, or society and history, or
human experience. The basic, tacit presupposition of the philosopher's
activity is that "basically"—whatever "basically" eventually turns out to
mean—people want to know what they are doing and they don't want
to contradict themselves. Clearly this assumption is on to something important about some aspects of human life, but equally clearly, especially
if classical psychoanalysis is at all on the right track, it isn't universally
warranted in anything like its simple form, and it requires very significant
qualification before it can be used as anything like a guide to a proper understanding of much human behavior. One doesn't, however, even need
to appeal to psychoanalysis to see the limitations of the philosopher's

---

I am particularly indebted to Zeev Emmerich and to Richard Raatzsch for discussions of
the topics treated in this essay, a shortened version of which originally appeared in *Journal
of the Royal Society of Art* (September 2008).

[1] Plato, *Apologia Socratis* 31c4–32a3; 29c6–30c1.

built-in bias in favor of self-knowledge and consistency, at any rate when it comes to collective human action.

In the run-up to the invasion of Iraq, a group of experts on the Middle East met with Tony Blair to warn him of the possible untoward consequences of a decision to invade. The situation in Iraq, they claimed, was complex, and it would be easy to upset the delicate balance that existed between the various political, religious, and national groups; one would have to have a very clear idea of what one planned to do, how one would organize the occupation and reconstruction of the country, and so on. Blair is said to have listened with evident lack of interest and increasing annoyance, and to have repeatedly interrupted the experts with the rhetorical question, "But Saddam is evil, isn't he?"[2] In his own later formulation, his political credo was "All I know is what I believe," where "believe" is not so much an epistemological, as a religiously based moral category, the equivalent of George W. Bush's "gut feelings." Some philosophers call these "moral intuitions"; they are construed as strong, relatively unreflective, individual moral reactions that individuals have to specific situations.

"Moralism" in politics is the view that the distinction between good and evil is clear and easy to discern to all men of good will, that is, to all those who are not themselves morally corrupt, and because this is the case, it is inadvisable to try to get too detailed an understanding of any given situation. Merely accumulating factual knowledge, one might argue, is not in itself making a moral, much less a political, judgment. Starting from this claim one might go on to assert that too much knowledge could actually be politically dangerous in that it could divert attention from the really important task of taking a clear moral stand. Excessive knowledge of the details, except in so far as it concerns the implementation of a decision already made, might tend to obscure the bright line between the side of the angels and the forces of evil, or to undermine one's resolve. The genuinely admirable moral agent sees the salient moral features of a situation quickly and immediately, faces up to the situation resolutely, and acts decisively to implement his "intuitions."

A politics centered around this kind of moralizing has some strengths, among which is the fact that it does mirror the structure of certain emergency situations in which we sometimes find ourselves. Sometimes we really cannot avoid choosing under great pressure of time in an irreversible way between alternatives imposed upon us by the world in which we live. Emergency situations, of course, really do exist, but one should also not overlook the fact that it is often in the interests of particular politicians to present certain non-urgent situations as "emergencies," for instance in

[2] Jonathan Steele, *Why They Lost Iraq* (Tauris, 2008).

order to prevent extended scrutiny of the policies they wish, for whatever reason, to adopt in these situations. Despite its advantages, then, as a basic attitude toward politics, the moralizing way of thinking also has very significant weaknesses. It encourages people to misconstrue what are in fact conflicts of interest as matters of principle; it inclines them to project a rather simpleminded binary distinction (good/evil) even onto situations which are by no means simple or unambiguous; it devalues understanding, tolerance, readiness to compromise, and the attempt to find new modes of living and acting in which existing forms of hostility will be defused. There may be situations of great danger and urgency in which this dimming of the light that our cognitive faculties can throw on the world is something we must tolerate, but the moralist characteristically fails even to see that this is a price we are paying. Without the imaginative deployment of our cognitive apparatus we are blind. The most valuable kinds of political imagination are precisely those that depend on both empathy and an ability to envisage concrete changes to the present situation rather than on direct moral reaction to the surface properties of events. Unwillingness to get a cognitive grip of the details of the given situation is unlikely in the long run to be a good thing. Finally, the moralizing approach tends to assign potentially infinite value to the struggle against certain (often rather arbitrarily determined) visible forms of evil. If the task at hand is of infinite importance, some fabrication of evidence, suborning or intimidation of civil servants, infliction of "collateral damage" on innocent populations, etc. are forgivable offenses. What weight, after all, could a few lies have compared with success in defeating Global Evil?

Still, few would consider this primitive moralism of *mere* intuition to be a fully adequate account of the ethical dimension of human action in all cases and in all respects. There must be at least some minimal role for reflection, foresight, comparative assessment of different possible plans of action, etc. Internal consistency of speech and coherence between speech and action are also, in one form of another, recognized as minimal conditions of morality. One must, it is often thought, at least, apply to oneself the standards one's intuitions cause one to impose on others.

Charges of inconsistency are frequently leveled in politics against individuals and governments. Thus, at the end of April 2003, spokesmen of the U.S. government warned the Islamic Republic of Iran against trying to expand its influence in Iraq. The United States, they asserted, would take the high moral line and resolutely oppose the evil of "foreign interference" in the internal affairs of a sovereign country. Given that the United States had just invaded Iraq (against the explicit will of the Security Council), toppled its internationally recognized government, and was occupying its territory with a large military force, many commentators pointed out that this delicacy on the issue of "foreign interference" seemed surprising. Many wondered whether a policy that combined a unilateral invasion of a sovereign country with preaching to others about the importance of the principle of noninterference in the affairs of other states might not be said to exhibit some kind of moral deficiency, regardless of the "intuitions" on which it was based, because it is so inconsistent. Similarly, it might be seen as problematic that Tony Blair's claim that he desired to fight the good fight against evil was subject to such striking variations in its intensity in different cases. This impulse had a particularly powerful hold on him in cases in which acting on it coincided with his view about what would advance his own interests. Thus, in the case of Iraq, he expected a politically useful "Baghdad bounce" after a quick military victory. On the other hand, the flame of his righteous indignation did not seem to burn as bright when it came to issues that were not part of his project for self-promotion, such as effective condemnation of Guantanamo Bay, of "extraordinary rendition," of dodgy British arms deals with Saudi Arabia, or the implementation of his own government's ban on tobacco advertising in motor sport (after a large donation to the Labour Party by the Chairman of "Formula One" racing). So either Blair's differential moral intuitions about Saddam Hussein's penal system, on the one hand, and Guantanamo Bay, on the other, were put into practice only after they had been fed into a complex decision process in which a result was reached by some process involving a careful calculation of the potential benefits and costs of various forms of action, or Blair's moral intuitions were themselves the result of a prolonged exposure to the formative effect of sustained ratiocination directed toward determining what courses of action would be most likely to advance his own interests. In either case, the sharp distinction between moral "intuitions" and the results of reflective processes on which the significance of "intuitions" is supposed to rest is corroded. A third possibility, that there was a pre-established harmony between Blair's moral intuitions and what would be of benefit to him, would require one to believe either in preternatural good luck or in some kind of divine providence. As a devout Christian, perhaps Blair believed in providence, but for those without this faith the third possibility is implausible.

One reaction one might have to the above is to see in it a mere further indication of human frailty or hypocrisy. That people do not always live up to the moral standards they publicly affirm (or even to the standards they genuinely espouse) is not news. Failure of consistency of action is often not easy to recognize, and ignorance is then a kind of excuse. Perhaps it is right to extend the benefit of the doubt to the U.S. officials who lectured Iran in 2003 by assuming that they were genuinely so obtuse and provincial that they did not see any incompatibility between the doctrine they preached and the policy they were pursuing. Even the fact that politicians knowingly violate principles of moral consistency need not be thought to discredit either the valid standing of these principles or the necessity to be seen to be complying with them, and this necessity itself might be of some political importance. Even a figure as apparently incapable of shame as Tony Blair at least had the decency to try to give the impression of being slightly embarrassed when the details of his transactions with the chairman of British "Formula One" racing became public knowledge. None of this, one might think, is really relevant to the general question of the role of morality in politics.

The above reflections are very plausible, but they still seem to leave the philosophical question open. Is consistency in the human sphere really so important? After all, politics is primarily about action, and only secondarily about thoughts, beliefs, or reasons. Consistency, however, is most naturally construed as a formal property of systems, as lack of contradiction between the parts of such a system, and contradiction is paradigmatically a relation that holds between propositions or the respective contents of beliefs as articulated in declarative statements: "Saddam Hussein has missiles capable of reaching London" or "Saddam Hussein does not have missiles capable of reaching London." Consistency of beliefs is, of course, not unimportant, and it is the object of the distinguished traditional philosophical discipline of logic; but some, including notably Kant and his followers, have thought it at least equally important for human life to exhibit not merely an internal consistency in thought, but also some kind of consistency of action and coherence between thought and action. There is a strong tendency to construe that coherence on the model of a logical relation between two statements, because what better model do we have than logical consistency? However, "actions" don't always come packaged as determinate propositions, whose formal relations of consistency or inconsistency with other propositions is, if not easy to discover, at any rate possible to investigate. Actions are not propositions, and they have to be described and interpreted to turn them into propositions. However, even a correct description of an action is not that action itself. In addition, the process of interpretation by which a description is assigned to a particular action is by no means a trivial or unproblematic one. This is true even if the "action" in question is the action of making an explicit verbal statement, because in order to understand such statements listeners will almost certainly need to fill in much of the necessary background from the context. That always leaves room for different ways of understanding these statements. "I am your friend" and "It is not the case that I am your friend" is a contradiction (provided "I" and "you" refer to the same people in the two cases), but have I obviously contradicted myself if I say I am your friend, but then refuse to lend you money in some particular situation? I may simply be

[margin annotation: Actions ≠ Propositions]

hard-hearted and stingy. If I say I will help you, should you "really" need it, does that mean I will do *anything* to help you, or that I will help you even if I come to realize you have become involved in a dangerous but shady transaction? This is one of several fatal flaws in approaches to ethics that put overwhelming weight on consistency as a sufficient condition for morality. For them to be plausible, it would have to be the case that every human action always came, as it were, with a visible tag attached, an explicit statement which clearly specified the nature of the action in question and the reason the agent had for performing it. That, however, is not the way human action works.

To repeat, the very idea of "contradiction," taken strictly as a logical term, has no direct application to actions. This is not a point about logic, but about human action. Two actions can, of course, *conflict* in any number of ways. To use Kant's example, two brothers, Lord X and Lord Y, may both be good Christians in that each wants what his brother wants: Milan. They can both "want Milan" (i.e., want to possess and control the city), and they can fight, either diplomatically or militarily, for control over it, but an action does not in itself become even a candidate for standing in a relation of contradiction or noncontradiction with another action until both actions are artificially "prepared" by being described in a canonical way. It is not the physical shock of Lord X's and Lord Y's cavalry in the Po Valley which constitutes a "contradiction" but the description of that shock in a very particular way. It is no contradiction to say that Lord X's cavalry were trying to move from point A to point B, and encountered Lord Y's cavalry, who were trying to move from point B to point A. To speak of a "contradiction" one would at least need to describe what was happening in a statement like "Lord X is trying to make it the case that he (reflexive, i.e., Latin: *se*) controls Milan and that Lord Y does not control Milan" and "Lord Y is trying to make it the case that he (*se*) controls Milan and that Lord X does not control Milan." Note how complicated and convoluted this formulation is, but note also that even this complex interpretative process has not visibly generated anything that one could call a contradiction. Lord X has a completely coherent project and so equally does Lord Y. To generate a contradiction one would have to move out of the real world altogether, in which Lord X and Lord Y are two distinct persons, and attribute the conjunction of projects of Lord X and Lord Y to the same person, say Z. About the hypothetical Z then one might say that what he wants is a contradiction: that Lord X control Milan and not control Milan, and that Lord Y control Milan and not control Milan. What status does this hypothetical Z have?

Some have wished to approach this problem by following what seems to have been Kant's view. Kant (falsely) took it to be the case that any agent, or at any rate any agent who was acting freely, always acted on a quasi-propositional "maxim" which he (or she) could clearly formulate, and this formulation gives one an appropriate canonical description of the action, which can then be tested for consistency with other possible maxims. Thus a person who commits suicide might be acting on the maxim "If the continuation of life promises more pain than pleasure, I will shorten it."[3] Kant's reasons for holding that people must be seen as generally acting on maxims that can be thus clearly and univocally formulated are buried deep in some of the more implausible recesses of his rococo metaphysical views about the nature of freedom, and have no plausibility without the support of these metaphysical views.[4] To readers of Gide, Camus, Freud, Joyce, and Svevo, and to anyone nourished on a diet of films by Godard, Bunuel, and Antonioni, it must seem extraordinary in any case that anyone could ever have held the view that real human agents who are acting freely are always acting on maxims.

At best, then, the above considerations suggest that agents can (sometimes) be treated *as if* they were acting on any one of a variety of explicit maxims. The status of this "as if" is completely unclear, and it is also unclear whether the inherent indeterminacy it designates is something that can in principle be overcome or something deeply rooted in the nature of human action. In fact, barring further metaphysical assumptions, the "as if" just means that other people can attribute to agents such "maxims" i.e., such purportedly canonical descriptions of action. Just as other people can describe my action in a variety of ways, so, too, I can describe my action in a number of ways. No one description, not even one I honestly give of my action myself, can claim any absolute canonical status. So it is a political struggle how the particular description of some relevant action is produced, who produces it for what purpose, and what its exact content is.

Action, then, has to be conceptually "prepared" (in the way a taxidermist "prepares" a specimen, i.e., treats the corpse of an animal before stuffing and mounting it) in order to put it into a form in which it is even potentially in contradiction (or not) with other similarly "prepared" statements about actions. This "preparation" takes the form of giving the practice or action a specific description. Without such a description, notions like "contradiction" have no purchase, but this shows that the real work in criticism is being done by the specific kind of description being given of the complex under discussion, not by the principle of "noncontradiction."

---

[3] See Immanuel Kant, *Grundlegung zur Metaphysik der Sitten* (Hartknoch, 1785), pp. 53–54.

[4] See Rüdiger Bittner, "Maximen," in *Akte des 4. internationalen Kant-Kongresses*, ed. G. Funke (de Gruyter, 1974).

Furthermore, apart from the difficulties just mentioned, what is supposed to be so wrong about contradicting myself? I might well have empirical reasons in particular situations for not contradicting myself. For
instance, if I promise to give you £10, and then refuse for no good reason to honor that promise, I have done something reprehensible, but the
reason I have done something reprehensible is not self-evidently that I
have contradicted myself, rather than that I have disappointed you in an
expectation I have caused you to have acquired. Similarly, suppose I am
very hungry and know that I need food urgently. I see a loaf of bread,
but instead of eating my fill, I for some reason form the two contradictory propositions "This bread is to be eaten" and "This bread is not to be
eaten." Perhaps I have a paranoid suspicion that the bread might be poisoned by my malicious neighbor. In this case I might eat the bread, not
eat the bread, or engage in some complex activity designed to express the
contradictory nature of the two propositions. Perhaps I wolf the bread
down, and then cause myself to vomit it back up immediately, or pull the
bread toward my mouth, but then push it away before eating it. If I perform any of these bizarre actions, I am probably acting to harm myself
(unless my paranoia is justified and the bread really is poisoned), but the
reason for that is not that my behavior can be described as contradictory,
but that I am not getting the bread I need. The very clumsiness of the
description I have given of this imaginary situation is, I would submit,
itself an indication of the inherent looseness of fit between propositions
and actions.

The more we move away from the glassy realm of explicitly formulated
propositions, on the one hand, or of immediate and urgent imperatives
to act, on the other, for instance, as we enter the realm of the imagination, of human desires, ideals, emotions, hopes, projects, the more clearly
we enter the world which most of us inhabit much of the time. Here
things are left indeterminate, contradictory beliefs are entertained, trains
of thought are left unfinished, conflicting emotions are tolerated (or even
enjoyed). This is the world of Virginia Woolf, but also of the Montaigne
who wrote: "Tant y a que je me contredits bien à l'aventure, mais la
vérité . . . je ne la contredy point." "As much as I might occasionally happen to contradict myself; the truth I never contradict."[5]

These difficulties, and some others, have motivated some simply to
throw up their hands, abandon moralizing approaches to politics altogether, and turn to "realism."[6] The whole apparatus of appeals to

<hr>

[5] Michel de Montaigne, "Du repentir," in *Essais*, ed. A. Micha (Flammarion, 1969),
vol. 3, p. 20.

[6] "Realism" in political theory is a term that is used for a wide variety of different positions. I use it in what follows to refer to the more hard-edged versions of realism. The

"values," moral principles, or ideals, the "realist" holds, is mere window dressing. Power and material self-interest are all that matter. Everything else is mere pretext for the increase of power and the advancement of one's own interests. The only limits are what you can get away with, so it is not surprising that so many politicians are adroit and vigorous in the employment of the moralizing flannel, but their high-minded discourse is of merely instrumental significance. On the "realist" view, when a contemporary government deploys the effectively vacuous vocabulary of "freedom," "democracy," "international community," "human rights," the only cognitively relevant thing going on is that it is trying to advance its power and the material interests of its real constituents, usually a small group of stratospherically wealthy representatives of the world of business, finance, and industry.

One insurmountable internal difficulty with realism is the difficulty in specifying what is meant by a "material interest" or indeed "power." If "power" means, as it is surely natural to take it as meaning, "ability effectively to get things done," then political scientists are right to distinguish at least two distinct kinds of power: the "hard power" of standing armies, police forces, courts and prisons, agencies that can, if necessary, force recalcitrant agents to act in a certain way, and "soft power," the ability to get things done by less directly coercive means: persuasive talents, the ability to grant or withhold economic or other benefits, the influence that arises from exemplary action that invites emulation. One kind of power is sometimes incompatible with another. Thus the Red Cross has the effective power to do various things, e.g., visit prisoners in war zones, in part precisely because it has no coercive apparatus at its disposal, and thus cannot possibly be a significant "hard-power" participant in conflicts. Which powers do governments always seek to maximize? To answer: "hard power" seems wrong. One of the first things New Labour did when it came to power was to transfer from itself to the Bank of England various by no means insignificant powers to regulate the British economy. To answer: "soft power" seems to invite back in through the scullery door those moralizing conceptions (exemplary action, reputation for rectitude, high purpose, and so forth) that the realist had originally ejected through the front gate.

"Material interest" is also an accordion-like concept the extension of which can be expanded or contracted almost *ad libitum*. Is the propagation of French as an international language a "material interest" of the French Republic? Is the support of Orthodox communities in the Balkans a "material interest" of the Hellenic Democracy? For the "realist"

"realism" I myself defend in my *Philosophy and Real Politics* (Princeton University Press, 2008) is not of this hard-edged sort.

thesis to be illuminating it would have to be the case that one could in some way specify what sorts of things were "material interests" prior to and independently of seeing what sorts of things political groups actually pursue. Otherwise one would run the risk of the kind of circularity one occasionally finds in theories of human action: States always act to further their material interests; in cases in which they appear to do something, X, which is *not* in their material interests, this appearance will turn out to be an illusion, because why would they have done X, if they did not think they had a material interest in X? One might think of this argument as instantiating an illicit shift from (a) "Whatever states do must be in their material interest because why else would they do them?" to (b) "States always do those things which can independently and antecedently be identified as being in their material interest." Or in some other versions of the argument one might encounter a shift from "States always do what *is* in their material interest" to "States always do what *they think (or believe)* is in their material interest." Are "material interests" supposed always to be so easy to discern that error is rare, so that one need not distinguish what truly is in someone's (material) interest and what that person takes to be in his or her (material) interest? If not, whose perception is supposed to be definitive? In general, if one allows the extension of "material interests" to be too wide, then anything would seem to count as a material interest and the realist scheme provides no genuine understanding. On the other hand, if the concept of a "material interest" is taken in too narrow a way, for instance as bread, medical care, and housing, then the claim that governments *always* pursue material interests is surely false.

The most important political philosopher of the twentieth century, Max Weber, thought long and hard about the relation of moral conceptions to the responsible business of real politics.[7] Weber thought that anyone who wished always to have tidy solutions in politics had made a bad mistake in choosing to be born as a human being. This is not an incitement to nihilism, but merely a remark about a common misunderstanding of the nature of politics. Even to think about politics as *exclusively* a collective attempt at "problem-solving" is a huge mistake. There may be some subordinate parts of politics, especially the highly routinized subareas of administration, that do look very much like standard problem-solving. Question: How to reduce traffic in the city without extra cost to the city government? Answer: Impose a congestion charge. Here there is a relatively clear difficulty (congestion) that can be described fully beforehand, and one can also antecedently specify the conditions which a "solution" would need to satisfy. Sometimes the solution to a problem

---

[7] Max Weber, *Politik als Beruf* (Duncker und Humblot, 1977).

can have the character of a singularity. Weber, in fact, was a particular admirer of what he called "*qādi*" justice, the informal arbitration exercised by a local judge (Arabic: "*qādi*") in some Islamic countries.[8] A *qādi* did not mechanically apply an existing written legal code, but used a wide variety of practical skills acquired through years of experience to confront what were often clearly unique and unrepeatable situations and change them so that they satisfied the relevant parties. How often do *two* feuding women each claim to be the mother of the same infant? So rarely that no existing code is likely to cover the case. Who then should get charge of the infant? The *qādi* would be the person to decide, and a good *qādi* would make a good decision. Weber thought that *qādi* justice, like the remarkably non-rule-bound justice practiced by genuine democracies such as that of ancient Athens, or some modern revolutionary tribunals, often "worked" admirably. It was often significantly more able to produce outcomes that really satisfied the contextually specific interests, and were compatible with the deeply held values, of all the participants, than more formal legal systems would be. Really significant political action, however, is action that, for better or for worse, neither simply conforms to existing rules, nor intervenes, like a *qādi*, to find craftsmanlike solutions to specific problems, but that changes a situation in a way that cannot be seen to be a mere instantiation of a preexisting set or rules. It creates new facts, violates, ignores, or even changes the rules. Such action may, like significant, original art, be extremely rare, but the fact that such disruptive change of the existing systems of action is always at least a *possibility* is one of the things that gives politics its special character.

Part of what politics is about is that we wish to be and live as people *of a certain kind*. We want to be good colleagues, good company, good Christians, good Europeans, or whatever. This means, among other things, deciding what role "moral" considerations, the pursuit of power, and the realization of what we take to be our material interests will play in our lives. In deciding this we are also deciding about the shape of the world into which the next generation will be born, and thus, to some extent, what sort of people they are likely to be.[9] In some very limited contexts honesty may be the best policy, and being a good team player, a pillar of righteousness, an honest broker, etc. may be materially profitable, but often it is not, and, in any case, we return to the question, what does "material" mean?[10]

---

[8] Max Weber, *Wirtschaft und Gesellschaft* (Mohr, 1972), pp. 157–58, 470–76, 563–66.

[9] This Nietzschean idea entered English-language ethics briefly in the work of Stuart Hampshire, particularly in his *Thought and Action*, but seems to have fallen out of fashion again.

[10] See Bernard Williams, *Truth and Truthfulness* (Princeton University Press, 2002), esp. chapters 3, 4, and 5.

What kind of people we want to be and how we can become those people are not really questions that are best described as "problems" because they lack the determinateness "problems" have. It is also completely unclear whether they have or do not have a "solution," or indeed what "solution" would mean in this context. We make it up as we live with as much intelligence and practical skill as we can muster with, if we are honest, little sense of completion, closure, or apodictic certainty.

Ethics is usually dead politics: the hand of a victor in some past conflict reaching out to try to extend its grip to the present and the future. There is nothing inherently wrong with this. Our past is an essential part of what we are, which we ignore at our peril. We could not completely leave it behind even if we wished to do so; but recognition of this necessity gives us no reason to romanticize it. Nothing stops us from making our own moral judgments on our past, on our present way of life, or, proleptically, on future action or its probable outcome, although the further away from present contexts of action we get, the less of a grip our apparatus of moral reflection will give us on the situations we encounter.[11] One should not, however, confuse trying to refine our moral categories with trying to understand what is going on in the world in which we live. There is nothing wrong with cultivating our own moral intuitions, but for them to have any value they must be minimally connected with the cognitive apparatus by which we track the world as it is. There is certainly no guarantee that the fit between these intuitions, which we in any case have reason to believe are historically highly variable, and the way the world is, will always be smooth and comfortable,so it would behoove us to be on our guard against trusting them too blindly.

[11] Bernard Williams, *Ethics and the Limits of Philosophy* (Harvard University Press, 1985) pp. 160–67.

IV

On the Very Idea of a Metaphysics of Right

SINCE THE VERY IDEA that there could be a "metaphysics" of "right" is by no means self-evident, what would motivate someone to think it was possible, advisable, or necessary to develop such a thing? One suggestion is the following: We notice that conceptions of "right" change dramatically from one society and era to another. Thus Roman law was based on a distinction between free persons and slaves. Slaves were considered to be "in the power" of their owners: they had no legal personality at all (*nullum caput habent*), and could be killed by their masters with impunity. The way this is expressed in one important Roman legal document is illuminating:

> In potestate itaque sunt serui dominorum. quae quidem potestas iuris gentium est: nam apud omnes peraeque gentes animaduertere possumus dominis in seruos uitae necisque potestatem esse. . . . Sed hoc tempore neque ciuibus romanis nec ullis aliis hominibus qui sub imperio populi romani sunt, licet supra modum et sine causa in seruos suos saeuire.[1]

> [And thus slaves are in the power of their masters. This power derives from the law of peoples, for we can notice among all peoples equally that masters have the power of life and death over their slaves. . . . But nowadays neither Roman citizens nor anyone else who lives under the rule of the Roman people may legitimately behave savagely toward his own slaves beyond measure and without cause.]

This passage is striking to a modern reader for three reasons. First, it affirms as a general legal principle that masters may kill their slaves.

I originally wrote the draft of this essay for a conference on Kant's *Metaphysik des Rechts* at the University of Tours, but was prevented by illness from attending that conference. Since my recovery I have had the opportunity to discuss and improve the draft as a result of discussion in the "Cambridger Philosophisches Forschungskolloquium." I am greatly indebted to my colleagues in that institution: Manuel Dries, Fabian Freyenhagen, Richard Raatzsch, and Jörg Schaub, and especially to Christian Skirke, who "presented" the text for discussion on that occasion.

[1] *The Institutes of Gaius*, translated with an introduction by W. M. Gordon and O. F-Robinson, with the Latin text of E. Seckel and K. Kuebler (Duckworth, 1988), i. 52 (p. 14).

Second, it "grounds" this in what it claims is something like an observed universal law of all peoples. And third, it then notes a change in what is considered to be "right": it is now no longer considered to be permissible simply to kill one's own slave for no reason. Most contemporary European theorists think that slavery is not conformable to "right" at all, and they are then tempted when looking back at older Roman practices that permitted masters to kill slaves to say something like: "It may have been legal at the time, but it was still, even then, not conformable to 'right.'" They may then further be tempted to think that what is "right" must be specified relative to a rule—this is by no means a self-evident truth—and that they need to ground or justify this rule in some way. One can't easily see how this can be done by reference either to any form of positive legislation or to a *consensus omnium*—the Romans appealed to *that* to justify slavery, after all. If, therefore, one wishes to continue to hold that beneath the visible welter of highly diverse and contradictory historically instantiated legal codes and opinions about what is "right" there must be one correct answer to the question what "right" requires, an answer which can be justified with certainty and thus known to hold always and everywhere, it is tempting to posit some hidden universal feature shared by all people, whether they know it or not, which could serve to ground a certain, universal, definitive doctrine of "right." Since nothing empirical seems to have the requisite properties (universality and ability to serve as a justification for definitive judgments of right), the doctrine sought must have the character of a "metaphysics." Kant thinks he has found such a universal, right-grounding feature in a metaphysically construed concept of "freedom," as when he writes:

> Das Recht ist also der Inbegriff der Bedingungen, unter denen die Willkür des einen mit der Willkür des anderen nach einem allgemeinen Gesetze der Freiheit vereinigt werden kann.[2]

> ["Right" is the epitome of the conditions under which the free choice of one person can be combined with the free choice of another according to a general rule of freedom.]

I wish to object to three aspects of Kant's position. First, I object to the very idea that it is possible to give a final, definitive "justification" (*Letztbegründung*) of any set of "rights" (or, for that matter, of any other claim, although I will be concerned only with claims about what is "right" in this essay). Various rights-claims can be justified in particular contexts, for which the notion of "justification" is clear, but to ask for a justification apart from *any* context, and that is what the Kantian request

---

[2] Kant, *Metaphysik der Sitten*, in Kant, *Werk-Ausgabe* (Suhrkamp, 1977), vol. VIII.

for an "ultimate" justification amounts to, does not make sense. Second, I wish to suggest reasons for thinking that Kant's doctrine of freedom is implausible. Third, I wish to object to a certain general way of looking at human society which is, it seems to me, an integral part of the Kantian worldview and which predisposes people who accept it to find other parts of the Kantian position plausible. This is what I will call the "rule-governed" view.

I will start with the third of these. One can look at certain human interactions in two distinct ways. If I look into a room and see two children seated before a board consisting of squares on which are placed some stylized wooden figures, I might say either of two different things:

a) A game of chess is in progress.
b) The children are amusing themselves in there perfectly amiably.

Similarly, in a large room in a court building various people, some oddly dressed in horsehair wigs, are speaking in turn and passing papers around. I may say:

a´) The trial of a commercial dispute is taking place in there.
b´) Mr. X is trying to get the better of his rival Mr. Y.

In both these cases, the first description describes the interaction as an instance of a set of rules, principles, or formal procedures ("chess," "trial") and the second does not, but rather cites the motives, intentions, and goals of the agents involved, the general way they are interacting ("amiably"), the powers they are trying to exercise, and so forth. One can try to approach human societies *in general* by emphasizing the first kind of description or by focusing on descriptions of the second kind. I'll call the first way the Kantian or rule-centered approach. This approach begins from the observation that most human societies do not seem to be merely random collections of individual events, but that these events seem to exhibit certain regularities. In southern England people drive on the left side of the road; when one crosses the Channel, however, they all suddenly begin to drive on the right-hand side. In France, people who sit down to eat together often say "*Bon appétit*," in Croatia they say "*Dobar tek*"; in Britain they say nothing. It might seem tempting then to think that an especially good way of understanding a society consists in construing it as a set of events that can and should be described and understood relative to a closed, unchanging system of rules. Much recent political philosophy, especially work that has been deeply influenced by Rawls, is an instance of this approach. The second approach I wish to distinguish has a very long pedigree going back at least to Thucydides and continuing through to the so-called "realists" in the modern academic discipline of "International Relations." This second approach is centered not on rules but on human agency and power, the agency of individuals and groups. I'll call it the agent-centered view.

If one proceeds in the first of the two ways I wish to distinguish, the underlying idea is that just as a particular game of chess can be best understood as a particular, concrete enactment of certain ideal rules which all other games of chess also enact, so there are some rules that all social interactions in that society instantiate, and understanding these rules constitutes in some sense the final framework for understanding that society.

It is important to be clear about what part of this claim is controversial and what part is not controversial. It is, I think, not controversial, or at any rate I am not interested in denying, that there might well be certain well-defined sectors of highly advanced industrial societies that can be seen to approximate such a closed system of rules, for instance, the legal system in a modern Western European country, or the system of university qualification. Such systems usually operate by being institutionally insulated and separated from the rest of society, and so, if one takes a temporal slice at a certain time and ignores the way in which such rules and the mechanisms for enforcing the rules are historically modified, they have a certain property of fixity and abstractness. To be sure, there are a number of profound and deeply puzzling questions that were raised by the late Wittgenstein about the very coherence of our notion of "following a rule." We usually think of a rule as marking out something like a path or track, which can be conceived as continuing indefinitely in an inherently determinate and fixed way into the future;[3] we then try to understand how agents come to perceive and follow that track. If this way of thinking about "rules" is incorrect, it would seem obviously to have very significant and almost certainly utterly destructive consequences for various traditional philosophical approaches, particularly for any form of Kantianism.[4] Despite these serious philosophical difficulties, I am not *in this paper* primarily concerned with attacking the very idea of following a rule or with any conception we might have of what it means to "follow a rule." Rather what interests me here is the further claim that one can sensibly extrapolate from individual cases of rule-governed subsystems to the society as a whole, and say that one can get an adequate understanding of the society *as a whole* by construing it as a single, huge, rule-governed system. From the fact that individual sectors might be amenable to description as rule-governed, it by no means follows that the same kind of claim can be made for societies as a whole. Inference from individual cases to the whole might be a kind of tempting illusion.

---

[3] See Ludwig Wittgenstein, *Philosophische Untersuchungen* (Suhrkamp, 1971), §218.

[4] I am especially grateful to Richard Raatzsch for helping me get an initial, minimal grasp on this Wittgensteinian point.

Thus, to take an example that was keenly debated in France during the nineteenth century,[5] it might well be possible in a highly developed commercial society to construe large swathes of human activity as the result of contractual agreements between individual agents or corporations, but this presupposes the existence of a more encompassing framework for agreeing on and enforcing such individual contracts, namely some rather complex system of communication, shared expectations, and some form of police and judiciary, and that framework could not itself be construed as resulting from mere prior agreement between individual agents. The "*liens sociaux*" that ultimately hold a society together, give it coherence, and make it possible to reach and rely on agreements made with others could not themselves be simply objects or results of some further contract. This is implausible for any number of reasons, among them because there would be no answer to the question, who would enforce such a contract?

It is important to distinguish between rules (in the sense in which I will use the term), regularities, and laws-of-nature. The notion of a regularity is simply that of a sequence of events that recur in a fixed order. Every time I get on the bus to go into the center of town, a certain man might get on that bus at the next stop to go into the center of town. That would be a regularity but it is neither an instantiation of a law-of-nature, nor of a rule, unless he decided each time to get onto the bus *because*, as we would say, I was on it. Rules are in some sense less than regularities and in some sense more. Thus, in traditional English grammar no sentence is to end with a preposition, and most educated speakers try at any rate to observe this rule. However, speakers, even native speakers, end sentences with prepositions all the time. We think of laws-of-nature as having a property of necessity. Thus if I am allergic to a certain kind of pollen, smelling a flower will make me sneeze. If humans are completely deprived of water for any significant number of days they will die. There is something in the nature of the entities involved, in this case in the biological configuration of humans, that brings it about that without water they die. The rules of chess do not have this character, but rather they are guides to action or to the evaluation of action. The rules of chess do not describe what always actually does occur. Beginners may well fail to observe them correctly; and if unscrupulous players do not try to violate them more often, for instance by trying to advance a pawn three squares on one move or by moving a rook diagonally, this is only because the rules are relatively simple and failure to conform to them is highly visible. At a certain point if too many rules seem to be violated, we might wish to say that the two people sitting at the board are not "really" playing chess,

---

[5] See Emile Durkheim, *De la division du travail social* (PUF, 1986).

but doing something else. That, however, is a separate issue, and it would seem a hysterical reaction to insist that two people are not playing chess on the mere grounds that one of them once made an irregular move. It is not so much that the rules of chess *are* in fact instantiated in most actual games of chess (although they usually are), as that, as we are inclined to put it, they "*should*" or "*ought to be*" followed. The players themselves must activate and instantiate the rules, although they could in principle do something completely different, such as play go, jointly admire the cat, discuss a recent book, or what have you.

Some philosophers have thought that there are different kinds of rules that might be exhibited in any given human society, and they have also thought it important to keep a clear distinction between these different types of rules. Thus, there are instrumental or prudential rules which we follow in trying to negotiate our way through the world. Examples would include such rules as "Eat lots of fruit to remain healthy." Then some philosophers think that there is a class of specifically moral rules and that these have a different structure. "Thou shalt not kill." Some add to this that these moral rules hold categorically or absolutely, and that the fundamental evaluation we should make of any human being is an evaluation of the extent to which that human being follows the rules of morality. Finally, there are legal rules, which in the first instance refer to ways in which people are enjoined to act subject to certain potentially co-ercive sanctions imposed by a specific designated social mechanism (the system of courts and judges). And, of course, there are any number of further kinds of rules.

One kind of rule-governed approach is an approach that succinctly reifies a set of rules as a bundle of "rights" and attributes these "rights" to certain members of the society. So if I have a "right" to the ownership of a certain piece of property, this means that people who might wish to do various things involving this piece of property will need to structure their behavior in certain specific ways if they wish their project to be successful. What these are will depend on the specific society in ques-tion because, notoriously, "ownership" designates a bundle of different rights—the right to use, the right to buy and sell, the right to control access to, etc.—the specific content of which varies greatly from society to society. In most recent Western systems, if I own a certain piece of land, this ownership can be associated with the rule "If you want to cross Raymond's land, first get his permission." To say that this is a rule is not to say that everyone will always follow it, or even that certain con-sequences will definitely follow from violating the rule—you may think you can cross without being discovered, or that I am a sufficiently relaxed person that although I have a formal right to prevent you from crossing, I will not be concerned to make use of that right, or that the system of policing and administration of justice is sufficiently inefficient to make punishment unlikely; and you may be right. This does not, on the other hand, mean that the claim that a "rule" exists floats completely free of the specification of *some* concrete existing mechanism for enforcement. The police, courts, and judges may not always and infallibly succeed in enforcing, or even attempt to enforce, the rules, but there are in the given society some sociological and institutional facts to which one can point to ground the ascription of the rule in reality. Even if the police are thoroughly corrupt, they swear an oath to enforce laws that are written down somewhere, they receive a regular salary, etc. The empirical basis may be paper-thin—one man in the village gets to wear a white armband if he makes a public promise to try to prevent people from grazing their goats in other villagers' gardens—but that does not mean it is nonexistent.

Many people think there is a further important distinction that must be made between rules people think they *do* follow (although perhaps not absolutely invariably: I do brush my teeth twice a day, but could I swear I have *never* once lapsed?) and rules they think they *should* follow (whether they in fact do or not: for instance, I think I ought to be kind even to obnoxious people, although I know I rarely am). I will call this distinction a distinction between rules of the first kind or type and rules of the second kind or type. Some of these rules of the second type may be enshrined in documents, canonical works of religion, philosophy, and literature, or legal codes. Having made this distinction, one can then further introduce the idea that we might say of certain groups of people that they thought they should follow rules which they ought not to follow. Thus, to return to an example from the ancient world, people did not merely treat slaves differently from free persons, but also thought they should treat slaves differently, and this "should" was grounded in a complex set of accepted rules, expounded at length in legal and philosophical documents which had canonical status. A modern looking back would say: They *thought* they should act in this way, but they ought not to have. This is a third kind of rule, one against which some observer measures the second-type rules the members of some given society accept (as the rules they "should" be following, even if they are not). In some exceptional cases, I may myself be able to adopt the position of the "other person" looking on at myself and my society and asking if type two rules are the ones I (and we) should be using.

If one decides to construe society relative to a set of rules, then, a number of different questions arise that need to be answered. I will distinguish three kinds of question: First, given that any number of distinct sets of rules are conceivable—in some countries (England and Japan, for instance) people drive on the left, in others (France and Italy, for instance) they drive on the right—how is a decision to be made on which set exactly is to be adopted? One might object to this that it seems to presuppose a fundamentally incorrect view of a human society. It seems to suggest that the rules people in a society follow are "decided on," but in many case this seems a completely inappropriate model, and the rules that exist seem to have been established by processes that seem to have a larger element of accident or to resemble biological processes of "natural selection."

Second, how does it actually come about that the given rules are instantiated? I will canvass two possible accounts of this. Either the agents all have an "internal" positive motivation to instantiate them, or they are externally enforced. One cannot press this distinction too far for reasons that I think are obvious, because part of the way in which external forms of enforcement work, if they work at all effectively, is by transforming themselves into internal motivations. The third kind of question concerns ways in which one can try to assess or evaluate the rules. One can ask whether they are efficient, serve their purpose well, are compatible with various moral intuitions, etc.

Proponents of the rule-approach ring changes on giving answers to these questions. There is, however, a second possible way of seeing a society. On this second view a society is not a closed system of action-events according to fixed rules, but a set of agents who have certain powers, beliefs, and interests. Social life is the action and the results of the action of agents and groups of agents who have various powers, and develop and exercise these powers through time in the pursuit of their interests and in accordance with various beliefs they have, including perhaps what we would call "moral" beliefs. The interaction in question is a series of the encounters of such agents and groups of agents with other agents and groups and with nature. Agents may *or may not* act in a way that instantiates a set of rules (in any interesting sense). One may immediately worry that the two "alternatives" I propose—the rule-centered approach and the agent-centered approach—are not really co-relative. The first alternative seems coherent enough, but the second might seem simply to be a grab bag of wildly different things, including views that emphasize agency, views that focus on power, views that *deny* with the late Wittgenstein that rule-following is a normatively determinate matter, and so forth. These do not, one might think, represent an alternative *theory*, but simply a way of gesturing at a variety of different kinds of reasons to oppose the rule-governed view.

Even if one grants that the second is not a strict single alternative but simply an open set of very different kinds of things that are held together merely by the fact that they are *not*-rules, all of the possible views the second approach encompasses will have in common that they will fail to put any emphasis on the purportedly *closed* nature of the system being described. This is an important contrast to the rule-governed model. Thus in Thucydides the Greek political world is not a closed system; "marginal" parts of it (Thrace, Sicily, etc.) come into focus and then go out again, according to the requirements of the narrative. That is, these places sometimes intervene in Greek politics (or are the objects of intervention) and sometimes are irrelevant. They are objects of interest depending on whether they are part of what happened and have to be mentioned in order to understand events, or not. As with most things of any historical significance there is probably no absolutely primordial origin of this second way of considering society, but a convenient starting point is Thucydides. His history of the great war between the Athenians and the Peloponnesians is enframed by a general account of the constitution of the major actors (the Peloponnesian Alliance and the Delian League), and the development of power in the Hellenic world. In this context he discusses the role of natural resources, the development of naval technology, and various forms of military and political arrangements, both cooperative arrangements and arrangements based on some form of domination of one party by the other, which affect the growth and exercise of power. Politics then is about exercising power to attain various ends; it is not an inherently rule-governed activity, but one better understood as the conjunction of different actors making context-specific judgments, taking advantage of unexpected opportunities, and innovating. There is nothing unnatural in exercising power (I.76), and part of the process of exercising such power might be to subject those under one's control to rules of one's choice. What these rules will be will depend primarily on two factors: first, on what the ruling power believes to be to its advantage, and second, certain traditional conceptions the ruler has about how people or cities should in general treat other cities or people. Thucydides is convinced that the first of these two is more strongly motivational than the first. So Athens, as the leader (*"hegemon"*) of the so-called Delian League, forced its "allies" (that is, "imperial subjects") to refrain from waging war against each other, and to settle commercial disputes in Athenian courts. From this perspective one can even see how certain minimal rules of equity might come to be established in particular cases within limited contexts. In a famous passage the Athenians tell their Melian counterparts that considerations of justice hold between those of roughly equal size and power (V.89). This then gives some kind of account of why certain rules hold among humans, uncluding rules which seem to instantiate justice or reciprocity. Between political entities that are relatively equal in power, some principles or rules might suggest themselves to minimize pointless mutual damage or destruction. These rules would, of course, be multiply conditional on the circumstances, and would be expected to change as circumstances change, although, of course, inertia is an enormously powerful and much underestimated force in human life, and so change will perhaps not be immediate. However, if you look at the configuration from the outside over a sufficiently short historical period of time, it might very plausibly be thought to instantiate an abstract set of principles or rules.

Note that this account gives rather clear and direct answers to the three questions that arose for the theory of rules. How do the rules get determinacy? The *hegemon* decides on one set rather than another (and he will do this by consulting some combination of beliefs about his own advantage, including considerations about what he can easily get away with, and residual traditional and moral beliefs he might have a commitment to). How are the rules instantiated? The *hegemon* (probably in collaboration with locally powerful groups) enforces them. It is sometimes suggested that this Thucydidean view is like that associated with the later philosophical school of Positivism, and that he does not permit the possibility of moral evaluation, but that seems clearly wrong. In the passage cited Thucydides allows the Athenian representative to give a perfectly coherent evaluation of Athenian actions that has resonance with various traditional Greek values. He says that Athenians were more self-restrained and moderate than they needed to be, and for that they deserve praise. It is hard to see this as anything but a moral evaluation.[6] One might say that one of the things one can learn from Thucydides is that the extent to which politics is rule-governed *or not* is itself an important historical variable, but not a completely independent variable, because its value is in part dependent on the relations of power that exist between the given agents who constitute the relevant "system" in question. The extent to which the rules will be the outcome of agents trying to instantiate traditional moral conceptions or the result of their attempts to act on their own interest is also historically variable, and overwhelmingly dependent on the level of relative power that exists. The "rules," then, are an epiphenomenon, not a part of the basic structure one would need to understand.

Lenin, who very definitely belongs to the tradition initiated by Thucydides, defines politics with characteristic verve when he says that it is concerned with the question that keeps recurring in our political life: "Who whom?" ("кто кого?") What this means in the first instance is that the impersonalized statements one is inclined to make about human

---

[6] The question of the role of moral evaluation in Thucydides is much more complex than my discussion here suggests. Thucydides' work is, after all, like a work of imaginative literature in that it contains within itself speeches which are attributed to various historical agents. It is no more obvious that one can attribute to Thucydides everything one of these agents is reported to have said than that one can attribute to Diderot everything Rameau's nephew says in the eponymous novel. I have a further brief discussion of this issue in my *Outside Ethics* (Princeton University Press, 2005, pp. 226–29).

societies are actually statements about particular concrete people doing things to other people. Although Lenin's formula is basically correct, it is perhaps too dense and needs to be developed or extended: actually, I would argue, it needs to be extended twice. First of all, the formula should read not merely "Who whom?" but "Who [does] what to whom for whose benefit?"

The second extension of Lenin's formula is connected with another important feature of our social life. We relate to other people not merely in terms of what they have done to us or are doing to us, but also with regard to what they *could* do to us. If I have certain effective powers, these may have a sufficiently intimidating effect on others that I get my way without ever needing actually to exercise these powers. To think politically is to think about agency, power, and interests, and the relation between these.

To be sure, the concept of power is in need of further analysis. It seems most enlightening to construe "power" as in principle connected with general concepts like "ability to do" (such as that I have the power of speech or of locomotion), rather than as designating exclusively a form of coercion (such as "the hostages remained in the power of the gang until they were freed by the police") or domination ("the Athenians reasserted their power over the island of Chios"). One cannot treat "power" as if it referred to a single, uniform substance or relation wherever it was found. It makes sense to distinguish a variety of qualitatively distinct kinds of powers. There are strictly coercive powers you may have by virtue of being physically stronger than me, and persuasive powers by virtue of being convinced of the moral rightness of your case; or you may be more powerful than I am by virtue of being a charismatic figure who is able to attract enthusiastic, voluntary support from others, or by virtue of being able to see and exploit a strategic, rhetorical, or diplomatic weakness in my position.

Despite their manifold differences, followers of Kant in contemporary political thinking are exponents of a rule-guided view, which I will try to reconstruct as an interconnected set of four claims:

a) There is such a thing as Reason as an autonomous faculty that operates centrally with rules and principles such as the principle of noncontradiction, and the results of the operation of which have the epistemic properties of categoricity, aprioricity, universality, etc.

b) In some sense Reason can be the Hegemon, i.e., it has some powers of determining rules, some authority, and some motivational force for all human thought and action.

c) Because of a metaphysical connection between Reason and freedom, the enforcement of the rules that have their origin in Reason does not have the property of being truly coercive.

d) There is such a thing as a (Kantian) Right, which is something like a reification of a set of rules of what I have called the third type. This Right can be the object of study, and one can use the result of such a study to criticize particular moral conceptions or legal codes in a determinate way that will have validity for everyone (i.e., for whatever is the contemporary equivalent of "all rational agents").

This Kantian view is subject to a number of interconnected objections, the cumulative effect of which is to make it difficult to see how one can continue to find it plausible.

First of all, as mentioned above, there is a general line of criticism of the whole notion of reason as "a rule-guided activity" in Kant's sense of that term. One of the strongest versions of this criticism depends on the late Wittgenstein's account of rules and rule-following. The details of Wittgenstein's view are highly controversial, but whichever way one understands Wittgenstein's argument, it seems lethal to all approaches based on some Kantian notion of society as a closed set of events taking place according to rules. Note, too, that Wittgenstein-style arguments about rule-following do *not* seem obviously fatal to approaches based on power and agency. If part of the objection to traditional (and Kantian) accounts of rule-following is that they do not allow us to understand how one could know when one was following the rules correctly and when one was not, *this* criticism does not hold for approaches based on power and agency. If the Athenians impose a set of rules on their subjects, we do have a criterion and thus can know whether the allies have followed the rule or not. The criterion is whether the Athenians accept the bit of behavior as rule-conforming or not. One can tell that rather easily: If the Athenian say nothing and continue to deal with the allies as they always have ("business as usual"), they have accepted what the allies have done; if they send ships out to burn the city and enslave the population, citing as their reason violation of one of their rules, they have not accepted the bit of behavior as conformable to the rules.

A second objection is perhaps related to the first without necessarily being quite as strong. For a Kantian approach to function Reason has to be universal to all agents in a sufficiently determinate form to constitute a possible complete framework for human life. This seems simply not to be the case for human beings. If one takes a realistic look at human life as it is actually lived, it is not even obvious that minimal principles like that of noncontradiction have straightforwardly universal application to it.[7] When

---

[7] See Michel de Montaigne, "Du repentir" and "De l'experience," in his *Essais*, ed. Alexandre Micha (Flammarion, 1979), vol. 3, pp. 20–33, 275–328.

Catullus writes that he loves *and* hates Lesbia, he is describing something which we have no difficulty in recognizing as an important feature of significant areas of human life and experience. To be sure, perhaps we have good reason to avoid direct contradiction in some restricted areas of *legislation*, but even if that is true it is not clear that it indicates anything about the universality validity of noncontradiction rather than something about the nature of specific forms of the institutionalization of human action and the limited nature of "legislation." That legislation should not contain contradictions might in other words indicate that legislation is not a good model for human life as a whole. Kant assumes rather than demonstrates that human action should be seen as a kind of legislation. To put this point in a slightly different way, there seems to be a gross mistake at the center of Kant's analysis. From the fact that in lots of empirical contexts it makes sense for us for any number of, mostly very contingent, reasons not to contradict ourselves, it is then concluded that noncontradiction is an absolute value in all contexts.

My third objection is that even if one grants that "Reason" is a human faculty which is in itself capable of yielding a sufficiently *determinate* set of rules and principles, it (and the rules it generates or endorses) has no automatic authority over human life, and the degree of motivational power it has will be highly variable, highly dependent on the context, and often extremely small. The distinction I have in mind between "authority" and motivational power is the following: If I am trying to decide what to do about a certain pain I have in a portion of my body, I can haruspicate, scry, try to cast my own horoscope, or consult a priest, a solicitor, a tax consultant, a random passer-by on the street, or a medical doctor. The notion of "authority" is connected with that of the relevance of one or another of these procedures. Depending on my purposes and my other beliefs I might think, for instance, that the medical doctor has "authority" in this case, or at any rate more authority than a lawyer or a tax accountant. From the fact, however, that I recognize the medical doctor as having a certain kind and degree of authority in cases like the one in question, nothing follows about how much real motivational power the consultation will have for me. There is nothing out of the ordinary, incomprehensible, or unheard of for me to find that I have no particularly strong motivation to believe or do what an acknowledged authority on some subject proposes to me in a "professional" capacity. I might have any number of what we would usually call "perfectly good reasons" to ignore the well-meaning and well-informed advice of experts. Why should my attitude toward the assertions of purported experts in moral and political "rationality" be any different?

Note that for the purposes of discussion here I am adopting a Kantian style of argument, assuming we can speak of "Reason" as if it were an *agent* who determines one thing or another. The basic terms in this area, however, are, and ought clearly to be understood to be, adverbial ("he acted rationally [in *this* context]"), not substantival. Actually, of course, Reason doesn't determine anything. In fact it is always some particular person or institution who speaks in the name of reason. Particularly in politics, it is, therefore, always apposite to think about and try to analyze the relations that exists between, on the one hand, the identity, situation, powers and interests of the person or institution which is making the claim to "speak with the voice of reason," and, on the other hand, the nature of the concrete claim-to-reason which is actually being made.[8]

If I have correctly interpreted the basic Kantian claim about "right," then one can see his concept of "right" as deriving from his concept of freedom. "Freedom," however, is anything but an uncontroversial concept. I would like now to discuss two distinct non-Kantian ways of thinking about freedom. If either of them has any plausibility, the Kantian notion of "right" will have to be abandoned.

The first alternative comes from Marx. In the English-speaking world we are used to following the lead of Isaiah Berlin and distinguishing two concepts of liberty, a "negative" concept that understands liberty as the mere absence of (external) obstacles or impediments to action, and a "positive" concept that has to do with self-governance, where that is construed as the ability to decide for oneself what to do or to give oneself the rule for one's own action. Berlin's distinction between positive and negative liberty was notoriously an integral part of his attempt to defend liberalism against various forms of socialism during the period of the Cold War. "Positive" conceptions of freedom—this is Berlin's central claim—have often been misused, and the basic reason for this is that the idea of freedom as giving oneself a rule for one's action allows one to introduce notions like that of "rationality" into the very nature of freedom itself. To be free, then, comes to be identified with "being rational" or following given rules, and coercing someone to follow rules can, then, with a certain amount of sleight of hand perhaps, be seen as "forcing them to be free." To prevent this a nontotalitarian society must, Berlin maintains, cling austerely to a purely negative conception of freedom.

Rather than following Berlin down this path to minimalist liberalism, I would suggest that Marx has a more sophisticated and cognitively superior account of freedom, one which deserves more attention than it has received. Marx distinguishes not two but three concepts of freedom. The first is one that is very much like Berlin's "negative liberty."[9] Marx con-

---

[8] See Montaigne, "De l'experience."

[9] See Marx and Engels, *Die deutsche Ideologie,* in MEW (*Marx-Engels-Werke* [Dietz, 1962]) 3.285–86.

nects this with a certain kind of philosophical and political anarchism—he is thinking specifically of Max Stirner—but you could equally think of it as the "freedom" of libertarianism.

The second concept of freedom Marx distinguishes is the ability a creature has to make its own decisions, or govern itself.[10] This is what Marx calls "bloße Selbstbestimmung des Willens selbst ohne jedes Resultat" and which he identifies with Kant's view. Kant, of course, is himself quite explicit in holding that the "freedom" he discusses is such a mere ability to determine the will; whether or not what I freely decide to do will in fact even be translated into actual action in the world is something about which I can have no knowledge, but is at best an object of a "postulate" of practical reason.

The third conception of "freedom" is the materialist notion that identifies it with power. "I am free" means "I am free to do . . . ," and that means concretely that I have the power or ability to do. . . ." To be more exact, Marx seems to think of the full notion of freedom as comprising the conjunction of the ability to determine what one will do and the power to do what one decides to do. Anything less than this is not freedom, but a mere shadow of that concept.[11] This part of Marx's analysis breaks dramatically with the account which Isaiah Berlin will eventually give of the concept of freedom. Berlin does not even countenance the possibility of construing freedom as power, but rather counts "power" as belonging not to liberty but to a wholly different subject, namely the conditions under which liberty can effectively be used.

Why should any one of these different concepts of freedom have priority over the others? I would like to suggest that Marx's third possibility ought not to be dismissed out of hand. After all, what reason would anyone have to be interested in freedom at all as a human ideal or aspiration if not that it is thought to be connected with actual attainment of something? I can, however, only really attain X if I have the power to attain X. No one actually wants to be *merely* externally unimpeded or self-determining.

The second alternative to a Kantian view of freedom can be found in the works of Rabelais: At the end of the so-called Picrocholine War, which is described in detail in *Gargantua*, King Gargantua wishes to reward Friar Jean for his good services by founding an abbey for him which will accord with his taste.[12] This institution is to be the very opposite of

---

[10] See MEW 3.176–78.

[11] See MEW 3.287.

[12] See François Rabelais, *La vie treshorrificque du Grand Gargantua, Pere de Pantagruel. Livre plein de Pantagruelisme*, in *Oeuvres completes* (Gallimard, 1973), ed. Guy Demerson, chapter 52.

an abbey according to any existing monastic rule, for instance that of Saint Benedict. The Rule of the common monastic life attributed to Saint Benedict is a text devoted to the practical task of organizing a common life for a group of humans who accept certain fundamental Christian doctrines. One of these is the doctrine of original sin. Original sin means that human will is corrupt, and any independent exercise of it is sinful. Monastic life gives a framework within which to some extent one can overcome this, by cultivating "humility" and subordinating one's will completely to the Rule (*regula*).[13] Thus, when Brother X says the canonical prayers at the canonical hour, there is a sense in which it is not the corrupt will of Brother X which is determining to say a prayer at this hour, but the Rule working through him. One becomes free from determination by one's own corrupt individual will, if one simply follows the rule blindly and undeviatingly.

The Abbey of Thélème is founded on exactly the opposite principles.[14] It is based on a conception of freedom which takes freedom to be an inherently non-ruled-governed form of behavior. We might say that I am free when I am spontaneous, but Rabelais prefers to say that free action is action not guided by fixed rules but by "bon sens et bon entendement," which is a judgment of what is *appropriate* in the circumstances in the individual case at issue.

Of course, Thélème is a utopian construct. Still, is there not *something* about it which makes it closer to our normal intuition about *Selbstbestimmung,* about a spontaneous, positive freedom which is not rule-governed, at any rate not governed by pre-given rules that can be specified with a high degree of context-independence than Kant's view is? The claim that there is an inherent connection between freedom and rule-governed behavior in Kant is simply a result of highly particular features of his metaphysics, particularly his views about causality.

In fact, humans have constantly shifting and deeply contradictory attitudes and desires, which we can render seemingly constant and consistent only at a very high price, a price few moderns are willing to pay. The realization of this is perhaps the most important thing that divides us, but it divides us *forever,* from a world in which the Kantian philosophy could be taken seriously.[15] We can't generalize all our maxims successfully, and

---

[13] Benedict, *The Rule of Saint Benedict,* ed. Justin McCann (Burns Oates, 1952).

[14] Rabelais, *La vie treshorrificque du Grand Gargantua,* chapter 57.

[15] "Bei der Anwendung von Prinzipien sollte man sich vor Durchbrechungen nicht scheuen. Man muß sich immer ins Gedächtnis rufen, daß man bei der Errichtung derselben zwar hinreichend viel Gründe besaß, aber daß dies doch nur hieß, daß die Gründe die Gegengründe überwogen. Durch Durchbrechungen läßt man diese zur Geltung kommen." Bertold Brecht, *Schriften zur Politik und Gesellschaft 1919–1956* (Suhrkamp, 1973), p. 178.

we don't have to. I can easily disapprove of and oppose a proposal to introduce gladiatorial games in the twenty-first century and yet remain neutral or even positive about them in Rome. My relation to Rome is not practical. Humans are not compulsively generalizing, or, if we are, we are also capable of seeing that this is a compulsion, not an argument. Or rather, we don't have to, *unless* we have to, that is, unless there is some specific reason about the kind of structure in the external world which we are trying to realize that makes a certain level of generalization necessary. One should not, however, confuse a "necessity" that has a complex origin in the practical relation of humans to a highly contingent world with the sheer necessity of logical noncontradiction.

Of course, no one would want to prevent human agents from trying to bring their own moral beliefs into some kind of order, and making of them a "system." However, it is important not to confuse this rather narcissistic activity with anything that might be called trying to engage *cognitively* (in the widest possible meaning of that term) with the real world.

Perhaps the psychological anarchy of desire and velleity that we find expressed in Rabelais and theoretically elaborated in the work of Montaigne could not serve in an unmediated way to "ground" a political order. But then, perhaps the whole idea of "grounding" a political order in the way in which one can "ground" a deductive inference by reference to premises from which it follows, is a misconception. We have a world of agents with different powers and with highly context-dependent views about how it is good for people to deal with one another. Most of us agree that wanton killing of the innocent is not a good way to deal with the world, although the exact meaning of this belief is unclear. What counts as "wanton"? What as "innocent"? If forced, we could probably come up with something further to say about why wanton killing of the innocent was not a good idea. Some parts of our argument for this claim might depend on reference to the consequences of permitting or forbidding this kind of action; other parts might refer to the way in which this prohibition fits in with other things we believe. The very idea of looking for an "absolute" ground to this does not make much sense.

I don't expect that the above remarks will actually convince people who already stand firmly in the Kantian tradition (or those who have a professional interest in rule-systems such as lawyers) to change their minds. It is a fact I fully acknowledge that the general idea of a closed form of human life guided by fixed rules—by "real rules" if at all possible, but certainly in any case subject to "ideal moral rules"—holds an almost invincible dominion over the modern imagination, even though in many individual cases we show ourselves very well aware of the fact that this is a fantasy. However, this idea is a profound mistake. The best I can hope is to plant the seed of suspicion about the contemporary reign of rule-systems, and perhaps suggest that an alternative way of looking at our moral and social world, as a historical configuration of differently configured agents with diverse power interacting in highly unpredictable contingent circumstances, is not excluded by the logic of our concepts.

Readers may find it strange that I discuss Thucydides, Rabelais, Saint Benedict, and Marx at relatively great length in a paper ostensibly about a concept in Kant, and that I did not expound more of the detailed internal architecture of Kant's view or engage in micrological exegesis of some Kantian texts. This way of proceeding is intentional, because I think the Kantian system is a *machine infernale* of enormous dimensions and extremely intricate internal structure with innumerable elaborate gears, cogs, flywheels, sprockets, bells, and whistles. The system operates and gains plausibility by inviting the unwary in and exhibiting a truly fascinating internal structure so that one loses perspective on the project as a whole. To change the metaphor, if one tries to shake hands with the Kantian, one can easily find one has lost an arm. In my opinion one needs to see Kantianism at virtually infinite distance, in the context of a number of views of a completely different kind, and, ideally through a Brechtian *Verfremdungsprozeß*, in order to see some major structural features of it clearly. I also think that seeing it clearly in that way will make it difficult to find it plausible, although obviously not everyone will agree with me about this.

V

The Actual and Another Modernity

Order and Imagination in *Don Quixote*

Two STRANGE FIGURES confront one another in one of those barren, timeless, imaginary landscapes in which gross anachronism is admissible. An elderly Spaniard, his hand resting on the hilt of his rusted sword, is undecided: who is the elegantly clad young man who bars his way? This unfamiliar young man is also armed with a sword. On his head he wears a plumed hat of black satin, with a white feather and gold embellishments. Nonetheless, there is a decidedly clerical look about him. Is he a nobleman? Or perhaps a cleric of some considerable standing? The Frenchman wipes his face, slightly reddened from his morning devotions at the altar of the God Bacchus. He is equally baffled. The comical eccentric who is examining him so closely is fiddling, for no apparent reason, with the visor of his old-fashioned helmet, which has been patched together from various bits and pieces. Does he perhaps intend an assault on him?

No chronicle or tale recounts this meeting between the ingenious knight Don Quixote of la Mancha and the formidable Abbot formerly known as "Brother John the Butcher" (Jean des Entommeures) from Thélème monastery, an institution founded by King Gargantua. No record exists in the *Grandes et inestimables Chroniques de l'énorme géant Gargantua*, nor in the *Segundo tomo del ingenioso hidalgo Don Quijote de la Mancha compuesto por el licendiado Alonso Ferdinández Avallaneda*. We do not therefore know the course that this meeting might have taken. But it is more than an idle thought experiment, thinking out a possible outcome for the meeting. It forces one to choose a position in the enduring debate on the nature of modernity; for since early Romantic times *Don Quixote* has been regarded as the first and archetypical modern novel, in whose structure one should also be able to read off the defining characteristics of the epoch. The belief implicit in early Romantic thought, that the

The article was originally published as "Die wirkliche und eine andere Moderne: Ordnungsstiftende Phantasie in *Don Quijote*," in *Mittelweg 36* 6, December 2005/January 2006, pp. 49–67. The translation is by Dr Keith Tribe.

analysis of a literary work did in some circumstances provide particular insight into important features of modernity, is perhaps less mistaken than it at first appears, if the constitution of modernity is itself linked to a particular kind of imagination.[1]

Different approaches do become slightly entangled here. One can first of all question whether *Don Quixote* really should be counted as the first modern novel—instead of, for instance, *Pantagruel*, which appeared sixty years previously. Is there such a thing as the "first novel"? And does it make sense to set up the history of literature as a competition over priority? Secondly, there is the claim that *Don Quixote* is the "archetypal" novel of modernity. But what indisputable features make *Don Quixote* and not, for example, *Pantagruel*, the exemplar? Thirdly, one could examine questions that relate not to forms of literary representation, but to the social world of the time. Does one understand life in modern societies any the better for viewing it through the perspective provided by the actions and afflictions of Don Quixote and Sancho Panza, or those of Gargantua, Brother John, and Pantagruel?

Ultimately one can question, from a philosophical perspective, what forms of life are actually possible in modernity, and of these forms, which conceivable alternatives might be considered preferable: an appropriate form of knight errantry, the kind of existence with which Alonso Quixano is reconciled in the book's final chapter? Or "la vie pleine de pantagruélisme"? Who, then, speaks for modernity? Don Quixote, Alonso Quixano, or Brother John?

There is today intense discussion over whether there is in fact any such thing as a unitary phenomenon of "modernity," or how such a phenomenon might be understood; but I cannot here engage with such debate in any detail. Enlightenment philosophers systematically formulated a *self-interpretation* of modernity that retains its authority today; they employed concepts such as "clarity," "lack of ambiguity," "objectivity," "sobriety," "consistency" and "reason" to characterize modern forms

---

[1] On the history of interpretations of *DQ*, see Jean Canavaggio, *Don Quichotte, du livre au mythe: Quatre siècles d'errance* (Paris, 2005). Other representative assessments: "Cervantes' novel . . . has brought into being the entire genre of the modern novel"—Friedrich Schlegel, "Geschichte der alten und neuen Literatur: Zwölfte Vorlesung," in *Kritische Ausgabe*, ed. Hans Eichner (Schöningh, 1961), vol. 6, p. 275; "Don Quijote . . . this first great novel of world literature"—Georg Lukács, *Theorie des Romans* (Luchterhand, 1963), p. 89; "Cervantes is likewise the founder of the modern era"—Milan Kundera, *Die Kunst des Romans* (Hanser, 1987), p. 12. Among the very few negative judgments is that of Friedrich Nietzsche: "*Don Q* is one of the most harmful books"—*Kritische Studienausgabe*, ed. Giorgio Colli and Mazzino Montinari (de Gruyter, 1967), vol. 8, p. 130; "damaging" certainly because of its conclusion; and also Vladimir Nabokov, who found the way that Cervantes wallowed in the portrayal of atrocities quite repulsive—see *Lectures on Don Quijote* (Harcourt, Brace, Jovanovich, 1983).

of consciousness and contrast them to earlier ones. It is thus no coincidence that René Descartes is generally thought to be the initiator and patron saint of the modern era; according to him, all knowledge depends upon *clara et distincta perceptio.* The indistinct and fantastic visions of the medieval era were to be dissolved by a luminous and incorruptible intellect, trained in analytical geometry. The bearer of this discriminating intellect, concerned with both clarity and consistency, is the modern subject: an autonomous individual who has liberated himself from all merely traditional bonds and has independently assumed responsibility for the organization of his own life. Since this individual is subordinated to the law of rational specificity, it is tempting to conceive the optimal organization of life as a form of rational self-legislation. Ideally, the modern subject lives according to clear and generalizable rules that he has himself established.

From the political point of view, the Peace of Westphalia established a system of unambiguously defined "sovereign" states in Europe, intended to replace the older, rich tapestry of overlapping competences. Every member of this rationalized state system could lay claim to a monopoly of the legitimate use of force within a specific, geographically defined territory that was recognized as such by other states. Under the auspices of a sober and mutual reciprocal assessment of historically existing possibilities and interests, modernity was increasingly characterized by the manner in which "autonomous" individuals faced "rational" states operating in terms of "reason of state."

From overenthusiastic reading of books of chivalry, we are told at the beginning of Cervantes's novel, Alonso Quixano's brain became so desiccated that he lost all reason and determined, entirely on his own initiative, to "revive the extinct order of knight errantry" (DQ II, ch. 16, p. 584).[2] Even though the hero of the book will comprehensively fail when confronted with the social reality of early modern Spain, Don Quixote's project is extraordinarily "modern." The creation of oneself from nothing, without regard to existing social conditions or supposedly "natural" facts (such as "good blood," noble birth, biological association to a particular clan, and so on)—for many historical theorists of modernity this is the modern ideal pure and simple. Don Quixote does in fact manage, by his own efforts, to promote himself into a higher social position than the one into which he was born. Of course he is at root a "Hidalgo," a man of honor to be addressed as "Señor," in fact as "Señor Alonso Quixano," but most definitely not a man of the higher nobility, no Don So-and-so from wherever (DQ I, ch. 1, p. 25). In

[2] Miguel de Cervantes Saavedra, *The Ingenious Hidalgo Don Quixote de la Mancha,* trans. John Rutherford (Penguin Books, 2000), all references to *DQ* being to this edition.

the first part of the novel he gets himself knighted by a rural innkeeper whom he is able to talk into staging the requisite ceremony (DQ I, ch. 3, p. 40). So he is in every respect a "self-made Don."

Now it is entirely possible, in fact rather probable, that the reality of early medieval Europe was no different. What later counted as an ancient house and the *non plus ultra* of "good birth" would in all likelihood go back to some bastard son or other who had been blessed by Lady Luck and a ready pair of elbows and fists. By contrast, what Don Quixote's initiative sought to renew had been no part of medieval reality, but was instead an imagined fantasy world whose literary form he had discovered in tales of chivalry. The "Knight of the Sorry Face" does not want to be like Charles the Great, Dietrich of Bern, or "Guillaume le Bâtard" (otherwise known as William the Conqueror); he wants to be like Amadis of Gaul. The stranger who one day appears at court and ends up saving the realm; or alternatively, an unassuming, plain man who puts the enemy to flight in the decisive battle—only in literature does it turn out that these figures are "really" sons of the old king, long thought to have been lost through some unlucky exploit.

Don Quixote's project is also "modern" in that his training involves neither an orientation to actually existing models nor participation in actual practices and disciplines: he simply reads books. Even if antique legend has it that Alexander of Macedonia slept with a roll of the *Iliad* under his pillow and so consciously sought to surpass the heroic deeds of Achilles; and even if in the Christian era *imitatio Christi* was at least in part communicated as an ideal to the literate—hence in the early Middle Ages the clergy—through reading; medieval knights were nonetheless for the most part illiterate, unlike Don Quixote. The literary project of individual self-creation, a program that Don Quixote pursued with the utmost energy, was a path that would not have been open to them.

Linked to this is another "modern" aspect of Don Quixote: his fetishization of the rules governing chivalrous conduct. How was it possible to work out, in a situation where the historical and social reality of chivalry had vanished, how a knight would have had to behave in the many unforeseeable constellations of modern life? How, to take just one example from the novel, should Don Quixote converse with the "two young women . . . of easy virtue" (DQ I, ch. 2, p. 32)? Alonso Quixano therefore puts together a codex of general rules and procedures for himself to which he will then slavishly adhere. So long as he follows "the rules" of his new, self-elected rank he need have no concern, and further need not trouble himself—as a good Kantian—about the likely consequences of his rule-governed conduct (DQ I, ch. 22, pp. 185–86; chs. 29, 30). Erich Auerbach has acutely pointed to the fact that Don

Quixote is never afflicted with inner doubts, indecisiveness, or moral uncertainty.[3] A good Kantian just *does not know* whether he has a free will or not. He can never be cognitively certain whether a decision that he has (apparently) made really follows from his obedience to the law, or from his own sensuous drives. Nor has the Kantian any idea whether any one of his conscious decisions will have the slightest impact upon the world. He is nonetheless quite convinced that moral law applies to him unconditionally. In a similar fashion, Don Quixote knows that he can never rely upon his sensual perceptions, for the perceptible world is ruled by evil forces hostile to him. His equanimity remains, however, unshaken by this knowledge. Even if all appearance is to the contrary, Don Quixote knows that the barber's basin that he has appropriated is really Mambrino's helmet. So he can feel quite "at home" in his world, for the division between the wise, benevolent counselor in worldly matters and the mad knight errant, between the real world and his imaginings, is so deep, yet so consistent, that both spheres can coexist without the slightest perturbation.

The enterprise upon which the Knight of the Sorry Face embarks might well be a paradoxical one, and it is almost certainly unrealizable; but I think we should take care that we do not immediately regard it as "contradictory," dismissing it in this sense as meaningless or even plain crazy. Of course, someone from the early seventeenth century cannot, unlike any reader of a historical novel, leaf back into the ninth century and live in the early Middle Ages.[4] But there is no reason to exclude the possibility that there might in the seventeenth century have been good reason for holding certain ninth-century institutions in high regard, or from wishing to revive analogous institutions that were perhaps better suited to the later century. Even Jean-Jacques Rousseau argued for the reintroduction of political institutions that had arisen in the ancient "free states" of the Mediterranean world, but which had disappeared in late antiquity.[5] Rousseau's opponents might have regarded his proposition as inexpedient, above all as anachronistic, but in no respect impossible or even crazy.[6] Nor was Robespierre a Don Quixote, but a thoroughly effective actor who had to be taken very seriously in the revolutionary politics of his time. One can, without becoming caught

[3] Erich Auerbach, *Mimesis: Dargestellte Wirklichkeit in der abendländischen Literatur* (Franke, 1971), pp. 319–42, especially pp. 330–31.

[4] See also Bernard Williams, *Ethics and the Limits of Philosophy* (Harvard University Press, 1985), ch. 5.

[5] Jean-Jacques Rousseau, *Of the Social Contract*, in *The Social Contract and Other Late Political Writings,* ed. V. Gourevitch (Cambridge University Press, 1997), book IV, ch. 5.

[6] Benjamin Constant, "De l'esprit de la conquête et de l'usurpation," in *Benjamin Constant: De la liberté chez les Modernes,* ed. Marcel Gauchet (Denoël, 1980), pp. 186–95.

up in any contradiction, individually, consciously, and "planfully" seek to bring about a social condition in which people live less consciously, less planfully, and less individualistically, just as one can, without any inconsistency, plan and execute a change in one's own character that excludes any possibility of any such future planful alteration.[7] Whether an intended alteration is desirable or not is determined by reference to the concrete individual case. There is no foundation for the charge that plans of this kind would disqualify themselves on account of their inherent *logical* faults. Consequently the objection that Don Quixote's project is a contradictory one is quite invalid. In actuality such criticism is just as questionable as the familiar, allegedly contradictory, arguments advanced against suicide, or against the decision of free persons to sell themselves into slavery.

So in what sense of the word is Don Quixote mad? There is no doubt that he has rather remarkable tastes, and cultivates curious inclinations and preferences. Quite obviously Don Quixote's indifference curve is different from those of his contemporaries—and of ours. Without any pressing reason he willingly sets off for barren hills, remains there for days living on meager rations, although he could just as well have stayed at home and had his fill. To Sancho's great amazement such deprivations do not seem to bother his master at all (DQ I, ch. 25, p. 219). Moreover, Don Quixote is credulous, does not seem capable of distinguishing fiction from true stories, and is often very unrealistic when it comes to deciding between what is really possible, and what not. He suffers from *idées fixes*, unusual taboos, and unbending behavior. On top of this, he reacts very sensitively as soon as one of his mad ideas is questioned. Here he is inclined toward unexpected, sudden expressions of rage. Nonetheless, apart from the bizarre imaginings related to all things involving chivalry and knight errantry, he is peaceable and affable, a man of healthy common sense (DQ II, chs. 16, 17). "A matter of knight errantry" is a very extensive category for Don Quixote, and in such matters he is subject to serious errors of judgment. He takes a flock of sheep for a "vast army" (DQ I, ch. 18, p. 139), windmills for giants (DQ I, ch. 8), a statue for a virtuous lady (DQ I, ch. 52), various inns for castles. He stubbornly maintains through a lengthy exchange that an object lying in front of him, openly and in clear view, is a "helmet," while for everybody else it is a barber's basin (DQ I, ch. 45, pp. 418–20).

---

[7] On the concept of "character planning," see Jan Elster, *Sour Grapes* (Cambridge University Press, 1983).

Imagination and Politics

As we know, our thoughts are not always free, nor our judgments, something of which we need to be especially aware if we want to avoid having a reputation of being mad. This casts doubt on the romantic equivalence of human imagination and absolute liberty. This equivalence is founded upon a fundamental misunderstanding, for imagination constantly processes given material within a force field created by both external and internal factors. Even the most vivid imagining needs some material that comes ultimately from either actual or inner experience. Not even the most gifted thinkers and artists are able entirely to shield their imagination from the ceaseless torrent of their own desires and impulses. There are overpowering imaginary constructs of such seductive power and attraction that they can prevail for centuries against all resistance. Among these ideas, in modernity there can be found the theory of the social contract, together with its philosophical vanishing point in the form of a theory of "ideal discourse." This theory has been subjected to the most ferocious criticism advancing devastating arguments, but it will still not lie down. Quite probably this is because unusually strong human desires and interests are at play here and are linked to enduring, effective institutional arrangements, together with related patterns of thought and perception.

For a very long time religion was the lens which focused human imaginative energies and directed them to particular objects of desire. Over the millennia humanity has been interested in ever-more complex elaborations of religious delusions that also, depending on the flow of changing historical circumstances, sometimes gained political significance. In seventeenth-century Europe these fixed ideas began to be sloughed off, and they gradually lost their dominant power. The Dutch humanist Hugo Grotius prompted astonishment and disgust in equal measure when in the prolegomena to his *De jure belli et pacis* (1625) he proposed that those prevailing natural laws which engendered the system of rights and the international commerce of peoples would still be valid if one assumed that there was no God.[8] This infamous "*etsi*" clause ("etsi daremus . . . non esse deus . . .") was the subject of such vigorous debate because even Grotius's contemporaries recognized that it made possible the complete liberation of law and politics from theological and religious tutelage. Grotius's "*etsi*" construction[9] was indeed a massive theoretical

---

[8] See Richard Tuck, "Grotius, Carneades, and Hobbes" in *Grotiana* New Series, vol. 4 (1983); also Tuck's *Natural Rights Theories: Their Origin and Development* (Cambridge University Press, 1979).

[9] Hugo Grotius, *De jure belli et pacis*, Prolegemona §11.

achievement, which the occidental imagination took up and deployed against an ossified version of itself. Grotius was himself a practicing and devout Christian, although an extremely active heir to the long historical process in which Christianity had stimulated human imagination into the creation of an uncommonly demanding God: a God who, in the Christian tradition, has created all nature, so that each of its laws is at the same time His law. Hence the real historical significance of Grotius is to have first developed this Christian system of illusions in his chief theoretical work, only to mark it off and in the space that he thereby created imaginatively form a system of "natural laws" that would hold even if there were no God. Grotius's reflexive imagination opened a broad avenue that proved so very accessible that the theory of politics—at any rate in the diverse versions of social contract theory—tended, even centuries later, to settle into the same tracks, as for example with John Rawls.[10]

Imaginary constructs can under some circumstances have a force capable of creating realities that go far beyond the structuration of merely subjective spheres of action. The modern state could for instance not be ignored given the manner in which it concentrated powers in an early modern Europe that was hostage to the constant feuding of ecclesiastical, feudal, and communal authorities. The development of the state required a conceptual innovation that we are today barely able to appreciate, since it has in the meantime become part of our political theory and reality. We should not, however, forget that the artificial conceptual construct "State" denoted the supposedly abstract site of independent authority that could not be equated with the charismatic authority of a successful warlord, nor with the traditional status or actual command of a dynastic ruler, nor finally with the will of the entire population. Quentin Skinner described this as follows:

> [O]ur modern conception of the state . . . has come to embody a doubly impersonal character. We distinguish the state's authority from that of the rulers or magistrates entrusted with the exercise of its powers for the time being. But we also distinguish its authority from that of the whole society or community over which its powers are exercised.[11]

The state as first created in the seventeenth century was a conceptual construction aimed at the establishment of a new authority, and was far from being a direct expression of popular will. It was rather intended

[10] See Raymond Geuss, "Weder Geschichte noch Praxis," *Mittelweg 36* February–March 2003, pp. 76–88.
[11] Quentin Skinner, "The State" in Terence Ball, James Farr, and Russell L. Hanson (eds.) *Political Innovation and Conceptual Change* (Cambridge University Press, 1989), p. 112; and John Dunn, *Setting the People Free: The Story of Democracy* (Atlantic Books, 2005).

that it be able to prevail *against* the will of a political community. It was this partly reactionary accomplishment—the erection of a conceptual bulwark against republican theories of popular sovereignty—that was realized through the mobilization of the human power of imagination. Men should breathe life into the "great LEVIATHAN called a COMMONWEALTH, or State (in latine CIVITAS), which is but an artificiall man,"[12] They do this by furnishing this creature in their imagination with artificial powers quite distinct from the powers of "natural" individual humans, but distinct also from the power of a community conceived as a mere collection of its members. In Hobbes the close relationship between the introduction of the modern concept of "state" and absolutist politics became explicit. It also became plain that the reality of the modern state arose in part from a construction in imagination. The activated imagination is not a mere historical epiphenomenon, but instead becomes a significant constituent of a political reality formed in this way.[13]

Imaginary constructs are by no means always indistinct, nor are their outlines always unclear and blurred. Cervantes's imagination is for instance characterized by a very clear concern with disjunction. Logicians distinguish between exclusive and inclusive disjunction. The first denotes a situation in which there are two options, in which it is an open question which of the two is true or can be realized, but where it is also true that both cannot be true or realizable at the same time. "With the 20 euros that you have you can buy either a book or a bottle of wine (but not both, since the sum of money that you have is insufficient)." This case demonstrates a complete dichotomization of the possible. By contrast, the inclusive disjunction describes a situation in which it cannot be ruled out that both alternatives might be realized. "If your holiday really does last a week, then you can go to the park tomorrow or the day after (or tomorrow and the day after; it is entirely up to you)." Latin has the exclusive disjunction *aut*, for example, in Cesare Borgia's famous statement: "*aut Caesar aut nihil*"—"I wish to be either undisputedly supreme or nothing"; the inclusive disjunction is expressed by *sive*, as in Spinoza's formula "*deus sive natura*"—"You can call the origin of the world 'God' or 'Nature' or both" (or perhaps something quite different, since for Spinoza the various concepts were at root different names for the same thing, and the name is irrelevant).

The world of Don Quixote is structured by the exclusive disjunction, which is why it is subject to rigorous dichotomization: the piece of metal

---

[12] Thomas Hobbes, *Leviathan*, ed. Richard Tuck (Cambridge University Press, 1999), p. 9.

[13] Benedict Anderson, *Imagined Communities* (Verso, 1983). The book deals with the role of imagination in the creation of a "nationality," but his findings are equally applicable to the history of the nation state.

is *either* a barber's basin *or* Mambrino's helmet (DQ I, ch. 45), each interpretation excluding the other. In fact the entire novel reads like one *aut* sentence after another. As a consequence, by the end of the first part a certain monotony has set in as Don Quixote, yet again, takes a holy image for an eminent lady being held prisoner (DQ, I, ch. 52, p. 469). The second part introduces variations of narrative virtuosity on the *aut* sentence; for a change Don Quixote does not take an inn to be a castle (DQ II, ch. 59, p. 885); Sancho convinces a skeptical Don Quixote that the peasant girl reeking of garlic is in fact the enchanted Dulcinea (DQ II, ch. 10, p. 550); the lackey Tosílos takes the place of the seducer of Doña Rodríguez's daughter in combat with Don Quixote, but changes his mind once he catches sight of the daughter, throws the fight, and ruins the Duke's plans (DQ II, ch. 56, p. 866). In each of these cases the alternatives are clearly stated and it is implied that no special interpretative power is needed to judge the elements exactly: a sheep is a sheep and no warrior (DQ I, ch. 18). The world has clearly recognizable contours. Of course, contingencies might prevent us recognizing the truth when we see it, be it because it is hard to see in the dark (DQ I, ch. 16, p. 126), or because one has been deliberately deceived by others (DQ II, ch. 21, p. 628); or for some other, quite comprehensible reason. Accordingly, Don Quixote is demonstrably "mad." The moment that Tosílos removes his helmet it is quite clear to everyone else that here is the Duke's lackey, and not the "real bridegroom." Nor does the novel ever make the reader doubt that he is in possession of the truth. We are never forced to make some special effort and seek the truth by deploying the complex instruments of an elaborate hermeneutics.

The art of interpretation had not always been at such a discount. In a letter to Can Grande della Scala, Dante, for example, gave methodological guidance on the reading of his *Comedy*.[14] According to Dante, interpretation is an important and general art not simply one limited to the proper reading of written texts. The world itself is a giant work of art, authored by God. In his artistic activity the Creator makes use not only of words, but also of (historical) events. *History*—what actually happened, not the historical narrative of what happened—is God's writing. As an infinite and all-powerful spirit God endows each natural fact, and every single historical event, with endlessly different meanings that complement, rather than contradict, each other. According to Dante, God has created a *sive* world, and not an *aut* world. The proper interpretation of both nature and history consists in ever-deeper immersion in the observation of all connected events, teasing out new, previously unsuspected

---

[14] "Epistola X" in *Dantis Alagherii Epistolae: The Letters of Dante*, emended text with introduction, translation, and notes by Paget Toynbee, (Oxford University Press, 1920), p. 173.

shades of meaning. The writerly activity of the human poet, even that of the evangelist, can be nothing more than a pale shadow of the divine creative power, but it has a similar structure and aim. The *Comedy* is deliberately polysemic ("istius operis non est simplex sensus, immo dici potest *polysemos*, hoc est plurium sensuum")[15] and has in principle to be read like holy scripture. One needs to interpret both the words and the reality represented by the words ("nam primus sensus est qui habetur per literam, alius est qui habetur per significata per literam").[16] In this way many interpretations are formed, layered one on the other and congruent one with another. "Exitus Israel de Aegypto" means both the exodus of the children of Israel from Egypt (considered by Dante a historical event) and "allegorically" our salvation through Christ ("nostrum redemptionem factam per Christum"). Moreover, the expression denotes "in a moral sense" the turning of our soul away from sin and its entry into a state of grace ("conversionem animae de luctu et miseria peccati ad statum gratiae"),[17] while other "true meanings" would be revealed to the attentive reader. In God all these various interpretations find their unity; everything comes together harmoniously, even aspects of reality that might seem to us discordant, incoherent, or inconsistent.

For Dante the interpretation of the human world is a complex, fraught affair, for the intentions and resolutions of men are not immediately apparent to us. Even God's judgments are not self-explanatory. Why, for instance, does the suicide of Caton of Utica *not* lead to his banishment to hell? Only through close attention, repeated reading, reflection, prayer, and the like can one gain deeper insight, and one has also to wait on God's mercy to gain wider perspectives. By contrast, even more intensive scrutiny of the barber's basin in *Don Quixote* will avail neither the Knight of the Sorry Face nor the assembled travelers; nor would more exact examination reveal any divine truths. In Cervantes things are what they seem, and that is that. This impoverishment and restriction of interpretative plenitude by comparison with medieval hermeneutics[18] is perhaps the first step along the path that in the twentieth century led to positivism. That is certainly not the only path, selected by God, nature, or "history," upon which one could have set out in the seventeenth century. François Rabelais's writings, for example, point in the direction of a completely different modernity. Rabelais knows, unlike Dante, Descartes, or Cervantes, of no foolproof method, no *fundamentum inconcussum* of knowledge. Authority not susceptible to doubt is completely

---

[15] "Epistola X" §7.
[16] Ibid.
[17] Ibid.
[18] Michel Foucault, *The Order of Things* (Pantheon, 1970), pp. 29–33, 47ff.

alien to him. If pressed, Rabelais would recommend the "oracle of the bottle" ("drink")[19] or the rule of Thélème monastery: "DO WHAT YOU LIKE" ("FAY CE QUE VOULDRAS").[20] Rabelais did not share Dante's confidence that "ultimately" all interpretations would harmoniously fit together, nor was he interested in a strict dichotomization of the world.

The Death of Quixote

The closing pages of *Don Quixote,* Part Two provide what many readers consider to be the most disappointing reading experience in world literature. Alonso Quixano comes to his senses, dismisses his identity as Quixote, makes his peace with everyone, and dies in the bosom of the Church. This ending is so unsatisfactory for contemporary readers that it is hard for us not to be haunted by the question, how should the novel really have ended?

The first possibility would be a literary ending like that of old Attic comedy. If *Don Quixote* is a "comic" novel then one has every reason to expect the book to adhere to "comedic" conventions. This would mean that there would be a happy and rewarding ending for our protagonists that would also please us as readers.[21] Old Attic comedies often begin with the protagonist having a completely insane idea—the Athenian Dicaeopolis seeks in the middle of a war to reach an individual and separate peace with the Spartans (*The Acharnians*); the women of Athens seek to end the war by a sex strike (*Lysistrata*); Euelipides and Pisthetairos want to build a city in the clouds where they can be as "free as the birds" (*The Birds*). In the end, against all expectations, the fantastic plan succeeds, and its successful realization is celebrated. Why then shouldn't Don Quixote also be able to realize his crazy plan? He might come to the notice of the king, be ennobled, and go on to found a new order of knights errant. The exclusion of these options can be blamed on modern "realism." This dictates that a plausible ending will demonstrate the impossibility of individual resistance to the supremacy of social institutions.

A second "antique" possibility would be an "epic" ending, where the later fate of the main character is suggested, but not directly given. The *Iliad* does not end with the death of Achilles, but with Hector's

---

[19] François Rabelais, *Oeuvres complètes*, ed. Guy Demerson (Gallimard, 1973), book V, ch. 45.

[20] Ibid., book I, ch. 57.

[21] See Thomas Mann, "Meerfahrt mit Don Quijote," in his *Leiden und Größe der Meister* (Berlin, 1935), pp. 265–67; see also Dante, "Epistola X" §10.

funeral celebrations. Even Odysseus knows that after the end of the *Odyssey* there will be another journey, although its course is only vaguely suggested.[22] An open texture allows new stories to unfold around epic heroes like Achilles and Odysseus. If they keep on turning up as actors in new, different stories, this shows that Achilles and Odysseus have developed lives of their own as literary figures. They have been represented with such vibrancy and vigor that their original narrative context is left behind them, so that they are able to transfer into an entirely new one. The first part of *Don Quixote* does have such an epic conclusion. Here Don Quixote pays the price of "realism," beaten by the factual supremacy of existing social relations. He attacks a passing procession of penitents—an action that Sancho takes for an attack on religion itself— "What demons have you got inside your breast egging you on against our holy Catholic faith?" (DQ I, ch. 52, p. 470). Don Quixote is so severely wounded by one of the penitents that Sancho proceeds to "throw himself upon his master's body and pour over him the most piteous and laughable lament ever heard, in the belief that he was dead" (DQ I, ch. 52, p. 471). Eventually Sancho discovers that his master is not dead, but only bashed about, and is able to persuade him to return home by luring him with an irresistible suggestion: "let's go back to our village with these gentlemen, who only want what's best for you, and there we'll work out a way to make another sally that'll bring us more profit and renown." This time Don Quixote responds: "You are speaking sound sense . . . and it will be wise indeed to wait for the presently prevailing malign influence of the stars to dissipate" (DQ I, ch. 52, p. 472). He had certainly suffered a clear defeat, and did not dispute it; but he does not at this time have to *reconcile* himself to a false and perfidious reality—although battered, Don Quixote remains true to himself, his visions, and his principles. The third sally out is indicated with typically epic ambiguity. But who knows whether it will really happen? All that we have is a declaration of intent from Sancho Panza. Cervantes seems almost playful in the way that he ruminates over Don Quixote's future (and over his death) at the end of Part One:

> Don Quixote's housekeeper and niece welcomed their master, undressed him and laid him on his ancient bed. . . . The priest told the niece to make sure to pamper her uncle and have him watched so that he didn't escape again, and described what they'd had to do to bring him back home. And then the two women again raised the roof with their outcry; again they

[22] Homer, *The Odyssey*, trans. E. V. Rieu (Penguin Books, 1946), p. 347. A commentator has noted that "The vagueness of what follows . . . has caused much speculation." This vagueness is no fault, but rather a characteristic of the epic genre. W. B. Stanford, *The "Odyssey" of Homer* (Macmillan, 1964), vol. 1, p. 386.

renewed their cursing of the books of chivalry; again they implored heaven to cast the authors of all those lies and absurdities into the depths of the bottomless pit. All this left them bewildered and fearful that as soon as their master and uncle felt a little better they'd lose him again; and that was indeed what happened.

But although the author of this history has searched with the most meticulous care for an account of the deeds performed by Don Quixote during his third sally, he hasn't been able to find any information about them, not at least in writings by reputable authors. . . . But the author could not discover any information about how Don Quixote met his end, nor would he ever have known about it if good fortune had not sent him an aged doctor who had in his possession a lead casket which, he said, had been found among the foundations of an old, ruined chapel that was being rebuilt. In this casket there were some parchments written in Roman letters but in Castilian verse. . . . (DQ I, ch. 52, p. 474)

Why then should the second part not end like this, weaving together suggestion and calculated vagueness?

Since we appreciate epic clarity, we should assume that a writer would be happy if the vitality and plausibility of his fiction was demonstrated by other writers, who made the life history of one of his literary figures part of their own books. As we know, Cervantes reacted differently. In 1614 an anonymous writer, using the pseudonym Alonso Fernandez de Allevaneda, published a "continuation" of Don Quixote's deeds that Cervantes felt to be an insulting, gross parody of his book. That of all things it was the "false" *Quixote* that became a bestseller must have added insult to injury.[23] This definitely ruled out concluding the second part with a traditional epic ending. The principal character had to die, a demise that Thomas Mann rightly called "literary death by jealousy."[24] At the end of the second part Cervantes sought with all conceivable literary means to keep the imagination he had shown at the end of the first part in check. He tried to re-impose his own exclusive authority on the creation that had outgrown him: "For me alone was Don Quixote born, and I for him" (DQ II, ch. 74, p. 981). Cervantes will decide Don Quixote's fate entirely himself, removing all ambiguity and all prospect of an open future. "Authoritarian personalities" are supposed to become aggressive when faced with ambiguity.[25] The reader gets the idea that there is something behind Quixote's death—the authoritarian gesture of

[23] Even in the eighteenth century Bertuch's very influential translation included a version of the "false" Quixote.

[24] Mann, "Meerfahrt," p. 264.

[25] Theodor Adorno, *Ästhetische Theorie* (Suhrkamp, 1970), pp. 201–2; see also Adorno's "Über den Fetischcharakter in der Musik und die Regression des Hörens," in *Dissonanzen*

an author concerned to protect his literary rights. And so we have to accept that the Knight of the Sorry Face has to die, and that his death has to be described. But why should Don Quixote "come to his senses" before he dies? Why this last humiliation, this "shameful denial of self at the end of his endeavour"?[26]

In fact Don Quixote's demise was prefaced with a whole series of defeats. Don Quixote's faith in errantry could remain unshaken when beaten by the Knight of the White Moon, even when he was made to promise to lay down his arms for a year, return to his village, and "stop looking for . . . adventures" (DQ II, ch. 64, p. 927). Occasional defeat for brave and famous knights can be found in other books of chivalry too. But when the Knight of the Sorry Face offers Sancho Panza money in compensation for the lashes he has to give himself to disenchant Dulcinea, this proposal is an important, moral capitulation to the supremacy of the new *Zeitgeist* (DQ II, ch. 71, pp. 962–63). The hidalgo Alonso Quixano is not unfamiliar with money, since we learn in the very first chapter that "he sold acres of arable land to buy these books of chivalry" (DQ I, ch. 1, p. 26). But otherwise money plays no part in Quixote's imaginary world of knight errantry. The innkeeper who has dubbed him knight has to remind him that next time he should have "something as obviously necessary as money or clean shirts," for "even if it wasn't written in the histories . . . there wasn't any reason to believe that [knights errant] travelled without supplies of both" (DQ I, ch. 3, p. 37). And the fierce dispute about Sancho's pay at the beginning of the second part (DQ II, ch. 7, pp. 528–31)[27] is not only about clarifying the personal relationship of Sancho and Don Quixote, but about the relationship between two economic forms. Don Quixote insists on his ("premodern") understanding of the relation between knight errant and his squire: "when one's head aches all one's limbs hurt, and I, being your lord and master, am your head, and you, being my servant, are a part of me, and for this reason any ill that affects me will hurt you, and vice versa" (DQ II, ch. 2, p. 499). He and Sancho are thus not two individual subjects independent of each other and free to dispose of themselves as they will, and who, if there is mutual advantage in it, can make a contract to provide quantifiable services. Of course Sancho should expect appropriate compensation for his service, but his pay will not take the form of a "fixed wage" to be paid monthly (DQ II, ch. 7, pp. 528–29).

(Vandenhoeck and Ruprecht, 1956), as well as his *Philosophie der neuen Musik* (Europäische Verlagsanstalt, 1958), especially the second part on Stravinsky, pp. 149–99.

[26] Friedrich Nietzsche, *Kritische Studienausgabe*, vol. 9, p. 156.

[27] See Caroll Johnson, *Cervantes and the Material World* (University of Illinois Press, 2000), especially ch. 1, sec. 1, "The Drama of Sancho's Salary."

Sancho will, depending on the circumstances, receive a governorship, or possibly a benefice (DQ I, ch. 26, p. 226), or the Kingdom of Denmark (DQ I, ch. 10, p. 81); in any case, a gift, and no contractual remuneration for services rendered.

Don Quixote's third defeat comes in meeting Don Álvaro Tarfe. This Don Álvaro Tarfe is a figure from the "false" continuation of the first part of the novel (DQ II, ch. 72). Astonishingly, Don Quixote allows this fictive personage to depose, before the village mayor and a notary, that Cervantes's Don Quixote is not the same as the "Don Quixote" of the false continuation (DQ II, ch. 72, p. 969). Thomas Mann responded with eloquence and enthusiasm to this passage:

> Don Quixote and his squire step out of the reality to which they belong, the novel in which they lived, and stroll, large as life, happily greeted by readers of their story, into a world that, like them, represents by comparison with the previous world of print a higher stage of reality.[28]

But one could also take this moment as a scene of shameful humiliation, as the point when the famous and universally recognized Knight of the Sorry Face needs to have his existence confirmed by a fraud, of all people.

Despite all these preparations Cervantes has to resort to a rather shoddy means of reconciling his hero to his circumstances. This is the healing sleep that Don Quixote has (DQ II, ch. 74, p. 976), but which remains unexplained. At a second remove one could ask whether what is superficially a simple failure—the contrived and obviously literary nature of this forced conclusion—might have a positive and realistic side to it. There is no question but that in such a country—where an absolute king, the Holy Inquisition, the Holy Brotherhood (DQ I, ch. 22, p. 184; ch. 45, pp. 422ff), and a sadistic and decadent duke (DQ II, chs. 30–57) rule over a mostly impoverished rural population, where torture is a common part of legal procedure (DQ I, ch. 22, p. 178), where it was taken for granted that "boys are disappointed when the condemned man they've been waiting for doesn't come out to be hanged, because he's been pardoned either by the aggrieved party or by the judge" (DQ II, ch. 56, p. 868), and where religious and ethnic cleansing was part of daily life—that in such a country there would be no place for a convincing reconciliation free of all illusion and aesthetically satisfying. The fact that Don Quixote's return to this normality is solely effected by an implausible act of literary *force majeure* is the revenge which reality takes on any form of acquiescence with such a world.

[28] Mann, "Meerfahrt," p. 231.

Another Modernity

The philosophical heirs of Hobbes, Descartes, and Kant have ruled the occidental imagination and thinking for too long. There was a short interval in which one could catch one's breath, linked to the names of Montaigne, Rabelais, Marlowe,[29] and Grotius. For one moment there was a prospect of a "modern world" in which there might be skeptical tolerance, the affirmation of life, and a conception of liberty not limited to disciplined self-regulation, the internalized policeman. A politics that arose from a realistic estimation of the possibilities of peaceful human coexistence also seemed possible. Certainly we did not have to wait long for the reaction: in the form of the modern state (Hobbes); Descartes's epistemology; and Kant's restoration of a vulgar Christian ethic based upon fideism. To recognize this as a reverse, to see it for what it was and is, is one of the most important tasks for political philosophy at the beginning of the twenty-first century. An indispensable part of this analytic task is to rewrite the history of modernity. Traditionally modern philosophy begins with René Descartes, the "discoverer of the principle of subjectivity," peaking in Kant's philosophy of individual autonomy. Contemporary Kantians such as Jürgen Habermas and John Rawls criticize details of the Kantian system, for instance the "monologic" conception of transcendental subjectivity, but otherwise merely trim Kant's basic insights to suit the needs of the present. We can find the first signs of this procedure in Hegel, whose *Lectures on the History of Philosophy* reverses the sequence of philosophers with whom he deals: first comes Descartes (born 1596), then Locke (born 1632), then finally Grotius (born 1583) and Hobbes (born 1588). It is not at all obvious that an ontological and epistemological proof of the human souls' immortality (*Meditationes de prima philosophia in qua dei existentia et animae immortalitas demonstrator*, 1641) should be considered "more modern" than Bacon's investigation of the role of induction in those sciences that can be rendered technologically useful (*Novum Organum*, 1620) or Grotius's attempt to separate the European Law of Peoples from theology (*De jure belli et pacis*, 1625). And when Hegel writes about Grotius: "His principal work is *De jure belli et pacis* 1625; no-one reads it any more, but it has had great influence . . ."[30] this comment is suggestive,

---

[29] "[Christopher Marlowe] affirmeth . . . that the first beginning of religion was only to keep men in awe . . . that Christ was a bastard and his mother dishonest . . . that if the Jews among whom he was born did crucify him they best knew him . . . that St John the Evangelist was bedfellow to Christ . . . and he used him as the sinners of Sodoma. . . ." "The Baines Note," in *Christopher Marlowe: The Complete Plays*, ed. F. Romany und R. Lindsay (Penguin Books, 2003), p. xxxiv.

[30] Hegel, *Vorlesungen über die Geschichte der Philosophie*, vol. 3, in *Werke in zwanzig Bänden*, vol. 20, ed. Eva Moldenhauer und Karl Markus Michel (Suhrkamp, 1967), p. 224.

to say the least. We too should engage with the high art of creative amnesia and apply it to the works of Kant, Rawls, and Habermas.[31]

Of course, novels are neither philosophical treatises nor political tracts. All the same, one of the possible political effects of the literary novel could be to free us from two powerful fixations: from the phantasm of an "absolutely autonomous subject" that underlies all variations of Kantianism; and from the fantasy of an overarching consensus that runs through all existing theories of a social contract. In contrast to such ideas, any good novel instructs us about the irreducible polyphony of modern society:[32] that everyone else, even under the most ideal conditions, will almost always firmly hold to opinions at variance with our own. At the same time the novel can show us how artificial and fragile the theoretical postulate of an autonomous subject is. In reading novels, it might dawn on us that we would best do without the fantasy of "a great Cyclops eye,"[33] whether it takes the form of the transcendental subject or that of a final consensus under ideal conditions.

The divided world of the *aut* was one to which Cervantes explicitly adhered. Even if Don Quixote had made the wrong choice at the beginning of the novel, he would eventually recognize his mistake and correct it. Of course the literary presentation makes sure that every reader becomes aware of the limits of this conception—even, perhaps, contrary to the author's intentions. For Alonso Quixano is not only mad, but extraordinarily admirable. This does not amount to a claim that behind Cervantes's artfully created *aut* façade there is an underlying *sive* reality upon which the reader, after considerable reflection, will stumble. "Mad" and "admirable" are certainly not properties that can ultimately be harmonized. The present-day reader of *Don Quixote* will rather sense a hidden similarity with *Gargantua and Pantagruel* that Cervantes did not himself intend. And according to that, the world is a place where things actually come together that do not belong together—neither in the here and now, nor in the human brain, nor either in the ideal speech situation, nor even in some world beyond this one.

The idea that novels might be dubious or dangerous was a common one in the eighteenth and nineteenth centuries, warning of the corrupting effects of reading novels (especially upon the tender souls of young women); moreover, this idea was not linked to particular morally questionable contents, but to the novel as a form. Since every novel is a printed text that invites repeated reading at a speed chosen by the reader and which, if in doubt, can be compared in detail with other texts, the genre of the novel

---

[31] See Harald Weinrich, *Lethe: Kunst und Kritik des Vergessens* (C. H. Beck, 2000).
[32] Mikhail Bakhtin, *Rabelais and His World* (MIT Press, 1968).
[33] See Friedrich Nietzsche, *The Birth of Tragedy* (Penguin Books, 1993), p. 67.

involves special structural possibilities for reflexivity, intertextuality, and the distancing of the reader from the read.[34] Novels can refer to themselves, for instance with a preface in which the author directly addresses the reader to introduce the narrative. The novelist has any number of possibilities: alluding to other texts, integrating them into his own text, or invoking them. He can seek to convince the reader of the veracity of his story, or prompt the reader to check for himself how true the story is. The reader of a novel finds himself urged to observe from a distance given social realities, and to reflect upon the values, rules, directions, and expectations thereby revealed. Stifter's *Nachsommer*, the lightly ironical but exaggeratedly morally conformist novels of Jane Austen, Saint-Pierre's *Paul and Virginia*—these are all as potentially subversive as Schlegel's *Lucinde* or Flaubert's *Madame Bovary*. For the theoretically sensitized lover of the novel this is a genre that—as long as it remains true to itself— constantly works with the reflexive instruments of ambiguity and irony, relativization and distance, and hence quite necessarily undermines the formation of consensus and the drive to conformity; politically it works against totalitarianism.[35] Irony, distance, and the endless play of "as if," sometimes expressed humorously, are antagonistic to the supposedly normative immobility of social consensus. They parody the seriousness and gravity with which socialized subjects are supposed to take the claims of such a consensus. The first theorists of the novel were convinced that the novel could not exist in a well-ordered society:

> I recall here what a famous thinker said—he was of the opinion that if police were entirely and completely effective (if the commercial state were completely closed and even the passport of the traveler contained a detailed biography and a true portrait) a novel would simply be impossible, for then nothing could occur in real life that could prompt one, or provide likely material. A view which, however strange it sounds, is not without foundation in regard to that flawed genre.[36]

Does this speak against the form of the novel, or against the idea of a "well-ordered society"? With some restrictions the early romantic judgment could be maintained in exact reverse. In this view *Don Quixote* would be one of the first novels of modernity, and the book would be archetypal in that—especially at the end of the second part—it provides

---

[34] Friedrich Schlegel, "Gespräch über Poesie," in *Kritische Ausgabe*, vol. 2, ed. Hans Eichner (Paderborn, 1967), pp. 284ff.

[35] Milan Kundera, *The Art of the Novel* (Faber, 1988), pp. 3–20; 157–65.

[36] Friedrich Schlegel, "Geschichte der alten und neuen Literatur: Zwölfte Vorlesung," in *Kritische Ausgabe*, vol. 6, p. 275. Schlegel is talking here only of a particular type of novel: "those in which the idea of the Romantic . . . coincides with that which is inimical to police."

a literary representation of the monumental restriction and impoverishment of human possibility inherent in the modern world as we know
it. The chivalrous life sought at the beginning of the book turns out to
be pure imagination, a mirage that Alonso Quixano not only ultimately
recognizes as pure fantasy, but which he repudiates and diminishes. All
the same, despite the probably dubious, sometimes reprehensible aspects
of the life of a knight errant, one cannot avoid the impression that a kind
of self-mutilation occurs at the end of the novel, although Cervantes cele-
brates this to excess as the return of reason and moral healing. This sense
underwrites the enduring actuality of the novelty right up to our own
times. Whoever might today prefer *Gargantua and Pantagruel* should
not forget that the social world in which we live is that of *Don Quixote*'s
second part.

VI

Culture as Ideal and as Boundary

NIETZSCHE, AS IS WELL KNOWN, was trained as a classical philologist, but it is, I think, often insufficiently appreciated that he remained intellectually true to this original choice of professions, albeit in his own highly idiosyncratic way, to the very end of his life. To be sure, from very early on Nietzsche understood "philology" as a discipline that was distinctively "philosophical" both in its method and in its content. The philologist cultivates an art of interpreting ancient monuments of civilization through the exact and subtle reading of obscure and difficult texts, and such practice is the best possible preparation for taking in hand one of the main tasks of modern philosophy, the critical diagnosis of contemporary culture. In addition, the "modern" philology Nietzsche came to know in the mid-nineteenth century had come to certain substantive conclusions that represented a philosophical challenge to some central features of the modern world.

To start with a discussion of the form of philological cognition, modern philology is a distinctly *historical* form of inquiry. Like every other systematic researcher, the trained philologist needs first of all to satisfy a series of quasi-moral demands, such as learning to subject his will to the asceticism of philological "science" and internalizing the requirements of "objectivity." The budding philologist has to cultivate the ability "to have his Pro and his Contra *in his own power* and to turn them on or off at will" (*KSA* 5.364),[1] and to sacrifice what he wants to be the case to the facts and to what could be demonstrated by the available relevant scientific methods. In addition to these general demands of rigor that are common to all cognitive disciplines, the philologist must also remain constantly aware of the historicity both of the topics and objects he is investigating and of the process of inquiry itself. In view of the temporal gap between ancient and modern times, giving an adequate epistemological account of historical philology would require at the very least a complication and, potentially, a complete revision of the neo-Kantian image of knowledge that was dominant in the middle of the nineteenth century.

---

[1] Work by Nietzsche will be cited by volume and page according to the *Kritische Studienausgabe* (*KSA*), edited by Giorgio Colli and Mazzino Montinari (De Gruyter, 1967).

The neo-Kantian subject is confronted with historically invariant objects which it must integrate into a unitary spatio-temporal system by subsuming them under causal laws. The philologist, on the other hand, has quite different objects in view and different cognitive interests, and must remain as aware as possible of the qualitative differences between antiquity and modern times. Not only were the concepts used by people in the ancient world very different from those used either in colloquial contemporary speech or in modern scholarly discussions, but they referred in many cases to a differently constituted social reality. To mention only three examples: The basic unity of modern politics is the state, but there were no "states" in the ancient world. Neither the Greek polis nor the Roman *res publica* or *imperium* were "states" in the proper sense in which that term is nowadays used, namely to designate an association that successfully exercises a monopoly of legitimate power through a specially designated administrative apparatus within a determinate geographic area. In addition, ancient forms of "religion" were very different from the monotheistic book-religions which dominate the modern Western conceptions: in pre-Christian Greece there were no canonical sacred books, no dogmatic confessions of faith, and no separate clerical establishment endowed with forms of legal jurisdiction. Finally, at the latest since the appearance of the second book of Foucault's history of sexuality,[2] it has been a commonplace to observe that even the apparently fundamental human phenomenon of sex was differently constituted and structured in the ancient world.

It was considerations like the above that led some historians in the nineteenth century to the conclusion that if history was to avoid thoroughgoing falsification of the past, the historian would have to make a systematic effort to work against the natural human tendency to be centered in the present. As against this, accounts of the ancients ought to strive to avoid anachronism at any cost. Not only should we refrain from attributing to the ancients our specific motivational structure and our opinions, attitudes, and value system, but we may not even apply to the ancient world basic concepts like "religion," "state," and "sexuality" without flagging some serious reservations about the use of these concepts.

If one takes this line of argument seriously, one can be tempted to think that one could and should try to understand, interpret, and evaluate the ancient world *simply and purely on and in its own terms*. It is, of course, perfectly proper to use individual Greek expressions like "polis" for characteristic ancient institutions even in modern discussion, provided they are explained in terms that make sense to a contemporary reader, but to try systematically to free one's account of *any* anachronistic term or conception is an incoherent project. Even if I were able to transform

[2] Michel Foucault, *L'usage des plaisirs* (Gallimard, 1984).

myself totally into an Athenian of the fifth century, this would be of no help to modern philology, because its task is not to explain the writers of antiquity to *other* members of ancient societies, but to our contemporaries. Philology is a form of translation, and is therefore of necessity as dependent on those *to* whom the translation is directed, as it is on those whose work is being rendered. Even if an Athenian of the fifth century was a fully competent participant in his form of life, he would not, by virtue of that alone, be capable of translating for us even his own linguistic utterances. The limits of what we can understand are for us the limits of the possible ways in which the ancient world can be comprehensibly represented to us.

Even in his early writing Nietzsche was determined to retain for modern philology the "practical" orientation of ancient rhetoric. Philology should not be construed as aspiring to be a "scientific" study of objects that are of no intrinsic interest or relevance to us, nor should it be taken to be a mere attempt to render some defunct form of life "comprehensible" to us; philology should stand in the service not of pure cognition but of "life." Nietzsche's thesis is that the specific form this "service of life" is to take is cultural criticism.

In the nineteenth century it was easy to fail to notice that philology's vocation was to be a form of criticism of culture, because the reality of everyday life for the practicing philologist was, as Nietzsche very astutely points out, the daily drilling of adolescents in the rudiments of grammar and lexis which took place in the humanistic gymnasia, the lycées, and the public schools of Western Europe. Nevertheless, Central European culture remained dependent on antiquity in two related respects. First of all, modern art, philosophy, and religion in fact arose in the ancient world, and even the most up-to-date nineteenth-century forms of these human pursuits retained as constituent parts of the way in which they were practiced conceptions that were actually deeply rooted in various ancient beliefs and attitudes. Second, the ancient world provided modernity with a standard against which we constantly measure ourselves. What Nietzsche calls the "constantly repeated accommodation of every subsequent era to the ancient world, the way in which each era measures itself against antiquity" (*KSA* 8.31), need not consist in taking antiquity as a positive model. Christianity derives a certain amount of its self-esteem from the fact that it considers itself to have "overcome" certain features of ancient customary morality, especially in the spheres of sexuality and family life, but this merely shows a different kind of dependency. Since orientation toward models and ideals drawn from antiquity is an internal feature of much European culture, to subject ancient society and its artifacts to any kind of substantive analysis was in the nineteenth century at the same time to take a position on contemporary culture.

The historical and social situation in which classical philology found itself during Nietzsche's lifetime was, on his account, one in which many people were vaguely aware that something was deeply wrong or even "perverted" ("*verkehrt*") with the contemporary world, although they could not exactly put their finger on what exactly that was and formulate it explicitly and precisely. If contemporary society is perverted in some fundamental way, one might worry that this would have a distorting effect on the very cognitive apparatus available to members of that society. At a trivial level, in a society in which slavery is an ubiquitous and integral part of all basic social relations it becomes that much more difficult, although never, perhaps, strictly impossible, to imagine life without it. If this is the case, how can it be possible for us to find a standpoint which is free of distortions like these and from which it will be possible to get a clear and critical view of the present? A Kantian has an easy time of it here because he can always appeal to a purported "transcendental" standpoint which is universally accessible to all and which provides a framework for evaluating all empirical institutions and arrangements, but the very possibility of such a "transcendental standpoint" is something Nietzsche never fails to reject. Every perspective is, on his view, a concrete perspective, having a specific historical genesis and location. Fortunately for us, the classical philologist by virtue of his linguistic and historical knowledge is in a position to present to us a concrete point of view which is distinct from our usual perspective, and to relate the past critically to the present. To be more exact, in a good philological treatise present and past are brought together with the intention of using each to criticize the other. "Antiquity is accessible to only a few people. . . . These few are critics of our contemporary world measuring it against antiquity, and they [also] measure antiquity against their own ideals, and are thus critics of antiquity" (*KSA* 8.35). It is this critical attitude toward both present and past which distinguishes those philologists who are aware of their true vocation from the majority of members of modern societies, who are unreflective. In particular, this commitment to criticism distinguishes *true* philologists from the people Nietzsche calls "*Bildungsphilister*," philistines who use their thin veneer of merely formal culture for the purposes of self-congratulation.[3] "*Bildungsphilister*" and their associates in the philological community have no interest in using antiquity and contemporary culture to criticize each other, but rather only in assimilating the one to the other in the most anodyne way possible, which of necessity leads to serious cognitive distortion.

---

[3] Nietzsche's own model is David Strauss (*KSA* 1.159–242), but a more contemporary model of this attitude would be Hans Georg Gadamer.

> The attitude of philologists [i.e., philologists as they now in fact are, not *true* philologists] toward the ancient world is one of making excuses for it, or of trying to prove the existence in antiquity of that which our times value highly. The proper point of departure, however, would be the reverse, namely to start from insight into the perversion of the modern world and then look back. (*KSA* 8.28)

Certain modern institutions, such as, for instance, Christianity, are "perversions" because the normal functioning of such institutions requires the repression of human vital powers and the imposition of limitations on the way in which certain human individuals could develop. In a good philological treatise the present would be revealed *as* something perverted, and by revealing it in this way philology would contribute, at least indirectly, to the liberation and development of repressed forms of human vitality.

If the prohibition on anachronism is treated in a completely unreflective way and understood as enjoining a complete abstraction from the present, this, even if it were to be possible (which it is not), would undermine the critical project of philology completely. Ancient and modern forms of religiosity cannot be allowed to diverge so far conceptually that they designate totally different things. If that were the case, they couldn't be fruitfully compared at all, and the idea of using one to criticize the other would not make sense. Since part of the point of philology, according to Nietzsche, is to use past and present to criticize each other, in *some* sense philology must be firmly rooted in the present, if it wishes to "serve life."

To put it another way, anachronism is to be avoided, but it is also clear that it cannot be absolutely avoided. If, *per impossibile*, it were to be possible to give an absolutely anachronism-free account of some historical phenomenon, such an account would also be utterly useless for the *critical* analysis (of the present and of the past) which it is the final goal of the philologist to give. Classical philology draws its life-sustenance from the attempt to deal with these tensions. The methodological problems of his own research, Nietzsche thinks, will force the philologist to confront and try to answer some fundamental philosophical questions. Unresolved antinomies are a breeding ground for philosophy and especially for philosophical forms of skepticism. The most relevant form of this for philologists is the radical ancient version, not what is usually called "skepticism" in contemporary parlance or by contemporary philosophers. The ancient skeptic was a philosopher who conducted his life in a particular way. When confronted with an opponent who asserted a proposition that had any cognitive content that went beyond what was given in direct sensory experience, the skeptic tried to demonstrate that one could with equal cogency argue for or against that proposition (see *KSA* 5.364; 2.20).

Since he in every case succeeded in this, he drew the conclusion that he ought to withhold judgment on the proposition. By thus withholding judgment the skeptic aspired to a state of mental and emotional equanimity (ἀταραξία) that was highly prized in the ancient world. Moderns may well wonder how such equanimity differs from spiritual death. In his *Untimely Meditations* Nietzsche speaks of the prerogative right of the young to hope (*KSA* 1.331–32), but a minimal amount of hope is probably a necessary component of any human life. Hope, however, is one of the possible opposites of absolute psychic equanimity.

The tendency to skepticism receives additional support from certain substantive conclusions which nineteenth-century philologists reached in their study of the ancient world. Classical philology is itself a typical and especially important part of modern culture, part of a huge apparatus modern societies create in order to understand and justify themselves. However, it is *also* part of the gradual historical process by which modernity undermines itself and dissolves its own foundations, slowly collapsing on itself.

> The time for religions that believe in gods, providence, a rational world-order, in miracles and sacraments is past; the time for certain forms of holy life, of asceticism is also past, because we too easily suspect a damaged brain or some kind of illness. . . . Who still believes in the immortality of the soul! Everything which was thought to carry with it a blessing or a curse and which thus depended on certain erroneous physiological conceptions, collapses as soon as these conceptions are recognized as mistakes. . . . *With reference to culture* this means the following: Up to now we were aware of only *one* perfect form of culture, the city-culture of Greece, a cultural form which was built on specific social and mythical foundations, and *one* imperfect form, the Roman, which was a form of decoration of life and was derivative on the Greek. Now, however, all these foundations, the mythical and the socio-political, have been transformed; what we call our "culture" has no substance because it is built up on states of affairs and opinions that are untenable and have almost disappeared.—To the extent to which we fully understand Greek culture, we will realise that its time is past. Thus the philologist is the *great Sceptic* in our cultural and educational establishment. That is his mission.—Happy the man who like Wagner or Schopenhauer has an inkling of the promising powers in which a new culture is beginning to stir. (*KSA* 8.37–38)

One might object that considerations like these are not sufficient to warrant a true radical skepticism on the ancient model. If philology shows that the foundations of modern culture are rotten, then why is this not a *focused* criticism of specific features that can be isolated and replaced? Focused, constructive criticism, however, is something completely different from skepticism. If the old cultural practices are unacceptable for whatever reason, why not try to create new ones? Nietzsche himself in *The Birth of Tragedy* seems to have something like this in mind when he describes the way in which the existing "culture of the opera" will soon be replaced by a culture centered around Wagner's music-dramas. Any attempt to weaken the skeptical potential of Nietzsche's view overlooks the fact that he holds that what the philologist discovers is not a simple defect of *ancient* cultures, but a general property of *all* cultures. For Nietzsche *every* culture is a construct of the human imagination, the foundations of which will not bear inspection.

> Task: the *death of the old culture* unavoidable: Greek culture is to be designated the original model and it is to be shown that all culture rests on presuppositions that are untenable. (*KSA* 8.83)

Nietzsche's philology-based skepticism finds an adequate expression in his "genealogies." His "genealogy of morality" starts from a series of observations that are typical of the kind of historically oriented philology he admired, for instance the observation that in many European languages the word "good" ("*gut*") has not one but two distinct opposites: in English, "bad" and "evil" (in German: "*schlecht*" and "*böse*"); and that the pair "good"/"bad" seems to be older than "good"/"evil." A genealogy is to dissolve a certain appearance: concepts that are in common use and present themselves as self-evidently univocal, internally coherent, well grounded, and rational to use are unmasked as historically contingent conjunctions of very diverse, perhaps even contradictory, semantic components. The apparent clarity is really confusion; apparent coherence and simplicity of meaning is unwieldy plurality; apparent rationality is arbitrary conjunction. These appearances are illusions created and maintained by a combination of direct force and force of habit. In the genealogy "real" history and "history of ideas" turn out to be inextricably interconnected; that is precisely part of the point. The concept of "morality" is actually highly ambiguous in part *because* the human phenomenon to which it refers is in fact constantly changing; it is a labile constellation of different forms of valuation which are historically continually shifting in an equally changeable institutional environment, or set of environments. The Nietzschean genealogy is a complex and devious history of certain human reactions, which gradually work themselves free from the contexts within which they are embedded, and attempt to deny their origin, in order to become normatively absolute. The claim to (normative) absoluteness which is built into the usual use of the concept is what is thrown into question by the genealogical account: how exactly can a concept with such contingent historical origins make such a strong normative claim?

Nietzsche criticizes some fundamental forms of contemporary culture very severely, but this criticism does not extend to the concept of "culture" itself. His treatment of "culture" thus contrasts strongly with his discussion of such phenomena as morality. His writings direct their fire not at individual moral imperatives or particular theories, but at the very idea that there is an absolute morality at all of the kind envisaged by Christianity. Nietzsche gives a genealogy of morality, but not of "culture." There seems, however, no obvious reason to think "culture" is a less problematic concept than "morality." Nietzsche didn't believe in God or morality, but one does wonder whether he didn't sometimes exhibit a slightly unnatural piety toward culture. "Culture in the service of life" is a sensible slogan if one knows what "life" means. If it means "*biological* existence" or "survival," then one has to ascribe to Nietzsche a rather uninteresting reductionist program of a type not very different from a number of others with which we are familiar. If "life" means not biological vitality, but a specifically human form of living, then the slogan looks dangerously like a tautology because the existence of a "culture" would seem to be one of the distinguishing features of a human, as opposed to a merely animal form of existence. (If Nietzsche had a *different* distinguishing feature or a range of potentially distinguishing features in mind, what are they?) If "life" means not merely *the* human form of life (i.e., *any* form of life that can correctly be called "human"), but one specific form of life, then we are turning around in a very narrow circle indeed. "(Victorian) culture should be in the service of the (Victorian) form of life" is not exactly a senseless recommendation because it might well be that a certain culture had lost contact with the wider form of life within which it was in some sense located, or it even might be that some major form of cultural activity was incompatible with the continued existence of the form of life within which it arose. Arguably, Nietzsche at one time thought that this was the case with Wagner's music-drama; Wagner certainly thought this. The corrupt feudal states of Central Europe would not, Wagner thought, be able to maintain themselves long once his music-dramas began to be performed. Still, if a form of art and a form of society are incompatible, why must it always be the case that the *society* must change? If one at this point continues: Because art represents human vitality which must not be repressed, then one must have an account of "human vitality" that does *not* define it relative to the given, existing form of life. Wagner's music-drama is *not* a contribution to increased human vitality, if "human vitality" means the cultural life exhibited by the tiny feudal courts of Central Europe: it has just been claimed to be incompatible with that. Why formulate one's hopes for a better future as hopes for a new *culture*? Is this self-evident? Why? "Culture" is a modern concept for which there was no real equivalent in the ancient world (or the Middle Ages). Despite his general acceptance of the prohibition on anachronism, Nietzsche uses this ambiguous, modern concept unselfconsciously as the key to understanding antiquity. What is special about "culture" that seems to give it its special status?

One can distinguish two families of usages of the concept of "culture" in the modern period. I will call them conceptions of culture "in the vertical dimension" and conceptions of culture "in the horizontal dimension." To begin with culture in the vertical sense, the English word (and the corresponding German term "*Kultur*") go back to the Latin substantive "*cultura*" and eventually to the verb "*colo*," which seems originally to have meant "live in" or "inhabit," then "till, cultivate," finally "look after, tend."[4] The "*agricola*" cultivates the fields. "*Cultura*" is originally used with a dependent genitive indicating the object of cultivation: "*horti + cultura*," "*agri + cultura*," "*arborum + cultura*." In all these cases the meaning is down-to-earth. To cultivate the fields, one must know the quality and condition of the soil. Is it sandy or rocky? Grapes for wine grow best on rocky *garrigue*, vegetables on sandy soil. To be a success at cultivation one must also know what one should plant, i.e., what one needs. If there is already enough wine, plant corn. If there is enough spelt and wheat, cultivate vegetables. In principle one can "cultivate" the gods (*"colere deos"*) in the same way as one "cultivates" the olive trees. Just as the peasant tries to treat the olive tree so that it becomes as useful as possible for human purposes, so he makes appropriate sacrifices to the gods to make them inclined to contribute to the success of human enterprises. To be sure, criticism of this archaic attitude by philosophers begins very early in the history of the subject, with Plato, who argues against it in the dialogue *Euthyphro*, but it is an open question how much effect such criticism had, and how quickly behavior and beliefs among rural populations changed. Since "cultivation" is clearly a value-based concept, the question immediately arises in whose interest (συμφέρον) the cultivation occurs. This, too, is a question which comes up for discussion very early in the history of Western philosophy, for instance in the first book of Plato's *Republic*. Does the shepherd look after his flock in the interest of the sheep in his flock? After all, what he does is in an obvious sense immediately directed at ensuring that they fare as well as possible. Or is the shepherd like the peasant who fattens his pig before slaughtering it?

In the course of history the term "*cultura*," with its associated genitive, comes to be applied to more and more abstract domains. Cicero seems to mark a turning point when, in the *Tusculans,* he speaks of philosophy as "*animi cultura*" (2.13). This also seems to indicate the beginning of a process of internalization in which "cultivation" becomes self-referential. If I cultivate a tree, the tree is distinct from me. If I cultivate my "soul,"

---

[4] *Oxford Latin Dictionary*, ed. P. G. Glare (Oxford University Press, 1982) *s.v.* "*colo*," "*cultura*."

it seems tempting to interpret what is happening as a process in which my soul is trying to cultivate *itself*. How should the soul know how to cultivate itself, if by hypothesis it needs cultivation in the first place?

The Christianization of Europe has further far-reaching implications for the concept of culture. If the Christian god is absolute, he would seem to require an absolute form of service perhaps in the form of self-cultivation, which can come to be called "*cultura Domini*" as in the inscription on the gravestone of a local ecclesiastical dignitary who is buried in the cathedral of Nietzsche's hometown, Naumburg. This Dr. Caesar Pflug, described as "deacon in Geusnitz and Gollßschau," is said in the inscription to have "nobly worked the plow [with a pun on his name: "Pflug" = "plow"] in the service of the Lord" ("in cultura Domini nobile duxit aratrum").[5]

By this point, then, "*cultura*" has moved semantically rather far from its origins. Originally the use of the term "culture" was embedded in the idea of the subordination of a determinate area to some higher goal—the soil subordinated to the needs of human nutrition—but gradually "*cultura*" comes to be used absolutely, without any associated genitive. This transition, however, might seem problematic because the genitive might seem necessary to make the various kinds of relativity which are built into the concept of "cultivation" itself clear. When I speak of "cultivation," it is natural to ask: *What* is it that is to be cultivated? Music? Urban parks? "Virtue"? *Which* virtue exactly? The dropping of the genitive makes it possible for unacknowledged value judgments to be smuggled into a purportedly value-neutral "absolute" concept of culture, so that one can make statements like "This population has no culture, because it has no

---

[5] The full inscription reads:

> [as a band around the edge of the stone]

> Sub hoc saxo conditur Reverendus //
> Magnific' et Nobilis: Vir:
> Dr. CAESAR PFLUG,
> in Geusnitz et Golßschau, ecclesiae //
> Numb. DECANUS,
> qui natus d. 7. Jul. MDXCVI //
> et pie obijt d. 24. Ianu:
> A.° MDCXXVIII laetus:
> Hinc carnis resurrectionem expectans.

> DER PFLUG
> Culturá in Domini qui nobile duxit aratrum
> CAESAR in hoc busti fornice corp' habet,
> Mens agit in caelo, tandem sub luce supremâ
> reddatur socius uterq', sibi.

> [Transcribed by the author]

endogenous forms of music" or "This group has no culture because it speaks a language which has never been written down." A further relativity resides in the specific values relative to which the success of cultivation is measured. Should a well-kept garden look as much as possible like a sharply etched geometrical figure, or should it look slightly asymmetrical, and like a piece of "nature"? How efficient is the process of cultivation? Relative to what standard of efficiency? Number of square meters of garden cultivated per day, per hour of labor, per unit of money invested? How successful are its results? Corresponding to the diversity of answers that can be given to these questions one can distinguish different levels or degrees of "culture." Nietzsche adopts the commonly used spatial metaphor and speaks of "higher" and "lower" cultures (*KSA* 2.187–237), locating them, as it were, on a vertical scale.

Despite Nietzsche's love of botanical metaphors, a human culture differs from a form of horticulture among other ways in that a human culture is capable of setting its own goals for itself: a species of plant can't do that. One can thus say that a "higher" culture, A, differs from a "lower" one, B, either in that A comes closer than B to realizing some model or paradigm against which both are measured, or because A posits for itself a goal or set of goals that deserve to be valued higher than the goals B sets itself. So A is higher than B in that A produces better poets or painters than B does, or because A produces high quality poets while B produces excellent cooks (on the assumption that poetry is more important than cuisine). The question still would remain who decides that poetry is more important than cookery.

"Culture" as an explicitly vertical concept thus has rather old roots, going back at least to Roman antiquity. In the nineteenth century a second family of concepts of culture established itself. Humans groups differ the one from the other with regard to their habits and customs, their folkways, traditions, ways of performing everyday actions, and characteristic beliefs, attitudes, values, and expectations. Members of some groups eat with knife and fork, members of others with chopsticks. Prima facie this is a mere descriptive difference, because there is nothing inherently better about using a knife and fork rather than chopsticks or vice versa. However, the eating equipment members of any society use and their table manners are generally structured so as to fit the way in which the food they usually eat is cooked and served. So the differences between groups are not merely a matter of individual habits or customs, but of systems of habits, utensils, and manners that all in some sense fit together, and can be thought of as forming a kind of whole. We call such a whole a "culture"; I will speak of "culture in the horizontal sense." Whereas culture in the vertical sense is defined by a hierarchy of above and below, culture as a horizontal concept notionally refers to a spatial location of different systems of activated possibilities that exist the one next to the others. There is a Chinese, a French, an Arabic culture, without it being the case that the meaning of the word "culture" required that one of these be thought to be in any way "higher" than the others. Specific cultures in the horizontal sense can also be thought to be subdivisions of larger cultural groups: there are Orthodox, Catholic, and Protestant variants of the common Christian culture of Europe. Finally cultures can overlap or form composites, such as, for instance, the so-called "creole" cultures in the Caribbean.

Even if it is the case that different cultures have vague, indeterminate, or shifting boundaries—Britain's "favorite" dish for some time now has apparently not been fish-and-chips, but some version of chicken curry— one must have some conception of the limits or boundaries of a culture in this horizontal sense in order for the concept to be intelligible. A "culture" in this sense has identity and substance at any given time by virtue of the fact that it excludes certain ways of behaving, attitudes, forms of thought. A Frenchman in a Vietnamese restaurant may well eat with chopsticks, but it is definitely not a part of French culture to eat *bifteck* with chopsticks, or by picking it up and eating it by hand rolled up in a plantain leaf. If one gives up *some* vague and minimal sense that "there are limits," one gives up the use of the concept altogether (which might or might not be a good idea in its own right, but that question is not at issue here). Nietzsche is keen to emphasize the great positive importance of the exclusion which a culture implies. In the second *Untimely Meditation* (*KSA* 1.330) Nietzsche writes that humans need a "horizon" in order to orient themselves. If there is no distinction between what is on this "side" of the horizon and what "beyond," human energies and aspirations threaten to become too diffuse. A "culture" is an artificial horizon, and the restrictions it imposes are also the conditions which make it possible that participants in the culture can lead a meaningful, valuable life.

"Multiculturalism" calls into question a number of traditional assumptions about culture. One can distinguish at least three types of multiculturalism. The first kind is organized around the descriptive thesis that modern societies have in fact lost some aspects or parts of the cultural unity and homogeneity they once had had, so that they now contain groups with fundamentally *different* cultures, that is, cultures in the horizontal sense that in fact exclude each other, both Somalis who practice female circumcision and liberal agnostics who abhor it.

The phenomenon of cultural difference within a single society which is presented by multiculturalists in this first sense as something new and unique is perhaps not as novel as they believe. Anyone who reads the satires of Juvenal can see that Rome in the second century was arguably no less multicultural than London in 2007. Juvenal's verse is pretty clearly motivated by the anxiety of a man who feared the influx of "foreigners" because of their possible deleterious effects on his own economic prospects. In contrast to Juvenal, multiculturalism in this descriptive sense is completely unproblematic for Nietzsche. First of all, Nietzsche very clearly saw that the apparent unity and homogeneity of *any* culture was a mere illusion. Not even "Homer" was the poet of a unitary aboriginal culture; after all, he used an artificial language composed of borrowings from various different existing dialects. Even the Homeric poems, thus, are documents of a Creole culture, or, to put it in the vivid way the young Nietzsche does, the word "Homer" is not a proper name designating an individual at all, but an "aesthetic judgment."[6] Second, Nietzsche has no objection in principle to a coalescence of cultures; in fact, one might argue that he affirms its unique positive value, as one can see from the anecdote about Benvenuto Cellini he recounts:

> *The statue of humanity.*—The genius of culture operates as Cellini did when he made his statue of Perseus: the fluid mass of metal was in danger of being insufficiently copious, but it *was supposed to be*: so he threw plates and bowls and whatever else he could get his hands on into it. In just this way that genius throws errors, vices, hopes, delusions and other items of poor or noble metal in, for the statue of humanity must come out and be finished; what difference does it make that here and there inferior material was used? (*KSA* 2.212)

Multiculturalism constitutes a serious problem only if one starts from the assumption that all human beings are of equal value and transfers this assumption to cultures. Thus arises a second sense of multiculturalism, the claim that all cultures are equally valuable or at any rate must, in some contexts, be treated as if they are equally valuable. This can be seen as a refusal even to recognize the differences in value which form the backbone of the concept of "culture" in the vertical sense. Nietzsche would have had nothing to do with this form of multiculturalism, but one doesn't need to be a Nietzschean in any interesting sense to see this form of multiculturalism as a crude and destructive illusion. "Radical relativism" is a ghost conjured up by philosophers when they wish to raise the profile of their own academic speciality.

There is, however, a third possible sense of multiculturalism. One can use the term to designate the lack of any unitary will imposing order, coherence, and sense on some domain. In this sense Benvenuto Cellini's

---

[6] See Nietzsche's early essay "Homer und die classische Philologie," which is not included in *KSA*, but can be found in the parallel *Kritische Gesamtausgabe*, ed. Giorgio Colli and Mazzino Montinari (de Gruyter, 1967), 2.1.248–69.

production of the statue of Perseus was not an instance of a parallel phenomenon: Cellini used various materials, but the assumption is that the process was dominated by *one* artistic will, his own. This third sense of multiculturalism is quite distinct from the second. One can easily grant that not all "cultural phenomena" are of equal value and yet deny that a society needs a single cultural will. Liberals may be tempted here to fall back on the old motif of the "invisible hand." There might be "anonymous processes" which are not consciously dominated by any individual or group, but through the operation of which a state of equilibrium is attained in which certain cultural activities simply die off, just as, purportedly, inferior goods that find no buyer in a free market simply stop being produced. Nietzsche would, of course, have had no truck with any conception which gave pride of place to "anonymous processes." If a unitary will, like that of Benvenuto Cellini, is lacking or is insufficiently strong to dominate the material, no work of art will result, but only rubbish. The same is true of "culture" as a whole, so that at one point Nietzsche even proposes the establishment of a "Ministry of Culture that gives mandatory directives" ("imperativische Kulturbehörde"; *KSA* 7.266).

On the other hand, Nietzsche was fully aware that the whole sphere of culture is in one sense a domain of mere deceptive appearances. Perhaps those who are directly engaged in cultural creation need to convince themselves that their actions and artifacts are subject to fixed, objective standards, and must think of culture as something unitary and paradigmatic, but philologists, historians, and philosophers will not be taken in so easily. No culture, either in the horizontal or the vertical sense, is absolutely unitary, closed, or merely self-referential. In the horizontal dimension every culture is internally related, positively or negatively (or in both ways), to something outside itself. Just as nineteenth-century culture explicitly stood in the constant shadow of ancient paradigms, so, to put it paradoxically, no culture is merely itself. The unity and paradigmatic status of culture in the vertical dimension is equally problematic. Is there *only one* way to cultivate "the plant 'man'" (*KSA* 5.61)?

The distinction between culture in a vertical and in a horizontal sense should not be confused with the distinction between culture (singular) and cultures (plural). While it is true that "culture" understood as a horizontal concept can usefully be used only in historical situations in which *different* cultures are under discussion, it is not the case that culture in the vertical sense necessarily presupposes a single, general standard or yardstick for evaluation. If the root meaning of "culture" in the vertical sense is "cultivate," there are also a variety of different ways in which one can cultivate anything, which cannot necessarily all be compared the one with the other. This is particularly the case in arts that have internalized and give special prominence to Romantic conceptions of "originality." Perhaps Debussy was a "better" composer than D'Indy or Ysayë, but who in 1920 could have said with any kind of authoritativeness which of Debussy, Schönberg, or Stravinsky composed "better" music? Adorno, to be sure, tried to argue in a complicated way that there had to be a single, final, comprehensive judgment in aesthetic matters, but his arguments, to the extent to which they are clearly discernible at all as arguments, are not very convincing, and they are certainly incompatible with some attitudes that were very deeply rooted in Nietzsche's thought, and of which Nietzsche ought himself to have been aware. Even an Office of Culture that gave orders which *had* to be followed ("imperativische Kulturbehörde") would be, from a philosophical perspective, a factory of illusions, and Nietzsche must have realized that. In the end one is therefore confronted with the same paradox that keeps recurring again and again in Nietzsche's thought: human beings are subject to certain illusions, which they can to some extent see through as illusions, but which are nonetheless utterly necessary for them to continue to live. The basic Nietzschean remains without an answer: how are we humans to deal with such *necessary* illusions?   Find better ones!!

Thucydides reports that in the first winter of the great war between the Athenians and the Peloponnesians, the Athenian general Pericles was chosen to give a funeral oration for those who had fallen in battle (II.34–46). He spoke about the relation between politics and culture—at least that is the way Nietzsche describes the subject of this oration, using "culture" is his usual anachronistic way. Politics and culture condition and support one another, but politics retains a certain priority. The real greatness of Athens consists in the political achievements of its citizens, who have "forced open for themselves with their daring access to every land and sea" and have set up everywhere "unforgettable monuments" of their power and their deeds. Such a city "needs no Homer to praise her" with beautiful words which delight "only for a moment" (II.41). Nietzsche's verdict on the sentiments expressed in this speech is devastating. The speech is a "huge optimistic mirage" (*KSA* 2.308). The purportedly freestanding "eternal glory" (κλέος ἄφθιτον) which derives from political success is just an illusion. Without Athenian "culture"—without Sophocles, Thucydides, and Socrates—who would care about the final fate of the Delian League? Pericles would have remained a minor personage mentioned in footnotes to works on the early history of the Balkans, if there had been no Thucydides, but it is also perhaps true that Pericles would not have been the man he was, had he not (falsely) believed, he had no need of a Thucydides. Despite all of this, it would be just as serious a mistake now to absolutize "culture" as it was in the nineteenth century to absolutize "morality."

VII

On Museums

THE COLLECTING AND exhibiting of natural objects and of artifacts has a long history. There are different kinds of collections, and they have varying origins, and serve a wide variety of different human purposes. Thus, for instance, in the ancient world temples sometimes served as repositories of various offerings, some of which were durable objects, such as the bloody armor of successively defeated opponents. The reasons the victors had for depositing these trophies are probably very complicated; the desire to thank a divine patron and commemorate a signal success may have played an important role, but also perhaps the desire to intimidate other possible enemies. Medical schools at least since the Renaissance have collected specimens of physically deformed, degenerate, diseased, and exemplarily healthy organs for training purposes; student physicians, it was thought, would best learn how to discriminate between normal variation and the abnormal by being synoptically presented with lots of instances of each.[1] Equally, since antiquity wealthy aristocrats[2] and, more recently, successful entrepreneurs have filled their residences with what they took to be beautiful or strikingly unusual objects for reasons of prestige or because they delighted in looking at them.

As the first of the above examples shows, some of what we would now call "collection" might originally merely have accumulated rather than having been intentionally brought together by any person or agency according to a plan with some specific purpose or rationale in mind. The priests in the temple might originally have been bemused or even irritated by the *detritus* deposed by successive generations of

This essay is an expanded version of a Comment I gave on Neil MacGregor's Tanner Lectures "The Meanings of Things" at Clare Hall, Cambridge, 16–18 February 2004. I am greatly indebted to Neil MacGregor for his highly informative and stimulating talks, and to several private conversations we had during his stay in Cambridge, and in particular for encouraging me to think more carefully about the Benin bronzes and their history.

[1] See G. Canguilhem, *Le Normal et e pathologique* (PUF, 1966). Also Foucault, *La Naissance du clinique* (PUF, 1978).

[2] See Margaret Miles, *Art as Plunder* (Cambridge University Press, 2008).

worshippers.[3] There will, of course, always remain a very important element of chance, randomness, the unpredictable and contingent, in any such collection, but at a certain point collecting may become a conscious project, and eventually institutional structures may be created to ensure persistent pursuit of the aims of the collection through time, protection and maintenance of the objects once they have been acquired, and appropriate forms of display. Some of the changing and various purposes that guided those who founded, endowed, supported, and maintained museums we would judge to have been, at least in part, benevolent and laudable, e.g., popular instruction (as in the Museum of Hygiene in Dresden); others we find less attractive and admirable, such as the sheer demonstration of power. In some cases purposes of which we approve are inextricably connected with purposes (and effects) which we find absolutely repugnant.[4] In addition to the intentions and purposes, conscious or unconscious and publicly acknowledged or not, which those who created and maintained such collections might have had, we can also often discover various ways in which these collections have actually functioned in various societies. The actual social functions will obviously often deviate significantly from those originally intended: thus, it is not unknown for collections intended for public instruction and moral improvement to come to serve as places of mere amusement or sexual assignation.

Originally the Greek word from which "museum" is derived had nothing to do with the collection and display of *objects*, and it did not necessarily have any reference to a particular place or space. A "museum" is

[3] Think of Ion in the play by Euripides of the same name, who is a slave-attendant of the temple of Apollo at Delphi. In one of the silliest sequences in ancient tragedy he sings to his broom ("Come, o young-burgeoning instrument of beautiful laurel, you who sweep clean the precinct beneath the temple . . . ," ll. 112–15) and describes his holy tasks as sweeping up (with the apostrophized broom), pouring out the holy water (ll.129–40), and shooting arrows to scare away the birds who would otherwise defecate on the many votary offerings to the god (ὡς ἀναθήματα μὴ βλάπτηται l. 177). He claims to be happy, but the thought cannot fail to occur to the modern reader that if he were less of a simpleton, he might prefer to have fewer offerings to clean and protect, and more time to do other things (such as getting a head start in his later vocation of populating all Ionia with his descendents ll.1571ff). In fairness, one should recall Nietzsche's point that we have only the written text of what was originally a work incorporating music and dancing. Whether or not the idea of Ion singing and *dancing* with his broom improves the overall aesthetic impression of the work I leave to the reader to decide, but it certainly is true that Barberina's silly aria about her lost needle is not generally taken to detract from the pleasure of hearing *Le Nozze di Figaro*.

[4] See Walter Benjamin, "Über den Begriff der Geschichte," in *Illuminationen: Ausgewählte Schriften* (Suhrkamp 1977), p. 254; Margaret M. Miles, *Art as Plunder* (Cambridge University Press, 2008); and Annie Coombes's marvelous *Reinventing Africa* (Yale University Press, 1994).

simply "that which belongs or pertains to the Muses," so it could be a place, a singing academy, an open space in which people assembled to dance, or a certain *time* at which the Muses could or should be especially cultivated (such as during certain festivals).[5] It is also apposite to recall that the Muses were not originally conceived simply as patronesses of what we would nowadays think of as the "fine arts." Rather their remit extended more broadly to encompass activities that we would classify as forms of "knowledge" rather than art. The ascription of one specific domain of competence, as it were, to each of the Muses does not belong to the most archaic period, but one of the more stable associations is of the Muse Urania with astronomy. So a rudimentary observatory, a clear space on the top of a hill from which one could observe the heavens, could be correctly called a "museum." Eventually in fact, the word "museum" came to be associated with the large foundation in Alexandria which was a library and what we would call a research center. The Alexandrian Museum was decorated with busts, statues, etc., but the papyrus rolls that were collected here were not displayed as *objets d'art* in their own right, but as texts to be consulted, i.e., as repositories of words. During the Renaissance collections of antiquities and other objects of interest were called by a variety of names: *studio, gabinetto, galleria*; the word *"museum"* established itself as standard term to refer to such collections only gradually.[6]

During the past two hundred years or so we have become inclined to distinguish more and more sharply between the "fine arts" (in the first instance, painting and sculpture),[7] crafts (including technologically advanced industrial forms of production), and forms of "knowledge" (in the first instance, natural science in its purer forms). In the modern world we generally construe "knowledge" as a set of interconnected propositions which can be accumulated, tested, transmitted by learning, and used in various ways, although characteristic modern forms of knowledge might require experimental apparatus, and be embedded in various intimate ways in complex kinds of machinery such as computers. The expression "fine arts," on the other hand, refers in the first instance to a domain of objects that sustain and invite intense, absorbing contemplation of the objects themselves and a pleasurable focus on their subtle

[5] See August Pauly, Georg Wissowa, et al., *Paulys Realencyclopädie der classischen Altertumswissenschaften: Neue Bearbeitung* (Metzler, 1894–1980), *RE* sub "μουσειον."

[6] See Paula Findlen, "The Museum: Its Classical Etymology and Renaissance Genealogy," in *Museum Studies*, ed. Bettina Messias Carbonell (Blackwell, 2004), pp. 23–50.

[7] The history of forms of classification of the "(fine) arts" is complex. See Paul Oscar Kristeller, "The Modern System of the Arts," in *Journal of the History of Ideas* 12 (1951), pp. 496–527, and 12, pp. 17–46. In the present context I will ignore music, dance, theatre, poetry, etc. for reasons that I assume will be obvious to the reader.

sensible properties, and then also to the skills needed to produce or appreciate such objects.

Correspondingly, in the present day there are roughly two kinds of collections of objects for public display. First, there are collections devoted to the fine arts, that is, collections of objects that deserve and will reward aesthetic contemplation. I will call these "(art) galleries." Examples include the National Gallery in London, the Quai d'Orsay in Paris, the Rijksmuseum in Amsterdam, and the Gemäldegallerie in Dresden. Second, there are collections of objects that are not themselves necessarily of great aesthetic value, but which illustrate or throw light on natural history, or on human history or culture. Examples of this kind of collection include the British Museum, or any of the great "Natural History" collections. I will use the term "museum" ambiguously: in a general sense to refer to either of these two kinds of collection, and in the narrower sense to refer specifically to the second kind of collection.

Up to now I have discussed one aspect of the museum: that it is a collection of artifacts; but the other aspect of our modern conception of a museum, namely that it is a collection intended for *public display*,[8] is equally important. There are, of course, extremely significant private art collections, and certain specialized research centers might have extensive holdings of objects to which only a very restricted group of persons have regular access. In addition, there might be various other limitations on the number of people who could be accommodated in a certain space or during a certain period of time—think of the queues to enter the Sistine Chapel. Finally, many museums are forced to charge admission fees that effectively restrict the number and the socioeconomic status of those who visit it.[9] Still, the commitment to some kind of wide access is deep-seated. Why? This presupposes that there is in principle some reason or reasons a large number and a wide variety of kinds of people might have or ought to have for visiting such a collection. One such reason might be that it gave them pleasure. Alternatively, the political powers or representatives of the society as a whole might think that they had an instrumental interest in promoting as many visits by as many people as possible. Thus the authorities might believe that visiting a Museum of Hygiene made the populace more aware of various dangers to public health, or that visiting a specially constructed National Museum would influence their political

---

[8] "Public," of course, can refer either to ownership or to access, i.e., a collection can be owned by an individual and yet be open to anyone to visit; similarly the state can own a collection, for instance an archive, and yet restrict access to it. I will discuss this further below, and see also my *Public Goods, Private Goods* (Princeton University Press, 2001) for some of the different senses of "public" and "private."

[9] Pierre Bourdieu, *La distinction* (Minuit, 1979) also considers other factors that restrict access.

views in ways they thought were desirable, such as by inspiring Love of
the Homeland and Hatred for the Enemy in time of war, etc. Considerations such as these form the basis of the claim to "public utility" many
museums make. Since in many countries museums are dependent upon
financial support of a direct or indirect kind from governments, and in
all sectors of modern life large institutions are expected to give *some*
account of themselves, claims to public utility are a serious matter. Is
there anything one can say in general about the possible sustainable and
presentable reasons for establishing and maintaining museums or about
their legitimate functions ?

In the first century BC the Roman poet Horace wrote a short tract in
verse on the art of poetry in which he formulated what came to be considered the classical conception of the aims of poetry:

> aut prodesse volunt aut delectare poetae
> aut simul et iucunda et idonea dicere vitae[10]

"Poets wish either to benefit or to delight, or to say what is at the same
time pleasant and useful for life." One could do worse than start by trying to construe collections of artifacts, including galleries and museums,
along these lines; among their numerous avowable purposes these two—
to benefit and to delight—have a certain salience.[11]

To reverse Horace's order, the first goal is the production of forms of
pleasure, enjoyment, delight, and isn't harmless pleasure prima facie a
perfectly legitimate and presentable goal? Although certain high modernist followers of Kant might wish to distinguish positive aesthetic
judgment from all empirical forms of enjoyment or pleasure, it seems
very difficult to maintain this distinction strictly if one wishes to have
any understanding of art as a social phenomenon.[12] Certainly art galleries, if they are good ones, produce at least in some people very vivid
and intense feelings of pleasure and delight, although one can perhaps
also wonder whether it is invariably "harmless."[13] I don't mean by this

---

[10] *Ars poetica* 333–34. I have always found this famous passage distinctly disappointing.
The use of "*aut. . . . aut . . .*" leads one to expect that some kind of quasi-existential choice
is going to be posed in stark terms: *either* benefit *or* delight. Then the third "*aut*" apparently
admits the possibility of doing both at the same time. Perhaps this is meant to be ironic, or
more ironic than I am willing to credit.

[11] There might be a third: to make people more "civilized," for which, see below. For the
classic philosophic discussion of these issues, see Friedrich Schiller, *Briefe über die ästhetische
Erziehung der Menschen*, in Schiller, Sämtliche Werke (Hanser, 1967), vol. 5, pp. 570–669.

[12] See Kant, *Kritik der Urteilskraft*, in Kant, *Werk-Ausgabe* (Suhrkamp, 1977), vol. 10;
Adorno, *Ästhetische Theorie* (Suhrkamp, 1970), pp. 14–31.

[13] Adorno, for instance, would not agree that the pleasure we take in art is always "harmless," but then it is not clear that this is not simply a consequence of his view that in the
modern world *nothing* is "harmless" (see his *Minima Moralia* [Suhrkamp, 1951]).

to suggest that Puritans were right to think there is anything inherently wrong with pleasure, but rather that we have some grounds to be slightly skeptical about the blanket claim that *all* of the pleasures of art are "harmless" until proven otherwise. We are familiar with forms of art that do not seem to us in the least harmless. I don't merely mean gladiatorial games or the lethal theatrical representations of ancient myth by condemned criminals in the Roman arena,[14] although we have no reason to think that these completely lacked an aesthetic dimension. Rather, I think there are two further reasons for suspicion about some kinds of aesthetic pleasure. First, we suspect that some works of art, especially representational works, will tend to reinforce existing stereotypes— positive or negative stereotypes—in a way that we now would find socially harmful or morally objectionable. The nobleman, churchman, or landowner in sixteenth-, seventeenth-, and eighteenth-century paintings is generally depicted in such a way as to encourage our admiration; mocking soldiers around Jesus are often given exaggeratedly grotesque "Semitic" features; and so on. Second, we have reason to suspect that some of the pleasure many people *in fact* take in art may be connected with their appreciation of various forms of exclusion.[15] One might not think there was anything particularly wrong with taking a pleasure from which others are excluded, and one might even think that it should be of no public concern if I take some extra pleasure in my awareness of the fact that others are excluded from the pleasure which I take. Still, we might think this becomes a public issue if the exclusion in question is deeply or systematically connected with other forms of exclusion, for instance exclusion from political power, or contributes to legitimizing otherwise unacceptable forms of oppression.[16] We are no longer so sure that aesthetic pleasure, if it occurs in contexts like these, can be fully insulated against them.

The second of the two goals Horace mentions is that which is beneficial or advantageous to us or to our life. There is an old tradition in

[14] See, for instance, Martial *Lib. spect.* 7.

[15] Matthew Leigh makes the point in his "Primitivism and Power: The Beginnings of Latin Literature" (*Literature in the Roman World*, ed. O. Taplin, Oxford University Press, 2001), p. 17, with reference to early Latin comedy, that "The value of certain jokes to those who get them is only heightened by the consciousness that there are others watching who are left entirely bemused." See also Pierre Bourdieu, *La distinction*. This is, of course, a deeply Nietzschean theme, although he presents the "discriminatory" aspect of art as a positive advantage rather than a criticism.

[16] This is one of the reasons the data cited by Neil MacGregor on the large number of visits to the National Gallery by ordinary workmen from central London are so surprising. In nineteenth-century London "exclusion" from participation in the enjoyment of art was *less* significant than one might have thought.

Western philosophy going back to Plato[17] which jumps to the conclusion that this must refer to some kind of knowledge. What is finally really advantageous or beneficial to us is to be able to lead a good life, and one can reliably lead such a good life only if one knows how to do that, that is, if one has a certain kind of knowledge. A central portion of the story of Western philosophy is devoted to trying to determine whether there is or could conceivably be such a form of knowledge-that-enables-one-to-lead-a-better-life, and, if there is, what it would be and how we could attain it. It does not seem difficult to see that factual knowledge of individual features of the world, or the general scientific knowledge which is provided by good empirical theories, would be beneficial, useful, or helpful in specific situations in which we must deal with particular difficulties. It is advantageous to know that penicillin will cure pneumonia, if one has pneumonia and potential access to a supply of penicillin; it is beneficial to know how to find directions by observing the night sky, if one is likely to find oneself wandering about, or drifting in a boat, alone at night. Knowledge of medicines and of how to orient oneself are forms of knowledge that clearly enable us to lead a better life: a life without pneumonia is better than one with pneumonia, and being able to find one's way about is better than being lost and disoriented. Some such knowledge can be used to help us change the world directly, and even factual knowledge that for one reason or another cannot be used to transform the environment directly, such as ability to predict the weather, can benefit us by allowing us to prepare for the inevitable in such a way as to minimize its disruptive effect, for instance by taking an umbrella or putting on a mac.

Many traditional philosophers have argued that this type of factual, instrumentally useful knowledge is not the only kind that is available to humans, and certainly not the kind that is of greatest significance to us. Many have claimed that there is a kind of knowledge which is associated with a general but noninstrumental improvement in the quality of the life I lead. That is, if I have this knowledge, my life is made better but not by virtue of the fact that I can control some element of my environment in a more efficient way.[18] To adopt a term popularized by Richard Rorty, philosophers have contrasted factual knowledge and edifying knowledge.[19]

---

[17] I discuss some of these issues in two papers: "Poetry and Knowledge" (*Arion* 11.1, pp. 1–31) and "Plato, Romanticism, and Thereafter" (*Arion* 11.3, pp.151–68).

[18] Some philosophers have also denied the existence of any nonfactual forms of knowledge; some would disagree with the tacit assimilation of "factual" knowledge and "useful" knowledge. As on most philosophical matters, opinions differ here greatly.

[19] Richard Rorty, *Philosophy and the Mirror of Nature* (Princeton University Press, 1979), pp. 315–94. Derived from Hegel, *Phänomenologie des Geistes* (*Werke*, vol. 3, p. 14; vol. 16, p. 7; also vol. 2, p. 558).

Edifying knowledge is knowledge of what would make my life a better life, or, alternatively, knowledge the acquisition of which would improve my life. This "or, alternatively" covers over the problem. It might be a property of the edifying knowledge in question that it cannot interestingly be construed as knowledge "of" anything specific. If that is the case, in what sense is it "knowledge"? Often this hypothetically posited edifying form of knowledge is understood as being connected with a transformation of the self, or of putting one's own soul in the proper order.[20] Useful factual knowledge enables us to transform and manipulate the world; transformative self-knowledge aids us in organizing, clarifying, and rendering coherent our own desires, preferences, and tastes, or in coming to a better conception of who we are, who we wish to be, or who we should wish to be, what we want, how we should act toward others, etc. Such knowledge is in one sense "beneficial"—what could be more genuinely beneficial to us than getting our soul into the right shape?—but it is not "useful" in the usual narrow way in which that term is used. Those who have this edifying knowledge can also be said to be "enlightened"—they know who they are, what they want, through what desires they should look at the world, etc.

One final complication to this picture is that although the general distinction between the instrumental or useful and the "edifying" seems clear enough, what I have called "the edifying" does not seem itself to be an internally unified category. It seems to lump together a variety of different things, each of which is perhaps not a strictly "useful" form of knowledge, but not all of which are plausibly supposed to be the same. Thus Plato, and following him many others, makes no clear distinction within the category of what I have called "the edifying" between knowledge that improves the quality of my own life, roughly speaking a knowledge that is an essential part of what it is for me to live a happy, fulfilling life, and a kind of *moral* knowledge, that is a form of knowledge by virtue of which I am "better" in my dealings with other people.[21] A "good life" that is, can be a life that is good *for me* (i.e., happy, satisfying, successful) or good *for the rest of you* (i.e., characterized by consideration for others, benevolence, public-spiritedness, etc.). Plato was keen to argue that only a virtuous or morally edified and edifying life—one informed by the moral knowledge of what is good—could be a happy life, but this is clearly false. A socially constructive life is not in fact necessarily a happy one for the agent, and "moral knowledge"—that knowledge by virtue of which I act

[20] Plato, *Apologia Socratis*.

[21] Plato, of course, thinks he is not "lumping things together," but that he has an argument for the necessary connection of these two things. Unfortunately the argument depends on accepting the doctrine of the transmigration of souls (*Republic*).

toward other humans as I ought—is not self-evidently the same as "feli-cific" knowledge—a form of knowledge that will make me happy.

Having embarked on the path of analysis by distinguishing the moral from the felicific, one might wonder whether one could move along it even further. Is there even any such thing as a unitary "moral knowl-edge," and if so, what would it look like?

At the beginning of Western ethics there stands a certain aristocratic Greek view of moral knowledge, which Plato is keen to consign to the rubbish-bin of oblivion. Certain people, it was assumed, did know how to act in a proper way and others did not, and proper behavior was to some extent something that could be said to be learned, although it also depended to some extent of natural aptitude (which was, however, some-times identified simply with "good birth"). Nevertheless, the most sym-pathetic reconstruction of what these pre-Socratic aristocrats thought would take them to have held that although one could learn to be a good person, one could not exactly be said to have been "taught." One learned how to be good by associating with the right kind of people (συνεῖναι, ὁμιλεῖν, etc.), thus acquiring by a kind of cultural osmosis the right habits of action, the right values, the right desires and forms of self-control, in the same way in which one acquired knowledge of one's first language, learning how to speak correctly by imitating those around one and as-similating their usage[22] without being given formal instruction by any particular person.[23]

Plato rejected this plausible and attractive view *in toto*, assuming rather a strict parallelism between learning and teaching. At least in this life if we learn something we must have been taught it, and taught it *by someone*; therefore there must in principle be specific teachers, and teaching takes place through dialectical discussion and takes the form of the transmission of propositional knowledge. The shoemaker who can make a good shoe for any foot does not really know what he is doing if he cannot give reasons for everything he does. From this the conclu-sion is drawn that no citizen of Athens can be a truly good citizen (and a good man) who cannot provide reasons for all his actions that stand up to the assault of Socrates' dialectic. The philosopher, the expert in ar-gumentation, is, so Plato finally concludes, the real purveyor of edifying knowledge, the person who can tell you how you ought to treat others and how you can live the best and happiest life accessible to you. The (as we would say, "morally") good person is the person who has this kind of knowledge; the same is true of the happy person. The best thing any person can do, therefore, is not to associate with the beautiful people of

[22] Plato, *Republic* 500c.
[23] Plato, *Meno* 86d–100b.

his society—in the ancient world these would have been people of "good birth," aristocrats: nowadays we might add to the mix rock stars, footballers, colorful entrepreneurs (even if unsuccessful), colorless but successful entrepreneurs in fashionable parts of the economy, etc.—hoping thereby to become like them; but to sit at Plato's feet, and take part in his dialectical exercises. The best society would be one in which philosophers like Plato were kings, which presumably means that they could not just reason with the other members of the society but *enjoin* them to act in certain ways and have those injunctions enforced.

This line of thought, however, does not seem at all convincing if it is intended, as it seems to have been at any rate by Socrates, to describe a sufficient condition for moral goodness. It may be correct that a person of a benevolent natural disposition may fail to act in what we take to be the proper way toward others because he lacks appropriate knowledge of how he must act in the world in order to realize his benevolence. It seems, however, equally clear that being a morally good person is not a matter exclusively of mastering and being able to defend a set of true propositions. Moral goodness requires both an intellectual component and a dispositional or habitual one.[24] Acquiring the intellectual skills and beliefs one needs may be a matter of natural aptitude plus active participation in something like the Socratic forms of inquiry, and, one might add, access to the latest results of established sciences, but building up the right dispositions, attitudes, and sets of values would seem to require a much more comprehensive discipline of learning how to act and react in a variety of real and imaginary situations—another reason, Plato might think, to make philosophers kings, not merely schoolmasters.

Suppose, then, that one can distinguish factual from two kinds of "edifying" or improving or enlightening knowledge: moral knowledge, a purported kind of knowledge that makes you a better person specifically in your dealings with other people, and felicific knowledge, mastery of the art of improving the quality of the life you lead. This still does not answer the question: Is there, however, really any such thing as "edifying" knowledge? Isn't this just a self-serving illusion, Plato's invention intended by him to glamorize the "philosophical" form of life he in some sense contributed to stabilizing?[25] Even if a form of inherently improving knowledge did exist, is there any reason to believe museums or art galleries could contribute to propagating or sustaining it? The fact that by far the greatest collector, museum builder, and patron of the arts of the twentieth century was Adolf Hitler, suggests that any positive

[24] A conclusion Aristotle draws.

[25] It is a complex issue to what extent it is historically correct to speak of Plato "initiating" a certain form of life. I can't discuss this here.

connection between the modern museum as an institution and forms of edifying knowledge is at best asthenic and adventitious.[26] The discussion up to now has been rather abstract, and so perhaps consideration of a concrete example would clarify what is at issue.

If one were looking for concrete examples of edifying knowledge of a kind that might be relevant to thinking about museums, one might start by considering the Benin bronzes,[27] and the effect they had of increasing the enlightenment of European consciousness at the start of the twentieth century. The Portuguese first encountered the Kingdom of Benin (located in the territory of present-day Nigeria) in the fifteenth century. Craftsmen in the kingdom seem already to have had a rather advanced knowledge of metallurgy, and during the sixteenth century began to produce brass heads and plaques of outstanding artistic merit, using the highly sophisticated *cire perdue* technique.[28] The center of this production was the royal court in Benin City. In 1897, one of the familiar late colonial stories played itself out in Benin:[29] In response to the massacre of a party of Europeans the British government sent a punitive expedition that sacked and burned Benin City, deposed the king, and took away with them virtually the whole corpus of traditional royal art. Many of the finest pieces of this traditional art ended up in the British Museum; much of the rest was sold by private individuals who were related to members of the punitive expedition or by the Foreign Office. In this way the museums in Berlin and Hamburg were able to acquire very significant collections. The public exhibition of these objects caused a great stir in late ninteenth- and early twentieth-century Europe by upsetting a great number of established prejudices about human history and the inherent cultural inferiority of non-European populations and societies. To be more exact, the art objects from Benin were thought to be disturbing for two slightly different reasons. First, the high level of technical skill and craftsmanship they exhibited was not compatible with deeply entrenched prejudices about African backwardness. So some attempt was made to claim that the bronzes were of Portuguese manufacture or were made by Africans who had been instructed by the Portuguese. Second, human sacrifice was practiced on a large scale in nineteenth-century

[26] See Frederick Spotts, *Hitler and the Power of Aesthetics* (Hutchinson, 2002), and Peter Reichel, *Der schöne Schein des Dritten Reichs* (Fischer, 1993).

[27] This is one of the examples used by Neil MacGregor in his Tanner Lectures.

[28] Confusingly, most of the "bronzes" are actually made of brass.

[29] For the history of the punitive expedition by a contemporary, see H. Ling Roth, *Great Benin: Its Customs, Art and Horrors* (Routledge and Kegan Paul, 1968). A more recent general history is A.F.C. Ryder, *Benin and the Europeans 1485–1897* (Longmans, 1969). For a good, although not comprehensive, overview of the brass art, see Felix von Luschan, *Die Altertümer von Benin* (Vereinigung wissenschaftliche Verleger, 1919).

Benin.[30] How could a human society both practice human sacrifice and cultivate such a technologically advanced and aesthetically subtle form of art? One hypothesis suggested was that nineteenth-century Benin was a degenerate descendant of an earlier higher civilization; the art had been inherited from this earlier lost civilization, and the human sacrifice represented the debased present.[31] The evidence for an indigenous origin of these artifacts was present almost from the very beginning and was recognized by some experts, but general acceptance of it required a very long process of struggle against what look in retrospect to be nothing but irrational if deeply embedded prejudices. However, the conclusion *was* finally generally accepted.

This example raises a number of questions about enlightenment. If one is looking for a special kind of edifying knowledge, distinct from other forms of knowledge, one might be tempted to think that knowledge of the Benin bronzes, at any rate, was not a good example. There seems nothing special about the kind of knowledge that is at issue here. It seems we have simply a set of historical facts: that these and these objects were in fact produced by native craftsmen working in an indigenous tradition in West Africa at a certain time. Perhaps the confrontation with this set of facts had some kind of enlightening effect in the given context, but it is not at all obvious that that tells one anything special about the kind of knowledge involved.

We now say that studying these objects was "beneficial" to late nineteenth-century Europeans, but not because it allowed them to manipulate some part of the world more successfully or efficiently, or because it satisfied some preexisting desire they had. It is true, to be sure, that the bronzes are so overwhelmingly engaging that they pleased those with aesthetic sensibilities immediately, but this is not the main thing people have in mind by calling the encounter with them "beneficial." It is beneficial because it could bring about a psychic change in Europeans and in the way in which they could see the world. To be sure, a certain kind of correct factual knowledge is required for this self-transformation to come about. It had to be true, and be known to be true, that the objects did come from Benin and were produced by local craftsmen there.

---

[30] Ryder suggests that human sacrifice was introduced in the seventeenth century by the first Beninian *oba* (king) to have been subjected in his youth to Christianity, with the implication that this fact might be relevant and significant. While this hypothesis is highly congenial to our modern sensibility, it depends on a rather weak argument *ex silentio*.

[31] See Annie Coombes (*Reinventing Africa*, Yale University Press, 1994), who discusses the various forms of resistance to acceptance of the indigenous African origin of the bronzes, and the complex and not always very admirable factors that lead to the eventual recognition of the truth. See also especially the discussion of the "degeneration " thesis in chapter 3. Contrast this with von Luschan's *Die Altertümer von Benin*.

However, this is just the necessary precondition for the change in question. This change, too, is not in any sense automatic—we have to work at it. Perhaps the edifying knowledge in question is a kind of skill in properly attending to appropriate facts and bringing them to bear on general attitudes. To be sure, in describing retrospectively what happened then as "improvement" or a "beneficial" development, we are appealing to various highly complex value judgments we would now make. Nevertheless, it does not follow that we are wrong to see the result as a state in which we have overcome some prejudices that made us less able to lead morally good and satisfying lives. This is not a case of the kind envisaged by Richard Rorty in which some kind of moral progress is attained by expanding one's sympathies, at any rate if "sympathy" is used in anything like its usual sense.[32] The exquisitely bloodthirsty Kingdom of Benin was not one to which any more or less detached observer would have felt impelled to extend the least sympathy. Rather it is precisely because the Benin bronzes are *both* technically highly accomplished *and* very strikingly beautiful that they could have the powerful effect they had in the late nineteenth century, despite the justifiable disapproval Europeans felt for the political system which produced them.

It was probably significant in changing people's general deep-seated attitudes toward Africa that the appreciation of the Benin bronzes did not require an antecedent transformation of taste. The bronzes were at least as skillful and beautiful *by prevailing European standards* as anything Europe could produce.[33] To be sure, once this had happened the way was perhaps paved for a more sustained and serious study of other forms of non-European art that could not so easily be fully assimilated to European canons, but required a change of taste. This brings us to two related further points. First, museums do not simply reflect existing taste and satisfy preexisting desire, but they change taste. That does not necessarily mean that people come to *like* what is displayed—they may come to dislike it intensely—nor does it mean that one can control and intentionally guide such changes of taste. How exactly taste changes is completely unclear. Second, the attempt to change or "cultivate" taste is, in one important strand of nineteenth-century theorizing, an important positive function of museums. They are not there simply to delight—satisfy existing preferences and desire—or to benefit, if that means either to be useful or to make us more moral or happier, but also for a third important purpose: to cultivate our taste, to make it more discriminating, polished, civilized,

---

[32] Richard Rorty, "Human Rights, Rationality, and Sentimentality," in *Truth and Progress* (Cambridge University Press, 1998), pp. 167–85.

[33] Note the contrast here to one classic modernist account of endogenous change of taste, Leo Steinberg, *Other Criteria* (University of Chicago Press, 1972).

sophisticated. There are obviously significant differences between these different dimensions along which taste can be cultivated. Taste is enlightened if free of prejudices—you try our snails, garlic, roast snake, octopus, or pork with an open mind, judging them, as far as possible, on their own merits without reference to the traditional cultural associations assigned to them by your own local group. Hume's discussion of the kinsman of Sancho Panza who could taste in a glass of wine the slight metallic tang left by a house-key that found its way by accident into the bottom of the barrel is the classic account of discriminating taste.[34] A sophisticated taste prefers the complex, the novel, and the subtle over the garish, the routine, and the excessively direct. Nevertheless for present purposes I will try to put aside these differences. To acquire a new, more enlightened, and more discriminating or sophisticated kind of taste is obviously not necessarily to be morally improved—although some of the early theorists clearly would love to claim this, and try by hook or crook to insinuate this conclusion—nor to be made happier,[35] although it might be argued that it opens up the possibility of a wider variety of possible experiences, which is generally, within limits, thought to be a good thing. On the other hand, if anything, a more sophisticated taste is likely to be more difficult to satisfy than a primitive one, and if happiness consists in satisfaction, sophistication and increased civilization will lead, as Freud thought, to greater unhappiness.[36]

The appeal to "enlightened taste" and the possible role of museums in the generation and support of such taste can scarce fail to call to mind for most of us a European movement—"*The* Enlightenment"—that is closely connected with the origin of many of the most illustrious modern museums. To put it with the kind of crudeness that limitations of space require, the Enlightenment can be thought to have two sides: a negative side directed at defeating a vicious enemy, and a positive side directed at the construction of a better human world. The hated enemy is religion: its infantile superstitions, its repressive institutions, and its gross deformation of the human character. More generally, being enlightened meant being free of prejudice, particularly religious prejudices. The central positive doctrine of the Enlightenment was the encyclopedic assumption that there was a single final system of all knowledge and that the knowledge in question would be *both* factual *and* edifying, i.e., deeply connected in some way both with useful application and with improvement of the quality of individual life and of social mores. One

[34] David Hume in *"Of the Standard of Taste" and Other Essays*, ed. John Lenz (Prentice Hall, 1965).

[35] Rousseau, *Discours sur les sciences ete les arts* (Gallimard, 1965).

[36] Sigmund Freud, "Das Unbehagen an der Kultur," in *Studienausgabe* (Fischer, 1974) vol. 9, pp. 193–270.

can see how on such a view the museum might have both a clear rationale and an obvious principle of internal organization. The rationale would be its contribution to the popular spread of knowledge, and its internal organization would be governed by the encyclopedic structure which human knowledge naturally exhibited. The museum, especially the so-called Universal Survey Museum,[37] could be the locus and embodiment of this encyclopedic dream. The "taste" one would acquire from engaging with all the forms of human knowledge and experience embodied in the displayed objects in the Universal Museum would have special standing, reasonably claiming priority over more provincial ways of reacting and judging.

We find parts of this way of thinking obsolete. The war against religion seemed to end in Europe when in the middle of the nineteenth century religion had ceased to be creditable in any serious way as a basic, independent mode of structuring our knowledge and life and when residual religious sentiments came to have the status of unimportant bits of folklore. Equally, however, we find it difficult to believe in the older positive form of Enlightenment, based on the existence of an encyclopedic form of knowledge that would be both factual and edifying.

Michel Foucault devoted much of his life to the attempt to distinguish sharply between the *doctrines* of the Enlightenment and the *ethos* of the Enlightenment.[38] The doctrines we know about; the ethos is the set of attitudes, habits, and practices connected with continual criticism and self-criticism, and in general an openness to new experience.[39] To criticize in the original sense (κρίνω) means to make distinctions, separate what does not belong together, and make judgments; it does not mean necessarily to reject.[40] Some of the powers that are associated with the ethos of enlightenment are the exercise of analytic abilities, of the imagination, especially the constructive imagination of alternatives to present ways of doing things, of discriminatory skill, and of judgment. What I want to propose is that there might be a post-Encyclopaedic notion of being "enlightened" of which Foucault's "enlightenment ethos" was an essential

[37] See Carol Duncan and Alan Wallach, "The Universal Survey Museum," in *Museum Studies,* ed. Bettina Carbonell (Blackwell, 2004), pp. 51–70.

[38] "Qu'est-ce que les lumières?" in *Dits et écrits*, vol. 4 (Gallimard, 1994), ed. Daniel Defert and François Ewald, pp. 571–78. See also "Genealogy as Critique" in my *Outside Ethics* (Princeton University Press, 2005), pp. 153–61.

[39] One might, of course, claim that this set of attitudes and habits is not *specifically* connected to the Enlightenment, that is the pan-European cultural and social movement of the eighteenth century. It is simply a modern version of the old Socratic doctrine that the "unexamined life is not worth living for man" (*Apology* 38a5: ὁ δὲ ἀνεξέταστος βίος οὐ βιωτὸς ἀνθρώπῳ).

[40] See also "Genealogy as Critique," in my *Outside Ethics*, pp. 153–61.

part, and I also want to suggest that it is difficult to envisage a realistic flourishing future for museums—or at least general survey museums directed at a wide public—if we can't see them as in some way oriented toward fostering this kind of enlightenment.

The most serious enemies of this form of enlightenment are not so much the feeble and decadent descendants of formerly robust religions, but rather the general idea that what our cultural institutions should do is give us or reinforce in us a natural sense of belonging, identifying with a prestigious collectivity, being at home in our world.[41] In Britain the institutional form which this ideal takes is what is called the "Heritage Industry." In its cruder forms this can mean placing social institutions like museums in the service of nationalism or other forms of communal or ethnic identification. The divergence between calls for criticism and enlightenment and calls for the reenforcement or creation of bonds of communal "belonging" is one of the many unresolved tensions which virtually all of our social and political institutions, not just our public collections of artifacts, must face, but museums stand in the very forefront of the struggle between these conflicting imperatives. There are particular difficulties for museums supported by public funds.

One of the original senses of "museum" was a space sacred to the Muses, daughters of Zeus and minor deities in their own right.[42] It was a grove or building which stood *outside* the usual world of human affairs, and by virtue of this standing as a religious space, it was surrounded by various taboos. Temple-robbing was not completely unknown, but the widespread, even though false, belief that the gods could take care of their own gave to the temple and its precincts a distinct status and could be thought to insulate it and its contents at least to some extent from minor forms of encroachment. What can the status of museums be, if their connection with even residual religiosity is broken? If the point of the modern museum was to "remove artifacts from their current context of ownership and use, from their circulation in the world of private property, and insert them into a new environment which would provide them with a different meaning,"[43] then this made good sense if one could presuppose the High Enlightenment project, and could say what that "different meaning" was. It was the location of the artifact in an edifying, coherent, progressive story of the enlightenment of human societies. If the Enlightenment worldview

---

[41] See Friedrich Nietzsche, "Vom Nutzen und Nachtheil der Historie für das Leben," in *Kritische Studien-Ausgabe* ed. G. Colli and M. Montinari (de Gruyter, 1967) vol. 1, pp. 245–334, and T. W. Adorno, *Minima Moralia* (Suhrkamp, 1973) § 18, pp. 40–42.

[42] Hesiod, *Theogonia* 75–79.

[43] Charles Saumarez Smith, "Museums, Artefacts, and Meanings," in *The New Museology*, ed. Peter Vigo (Reaktion Books, 1989), p. 6.

has become implausible, what other account do we have available? Can a (quasi-Foucauldian) commitment to the *ethos* of enlightenment suffice?

In the contemporary political context museums need positive legitimacy, that is, it needs to be shown not only that what they do is licit and permissible, but also that it is somehow very important and worthwhile. They also, however, need a kind of power, in particular the financial power which will allow them to carry on their operations. One special difficulty which modern museums face results from the fact that we have a relative poverty of possible sources of general legitimacy in the modern world. Who can say with authority that it is a good thing to have museums, and to have this kind of museum rather than that kind? Such legitimacy is percolated through one of three social institutions. First there are the authoritative political institutions: the Parliament, President, Chancellor, Congress, Diet, Chamber of Deputies, Prime Minister, etc. These are certainly in a position to grant a kind of highly visible recognition and endorsement in principle of museums and their tasks that will be likely to have some standing. The second institution is "the market." Few people are now (2008) still naïve enough to take the full "free-market" ideology at face value. A "free market" is obviously a complex and highly artificial social construct that requires continual political intervention to survive, not in any interesting sense "natural," and it is clearly as much a realm of systematic coercion as of freedom and individual choice. The question is not if, but how markets should be constrained and structured. Equally, since there is a vigorous market-demand for narcotics, mercenaries, polluting plastics and pesticides, pornography, etc., the connection between effective market-demand and any reasonable sense of "legitimacy" is tenuous. Still, if there were an articulated "market-demand" for museums, this would go some way toward giving at least a prima facie answer the question "why?"

The third potentially legitimating institution is "science," an abstraction realized in various bureaucratic agencies, independent laboratories, universities, international committees, etc. This particular pilot ship which once seemed destined to guide us safely and reliably into a vibrant future is now a bit derelict, having been dented and knocked about considerably by the contributions scientists made to the human destructiveness of World War I and holed below the waterline by Hiroshima. Nevertheless its intricate system of subdivided waterproof compartments has allowed it to remain afloat, deep in the water and making no seaway, but not yet quite consigned to the breakers' yard. "Science" in the sense in which it commanded some residual respect and retained some legitimatory power even into the late twentieth century, was, however, a pale shadow of Plato's "moral knowledge" (ἐπιστημή), and in it the tacit orientation of part of the enlightenment ideal—toward the importance of instrumentally *useful* knowledge—came to fruition in a way that makes it seem difficult to imagine that what is left of the prestige of "science" could make much of a contribution to legitimizing art galleries, or museums of any but the narrowest instructional kinds.

To move now from the sphere of legitimation to that of finance, there seem to be four obvious conceivable new sources of funding for museums:[44] political structures (particularly the central government), public admissions charges, commercial enterprises, and private donors. For many of the most visible museums in the UK, including virtually all of the large London museums, the second of these is consciously eschewed, presumably on the grounds that a decent society is one in which certain basic benefits such as personal security, health, education, and access to cultural experiences are provided to everyone as a matter of course without the expectation that those who receive these benefits or take advantage of them ought to pay a special fee for so doing. Although I do not pay a special fee (an "entrance charge") to visit the British Museum any more than I make some special individual payment to the doctor who gives me medical treatment on the NHS, the NHS is not "free," but funded by the general taxes collected by the British government. Should governments then fund museums, as they fund medical services (at least in Britain and other civilized and affluent countries)?

Given that one of the points of having museums at all—*one* of the points, not the *only* point—is to cultivate forms of taste and imagination, generate new aspirations, and perhaps even implant new psychic needs in the hope of improving political behavior, one must be rather careful to keep actual managerial control of museums by government agencies to a minimum. How much financial support will a responsible government give without any strings attached? Similar considerations apply to "private" donations and to the commercial enterprises museums run. There would seem to be limits to the extent to which a museum can allow itself to become dependent on such sources of funding without losing sight of its *raison d'être*.

Neil MacGregor has emphasized[45] the importance, at least for understanding the organization and operation of public museums in this country, of a specific British legal institution: the "trust." The objects in the British Museum are not owned by any particular person or persons or even by the British state as a whole, but are held and administered by a designated group of people—the Trustees—who are obliged to preserve and care for them for the benefit of the public, including future generations. This legal construction attempts to create a buffer between the museum and the potential ravages of commercialism on the one hand—because

[44] "New" meaning "abstracting from the fact that the museum itself and its holdings probably constitutes an existing accumulation of capital that could be realized."

[45] In his Tanner Lectures.

the holdings of the museum cannot legally be sold—and of the narrower forms of politically motivated manipulation on the other—because the Trustees are not chosen by or directly accountable to the government of the day.[46] A legal "trust" is a specific institutionalization of the more general phenomenon of human and civic trust which is the foundation of most societies. That such trust between people is not a natural state, but one which must be created, was one of Hobbes's basic insights, and one that survives recognition of its slim basis in the developmental psychology of humans. Trust is also notoriously difficult to reestablish, if once broken—who, after Iraq, ever trusted a thing Tony Blair said?—and it is healthiest when it is a two-way street. The public trusts the museum staff to preserve significant artifacts and present them in ways that are compatible with minimal standards of historical truth. Ideally, in fact, we make an even greater leap of faith and trust a museum to collect and preserve works we do not ourselves understand, and the significance of which is by no means evident to us. This goes beyond even Wittgenstein's famous comment that he did not understand the poetry of Trakl, but was convinced of its high quality, or the similar remark attributed to Mahler about Schönberg. We trust a museum to collect things (e.g., the collection of contemporary credit cards in the British Museum) of whose "high quality" or epistemic significance we are not convinced. We know mistakes will be made, but trust that they will be few and that in the long run it is best to leave these decisions to the judgment of the staff. The other side of this two-way street is that the staff of the museum should exhibit trust in the ability of visitors to make judgments on their own.[47]

One cannot force people to reflect, to be critical, or to confront the strange and rebarbative, and it is not even fully obvious what strategies will be most likely to encourage effectively those who begin to reflect to continue to do so. In fact, I think that the project of fostering the ethos of enlightenment is best served by making museums *less* explicitly didactic, at any rate in some respects, than some of them have come to be.

In a famous essay[48] Paul Valéry voices two complaints about museums. First, he says he feels constrained and coerced when at the entrance he is asked to give up his cane and forbidden to smoke, and feels that sense of coercion is incompatible with the appreciation of art. His second complaint is that the museum presents a "cold confusion" of heterogeneous

---

[46] Of course, this "buffer" is no absolute hermetic seal; no legal structure can give an absolute guarantee. If a museum goes bankrupt or a government wishes to be sufficiently ruthless, all bets are off. This essay was originally written partly under the impact of the assault by the Labour government under Tony Blair on the independence of the BBC in the aftermath of the disastrous decision to invade Iraq.

[47] On this see further *Whose Muse?* ed. James Cuno (Princeton University Press, 2004).

[48] Paul Valéry, "Le problème des musées," in *Pièces sur l'art* (Gallimard, 1934), p. 93.

objects all jumbled together.[49] These complaints clearly stem from Valéry's underlying commitment to the ideology of pure aesthetic experience that was given its first major formulation by Kant. Nevertheless one can agree in general with the first of these two grounds of dissatisfaction, although in the specific case of Valéry's cigar, one cannot but have sympathy for the prohibition. I want, however, to suggest that taking the resistance to the "authoritarian gestures" seriously should make us wary of Valéry's second objection: there is a certain value in *some* disorder, accidence, chaos. A museum *should* in some sense be a jumble, because the world is in some sense a jumble and a museum should be, among other things, a place to learn to exercise judgment.

In some modern museums, although the archetypical cases I have in mind are not museums I know in the UK, one has very intensely the sense of being controlled, regimented, lectured to, or preached at: "Enter here, this is Room One where you see xyz. Please notice α β γ, and now on the right observe ABC; these artifacts *show* that. . . ." *That* kind of apparently authoritative storytelling should not structure the forms of exhibition in a museum. Precisely if museums are supposed to be places which foster a certain kind of secular, cosmopolitan enlightenment, a cultivation of the imagination, and of the faculty of judgment, they should avoid making themselves too ordered and seamlessly coherent, allowing themselves to tell too singular and categorical a story. Museums are most importantly collections of artifacts, and that means of individual concrete objects. An object is not a story; it is a hard extra-narrative bit of formed matter. To be sure, it makes sense to us only as part of a story or perhaps a theory, but to try to eradicate the distinction between object and story or theory seems to me a bad mistake. One of the main points of having a museum in the modern sense at all is that the individual object has some kind of stubborn independence, radical otherness, and it is good for us to be confronted with this.[50] If there was no distinction

---

[49] It isn't clear whether the second complaint is directed primarily at the extreme profusion of objects in museums. There are simply too many on display, so that one feels overwhelmed. Or whether his complaint is that the presentation lacks order, or that the objects were too close together and it was thus difficult to have the right kind of aesthetic relation to them. In his prospectus Neil MacGregor distinguishes between collections of art objects and museums of cultures, and suggests that although most large museums will have both artifacts of inherent aesthetic value and objects of great historical and cultural significance, the emphasis will be on one of these two or the other. A museum of cultures will necessarily have a certain didactic coloration. In his lectures MacGregor also cites another of Valéry's complaints—that museums "turn Venus into a document"—which seems to refer to a state of confusion between aesthetic and didactic purposes. Is this necessarily a mutually destructive state or a healthy and potentially productive one?

[50] Also, contra Walter Benjamin (*"Das Kunstwerk im Zeitalter seiner technischen Reproduzierbarkeit"* [Suhrkamp, 1963]), the category of the "authentic" or the "genuine" is

between actually seeing some individual objects and reading a narrative or a general theoretical description, then there would be no need for museums, just for textbooks. Made-up, non-real, or imaginary examples are not enough to make the envisaged form of enlightenment attainable, and in particular no description (including literary description) will do the trick. In the case of imaginary examples one often *knows* the "correct" answer already, partly because in setting up such examples one is often (necessarily) mobilizing existing prejudices. More importantly, by the time a purportedly "real" situation or object has been *described*, most of the most difficult and important work of judgment has already been done. The case is described as a case of murder or fraud, or altruistic assistance. The description already directs one to look at certain things, or sometimes *not* to notice certain things . Part of the point of becoming a practically enlightened agent, however, is to learn what one can, and should, notice, and how one can, and should, describe what one notices. This is one of the reasons for thinking that the use of "literary examples" in philosophy, especially in moral philosophy, is not just grossly philistine, but so misguided as to be self-defeating. Literature is not life, and once the literary structuring has taken place, the more important part of the work is already finished, and what is left is mopping up. Perhaps that is all philosophy is good for, but one ought not to build this defeatist strategy into the very way one approaches thinking about human action.

Obviously this rejection of excessive didacticism should not be construed as implying that museums should try to re-create "the real experience." Part of the reason for that is that this is not in any case even in principle possible, and to think it is possible would be merely to fall prey to the other side of the very same dangerous illusion. If "the real experience" is not accessible, it is better not to pretend it is. The old style museum with detached labeled objects in cluttered vitrines was more honest in that it did not hide the fact that one had to operate on the exhibits with the theoretical imagination to *do* anything with them.

A very welcome development is the recent tendency of museums to give detailed information about themselves, and the origin and structure of their own collection. Reflecting on the power relations which allowed *these* particular objects to be collected in the way in which they were, and on the interests which lay behind this process, will not in itself cancel out the influence of this context of the collection, won't extract it from the web of power relations within which it is embedded, but it might be a way to foster, within limits, the ethos of Enlightenment.

---

vital to the museum. If it were not, why wouldn't the Greeks be satisfied with exact copies of the Elgin Marbles? Why is this? "The genuine" and "real" or "authentic" can always surprise us.

VIII

Celan's Meridian

IN OCTOBER 1960 the German Academy for Language and Literature in Darmstadt made what might seem to be a highly peculiar decision. It presented the prestigious Georg-Büchner-Preis[1] for literature to the forty-year old poet Paul Celan, a man who had never spent any appreciable amount of time living in an officially German-speaking country. Celan was born in 1920 over a thousand kilometers east of Darmstadt in the city of Czernowitz in the Bukovina. Bukovina had been the most easterly province of the Austro-Hungarian empire between the late eighteenth century and the end of World War I. In 1918 it was made part of the newly enlarged Kingdom of Rumania; today it is part of Ukraine. Celan's parents belonged to the German-speaking Jewish minority of

I am very grateful to the postgraduate students in the interdisciplinary M-Phil. Programme in Intellectual History and Political Thought at Cambridge who asked me to convene a seminar on literature and political history (Lenz, Büchner, Mendelstamm, Celan) in Lent and Easter terms 2004, during the course of which I was first able to articulate the basic themes of this paper. Phil Poole and John Rety gave me a first chance to try out some of the ideas in this paper in public at a session in the Torriano World Poetry Series at Torriano House, London, in April 2005. I would also like to thank my colleagues Zeev Emmerich for numerous helpful suggestions, Professor Fred Rush for inviting me to present this paper as one of the Notre Dame Philosophy and Literature Lectures (2005–6), and Professor Robert von Hallberg, who kindly invited me to present the paper in the History and Forms of Lyric Lecture Series at the University of Chicago. I learned much from the audience on these occasions.

[1]In 1923 the "Volksstaat Hessen" (as it then was) decided it would award a prize in the name of the writer and political revolutionary Georg Büchner to an especially meritorious Hessian artist—composer, writer, painter, etc.—and it very significantly also decided that the prize would be awarded every year on the 11th of August, the official anniversary of the promulgation of the Constitution of the Weimar Republic. Unsurprisingly, during the National Socialist period it was not possible for the State of Hesse to continue to award a prize with these particular political associations, so it was suppressed. After the end of World War II the prize was reestablished, but the power to confer it was shifted from the Hessian government to the newly formed German Academy for Language and Literature, and the field of possible recipients was redefined. Henceforth it was to be given only to writers, but would be open to anyone who wrote in the German language. For further details about the history of the prize, see Dieter Sulzer, Hildegard Dieke, and Ingrid Kußmaul, *Der Georg-Büchner-Preis 1951–1987: Eine Dokumentation*, ed. Michael Assmann (Piper, 1987), esp. pp. 13–37.

the province. They were both killed by the Nazis during the Second World War, but he survived, and after 1945 gradually moved west, first to Bucharest (1945–47), then to Vienna, where he spent less than a full year (1947–48), and this brief sojourn was the only time in his life when he would have heard the language of his poems spoken naturally as the unquestioned, sole vernacular on the streets. In 1948 Celan moved to Paris, where he eventually was appointed to a position as lector in German at the École Normale Supérieure. In the 1960s he began to have serious psychiatric problems. He tried to kill his wife and son with a knife in 1965, tried to commit suicide by stabbing himself in the left lung in 1967, and attacked a neighbor with a knife in 1968, when he was arrested and placed in a psychiatric clinic. He drowned himself in the Seine in 1970.[2]

Celan, had a number of distinct ways of identifying himself: as a (naturalized) Frenchman; as a communist—in the early 1960s he was writing about his "vieux coeur de communiste" and stating that his "hope was in the East"; as an anarchist and avid reader of Kropotkin and Gustav Landauer; as a Jew; as a native of the ex-Hapsburg province of Bukovina; and, most bizarrely, perhaps, as a "Russian poet living among the infidel Germans." In the 1960s he occasionally signed himself in private letters "Pawel Lwowitsch Tselan" and used the peculiar macaronic phrase "*russkij poët in partibus nemetskich infidelium*" to refer to himself.[3] This is strange, not so much because he calls himself a "Russian"—Celan's home city Czernowitz had, after all, been made a part of the Ukrainian Soviet Socialist Republic—but at the time of writing Celan had been living in Paris for over a decade, so if he was surrounded by German infidels this was in his literary imagination, not on the streets and in the cafés.

Celan was seriously polyglot, working in his early life as a translator from Russian into Rumanian, later publishing translations from French, Russian, Rumanian, and several other languages into German, and, of course, for most of his mature life earning his living by training students in Paris to translate back and forth between German and French; and his activity as a translator was clearly central to his conception of himself as

---

[2] Celan's body was found on 1 May in the Seine near Courbevoie. This has given rise to two speculations: the first that he killed himself on 20 April, Hitler's birthday; the second that he threw himself from the Pont Mirabeau, subject of the famous poem by Apollinaire about the transitoriness (and relative permanence) of human life and human affect. For further biographical details, see "Zeittafel," in Bertrand Badiou and Eric Celan, eds., *Paul Celan und Gisèle Celan-Lestrange: Briefwechsel*, with commentary by Barbara Weideman (Suhrkamp, 2001), vol. 2, pp. 385–500.

[3] *Paul Celan, Die Niemandsrose: Vorstufen, Textgenese, Endfassung*, ed. Heino Schmull, Michael Schwarzkopf, and Jürgen Wertheimer (Suhrkamp, 1996), p. 42.

a poet. On the other hand, he always insisted that poetry could be written only in one's mother tongue, and for him that was German.[4]

If one thinks about Celan's life it isn't difficult to agree with him that it was characterized by a series of radical displacements, ruptures, dislocations, and losses. The Bukovina which was his home had disappeared from the maps[5] and from history.[6] Under these circumstances it is not surprising that Celan felt a deep and lifelong need to try to orient himself in space and time, and it is also not completely surprising that what provided the main medium for that orientation was language, the one thing, he says, that "remained reachable, near, and not-lost amidst all those losses."[7] He wrote poems, he says, "to speak, to orient myself, to find out where I was, and in what direction I was headed, to project for myself reality" ("um zu sprechen, um mich zu orientieren, um zu erkundigen, wo ich mich befand und wohin es mit mir wollte, um mir Wirklichkeit zu entwerfen"[8]). This is clearly not an expression of commitment to any form of eighteenth- or twentieth-century philosophical empiricism or nineteenth-century literary realism, because in another oft cited public statement Celan *also* claimed that "reality is not, but has to be sought and won" ("Wirklichkeit ist nicht, Wirklichkeit will gesucht und gewonnen sein").[9] What exactly does he mean by stating that his aim in writing poetry is to orient himself by "projecting for himself reality"? What does he mean by "project"? He seems to assign the word a special significance, even writing at one point that "Poems are . . . perhaps projects of existence (Daseinsentwürfe)."[10]

---

[4] "An Zweisprachigkeit in der Dichtung glaube ich nicht," *Antwort auf eine Umfrage der Librairie Flincker* (1961), in Paul Celan, *Der Meridian und andere Prosa* (Suhrkamp, 1988), p. 30. Hereafter this work is cited as *MP*.

[5] *MP* 61.

[6] *MP* 37.

[7] *MP* 38.

[8] "In dieser Sprache habe ich . . . Gedichte zu schreiben versucht, um mich zu orientieren, um zu erkundigen, wo ich mich befand, und wohin es mit mir wollte, um mir Wirklichkeit zu entwerfen." *MP*, p.38.

[9] "Wirklichkeit ist nicht, Wirklichkeit will gesucht und gewonnen sein." ("Reality/ actuality is not; reality/actuality must be sought and won.") *MP*, p. 22. Particularly in the tradition of philosophy which derives from Hegel, "Wirklichkeit" is used as a technical term and designates not a state of the world considered as a mere fact, but the property of actively having some affect on someone or something else. So the poem has "reality/ actuality" (Wirklichkeit) when it is actually understood by the audience to which it is directed and has an affect on them.

[10] *MP*, 60. At this point in his lecture Celan is discussing the possibility of construing poems as being like "paths"—in particular paths that lead to a possible "encounter," either between two people (author and reader) or between the author and, *via* his encounter with someone else, himself. The "path" as an image of the process of thinking was, of course, a central one for Heidegger (a collection of his papers published in 1950

In accepting the Büchner Prize Celan gave the customary speech and used the opportunity to talk about his own poetic practice. He gave the speech the title *"Der Meridian"* and later had it published. I want to isolate and discuss three of the many strands in the extremely condensed account of poetry which Celan gives in this speech. First of all, there is what one might call "poetry as existential orientation," including in that category all the statements about projection of reality or existence. Second, there are the various things Celan says about poetry and the "meridian." Finally, there are the cryptic remarks about utopia.

To begin then with existential orientation, one of the phrases Celan uses to describe poems ("projects of existence") is also a technical term in a certain variety of philosophy in the twentieth century, existentialism, but one might wonder just how significant the use of the *phrase* "project of existence" is for Celan. Is Celan's use of this phrase just an accident, a relatively superficial assimilation of a form of speech he happened to encounter in his environment, or something more significant?

Celan was a keen, if autodidact, student of philosophy. After his death his library was donated to the Deutsches Literaturarchiv in Marbach, and it turned out to contain about 500 philosophical books in six languages, many of them with copious underlining and frequent marginal annotation.[11] The composition of this library, including volumes of works by the pre-Socratics, Plato, Augustine, Montaigne, Pascal, Descartes, Leibniz, Hegel, Charles Sanders Peirce, Nietzsche, and literally dozens of others, indicates that Celan had a particular interest in the history of philosophy, but he also had many twentieth-century works on

---

is titled *Holzwege*). "Holzweg" in everyday German means "the wrong track, a path leading nowhere." In his introduction to the 1950 volume, however, Heidegger is slightly coy about whether the paths on which he is travelling really "lead nowhere"; he says that these paths "generally" *(meist)* end in an impasse, which presumably means that they might occasionally lead somewhere. One might also note that although a "Holzweg" is not a well-travelled and marked out road, it is a path that preexists in the forest—not one that the thinker himself cuts, as it were, through jungle or virgin timber. Heidegger was trying to get away from a philosophy of subjectivity, and so also from the idea of the thinker (or poet) as a radical originator, creating something from nothing by the sheer force of his own subjective agency. The thinker, like the poet, does not create something out of nothing like the traditional Christian God, but is someone who "can listen" *(Erläuterungen,* pp. 36–39; see also *Holzweg,* pp. 296–343). The reference to the image of the philosopher travelling down the "Holzweg" is supposed to allow us to understand thinking better than the old dichotomies of "activity/creation" and "passivity/responsiveness" would. The "Holzweg" is there, but the philosopher must leave the highway and courageously travel down it on his own. Something similar is going on in Celan's notion of the poem as a "path" to a possible encounter.

[11] *Paul Celan: La bibiothèque philosophique,* ed. Alexandre Richter, Patrik Alac, Bertrand Badiou (Editions Rue d'Ulm, 2004).

his shelves, including books by Wittgenstein, Bergson, Russell, Feyera-bend, Husserl, Croce, Lukács, Althusser, Paul Ricoeur, and many others. There is one striking absence. This collection of 500 volumes does not contain one copy of a philosophical work by Kant.[12] It is hard to avoid the conclusion that Celan simply did not find Kant in any way useful or interesting. There were any number of serious, some would say fatal, objections raised to Kant in the nineteenth and twentieth century, but objections can always be answered—or at any rate by responding to them one can entangle the objector in a discussion. Gross disinterest, however, is something much more deep-seated, and, in a sense, unanswerable, than any objection. One can, of course, still speculate about the reasons for this. The speculation that immediately recommends itself to me is that Kant had a notorious blind spot about the phenomenon of human language. There are a few odd, and random, remarks, but, as far as I am aware, there is no sustained discussion in any of Kant's works of human communication. As various of his contemporaries, most notably Herder, immediately pointed out, Kant's "Reason" is a configuration of faculties that purportedly operates with concepts and judgments whose specific mode of linguistic expression is left completely undiscussed, as if it were irrelevant to the task at hand. A philosopher in whose work language as a concrete human reality with an important historical and social dimension, and human communication in the variety of its forms, were completely invisible was not likely to be one who recommended himself to Celan's attention.

Although there is one noteworthy absence in the library, there is also one grand and almost overwhelming presence. Celan and the philosopher Martin Heidegger belonged to a very serious and active mutual admiration society.[13] Celan in one text speaks of his "reverence" (*Verehrung*)[14] for Heidegger and addresses him as "Master-Thinker" ("*Herrn Martin Heidegger / dem Denk-Herrn*").[15] In particular, Celan's library contained over thirty books by Heidegger, some of them with personal dedications by Heidegger to Celan, and most of them very copiously annotated in Celan's hand. Similarly, Celan seems to have sent inscribed copies of all

[12] All there is is a popular collection of "Sayings" by Kant (*Aussprüche*, ed. Raoul Richter, Insel, 1923), an edition of "Kant on Books and Reading" (Norbert Hinske, "Kant über Lesen und Bücher," in *Inselalmanach auf das Jahr 1964*), and *Über Theorie und Praxis* (ed. Dieter Henrich, Suhrkamp, 1967) containing essays by Kant, Gentz, and Rehberg (as if they were equally weighty thinkers). None of these three volumes contains any underlining or marginal notes at all.

[13] See Hadrien France-Lanord, *Paul Celan et Martin Heidegger: le sens d'un dialogue* (Fayard, 2004).

[14] France-Lanord, *Celan et Heidegger*, p. 227.

[15] Ibid., p. 225.

his books to Heidegger, who reciprocated by reading them intensely and often annotating them.

The idea of the "project" is central for Heidegger's understanding of human existence. In *Being and Time* Heidegger claims that when traditional philosophers approached the study of human life they had generally been asking the wrong questions. They had asked, that is, "What am I?" or "What are we?" or "What is man?" as if one were asking a question of the same kind and structure as, say, "What is a triangle?," "What is a volcano?," or "What is DNA?" The more relevant human question is not "What am I?," but "Who am I?" (or, "Who are we?").[16] The difference between these two questions mirrors a difference between two attitudes I can adopt to a human life. It is, of course, perfectly possible, and in some contexts highly advisable, for me to think of my life, or for that matter someone else's life, as a sequence of natural events that occur—I am born; as a result of a complex interplay of genetically and environmentally determined processes my internal organs develop; I may fall ill because I am poisoned or exposed to a contagious disease or because some developmental process went wrong; I may recover or not. This is a useful way to think if I am trying to see if there is a particular medical intervention that will correct some organic malfunction. This sequence of thoughts is naturally associated with a series of particular what-questions: What are my symptoms? What poison was used? What antidote is available? And these particular, practical what-questions can reasonably be seen as in some sense motivating a set of more general theoretical questions such as, What is a poison? What is healthy functioning for a human being? What is disease?

There is, as I have said, nothing inherently wrong about looking at one's own life in the above way, but it does require that one adopt a kind of external perspective—what will be a disease for me would as a general rule also be a disease for you. One of Heidegger's major claims in *Being and Time* is that it is also possible to look at one's own life "from the inside," as it were, that is, as a human life I am living and must live in one way or another. This view from the inside is what is called "existential." In living my life, he claims, I am always trying tacitly to ask and answer the question "Who am I?"—we might say I am trying to "define myself" or "give myself an identity," although Heidegger would never use these particular ways of putting it because he thinks the use of the term "definition" has technical associations of verbal explicitness which it derives from its use in the philosophical tradition and which he rejects, and "identity" has unfortunate and highly misleading ontological connotations. If I am late and treat the taxi driver brusquely, that shows what

---

[16] Martin Heidegger, *Sein und Zeit* (Niemeyer, 1963), §9.

kind of person I am. If I realize what I have done, and feel ashamed of myself, the fact that I feel ashamed indicates that I have been asking and trying to answer the question. "Asking and trying to answer the question 'Who am I?'" need not be a verbal matter at all. I can define myself by acting "without saying a word," by *being* brusque. For that matter, I need not even act: the fact that I *feel* ashamed shows that I have been asking the question even if I have not formulated it as an explicit question to myself in so many words or even in so many thoughts on some particular occasion. Having established to his own satisfaction that human life is a continual process of self-definition by virtue of the asking and attempted answering of the question "Who am I?" Heidegger goes on to develop an account of the internal working of this process. The central part of this is a rethinking of the distinction between reality and possibility with which we are familiar in our everyday dealings with objects in the world. Kant (*KrV* B 627) expresses the everyday understanding of matters when he points out that there is a grave difference between having 100 "real" units of your favorite currency in your bank account and having 100 "possible" units, and there is, of course, a great difference between *really* having been poisoned and there being a possible state of things in which one had been poisoned.

In contrast to this, what I *really* am, or what I am "existentially," is to some extent constituted by my possibilities. So my human reality is changed if I know how to speak French or if I have had the Christian message preached to me, even if I am not at the moment actually speaking French or have rejected the Christian way of life. This does not, I repeat, mean that it makes no difference whether I am speaking French or not speaking French (because, for instance, I am speaking English), but it does mean that at some level it is a more important feature of my life that I am related in a certain way to the possibility of speaking French than whether I happen to be actualizing that possibility at any particular moment. To put it in a way that would be congenial to Heidegger, the reality of the life of a pagan who lived before the beginning of the Christian era is radically different from the reality of life of a twenty-first-century atheist in a way that is not reducible to the actions they perform, which might well not be that different. Heidegger uses the term "project" (*Entwurf*) to designate the relation I have to my own possibilities. Who I really am, is given by what I project as my possibilities.[17]

Celan is particularly keen, more keen perhaps than Heidegger himself, to emphasize that the projection of a set of possibilities that defines my own identity is not a process that can be understood as taking place in isolation by some kind of transcendental subject but is one that requires

[17] Ibid., §§31–32.

some kind of encounter between an I and a You. To project oneself onto
the possibility of speaking French, as Heidegger would put it, or to project the reality of French speech for myself, as Celan puts it, is not a
purely speculative or mental activity, but is connected with actual encounters with some concrete others who are speakers of French. The
process in which I actually construct an identity for myself cannot be dis-
entangled from that through which actual others construct an identity for
themselves, each as a "You" to me. Poetry is one kind of way in which
such an encounter, and indeed one of particular intensity, can in principle
take place, and so it has a special role in the constitution of identities.

That the poet is someone who initiates the possibility of a new communal form of living is another of the Heideggerian themes, expressed
with great clarity in his essays on the poet Hölderlin, especially "Hölderlin
und das Wesen der Dichtung."[18] This Heideggerian theme, too, had great
appeal for Celan. The situation for the poet Celan, however, was, if anything, even more extreme and difficult than that envisaged by Heidegger.
Heidegger's archetypical poet, the Swabian Hölderlin, could write a poem
entitled "Heimkunft: An die Verwandten" ("Homecoming: To My Rela-
tives" or "Homecoming: To Kindred Spirits"),[19] which Heidegger, himself
a Swabian, interprets both as a return to aboriginal "mother Swabia"
("Glückselig Suevien, meine Mutter") and thereby as the initiation of
some further unspecified Germanic future ("Diese Heimkunft aber ist die
Zukunft des geschichtlichen Wesens der Deutschen").[20] Hölderlin's poem
is full of references to his "*Landsleute*" (l. 43), to his mother (l. 73), and
his "dear ones" (ll. 76 and 84), and to the positive emotions sometimes associated with homecoming, especially "*Freude*" (ll. 75, 81, 95, 100, also
l. 25; note also "*die Frohen,*" l. 94, "*Freudiges,*" l. 2 , and "*das Freudige,*"
l. 106), but also "*Liebe*" ("*liebende Namen,*" l. 58; "*wenn Liebende wieder sich finden,*" l. 95; "*Unschickliches liebet ein Gott nicht,*" l. 99, is also
an instance because it is presented as an exception to the general condition
being expressed). The image of the Swabian poet among happy, loving,
fellow Swabians could be no model for Celan. German-speaking Jewish
Bukovina was gone, and no return there possible. In Paris the exclusive
language of his poetry[21] was not only not the vernacular, it was not even
the language he spoke at home with his wife and son—that, of course,
was French, not German. The German language, furthermore, was both

[18] Heidegger, *Erläuterungen*, pp. 31–47.

[19] Ibid., pp. 9–31.

[20] Ibid., pp. 22, 29.

[21] This is not strictly true, because there is one extant poem in French which Celan
wrote for his son: "Ô les hâbleurs," in *Paul Celan: Die Gedichte*, ed. Barbara Weidemann
(Suhrkamp, 2003; hereafter cited as *PC*), p. 526.

the much-loved language of his mother and one of the identifying criteria of his parents' murderers. As far as other Jews—"*Geschwisterkinder*" he calls them: "children of my brothers and sisters"—are concerned, Celan writes: ". . . they did not love me, and I did not love them" ("die Geschwisterkinder . . . liebten mich nicht und ich liebte sie nicht"[22]). Can language alone ground, or initiate, or render possible an encounter under such conditions? Can language alone create community even where the common bonds of a vernacular rooted in shared joyful experience (*Freude*) are broken? Even where there is no love?

Poetry is a concrete act of speaking in which a particular human being addresses others, and is understood by them so that a proper encounter takes place. When the poet addresses the audience, and is understood, the possibilities for *all* those involved change, and each has come to have an identity that is dependent on that of the other participants. Celan, that is, is the poet he is only if he has an audience who in some sense come to define themselves through what they hear and understand of him, and they have the identity they have only provided Celan defines himself to some extent in relation to them. Audience, then, is essential for poetry, and without an understanding audience a poet (like Celan) suffers a loss of identity.

If, however, the basically Heideggerian thought is right, then in some sense *every* act I perform is a definition of who I am—as a human being I am constantly asking and trying to answer the question who I am in everything I ever do. It would seem to follow then that everything is an existential gesture, and what, one might wonder, is so special about poetry? A first response to this is that what poetry is supposed to be about is not just reasserting an existing identity, important as that is, and not merely carrying out minor changes in existing arrangements, but some kind of *radical change of attitude, orientation, possibilities, or identity.*[23]

Thus suppose I am playing a game of chess with someone who is known to be a poor loser. Suppose further that I am winning, and pressing my

---

[22] MP 27.

[23] This is the point, I think, at which Celan departs from the theory presented in *Sein und Zeit*. The Heidegger of *Sein und Zeit* could not accept the distinction between routine, minor readjustment, and radical change of possibilities. For him, all my possibilities are given to me in "everydayness" and remain unchanged, even if I come back and reappropriate them "authentically." Their content does not change, merely the mode in which I grasp and live them. To be sure, virtually no one was ever able actually to cleave to the most austere version of the doctrine, not even Heidegger himself, as his speeches in 1933 demonstrate (see Guido Schneeberger, *Nachlese zu Heidegger* [Bern, 1962]). There seems an almost irresistible tendency for anyone who takes the doctrine of authenticity seriously at all to think that, despite Heidegger's explicit denials, it *must* have some effect on the content of the actual choices and possibilities open for me, and not merely on the way in which I embrace given possibilities.

advantage. My opponent and I may play along relatively predictable lines, or one of us may make a sequence of moves that represents a new and unexpected combination. This is what I mean by a "minor rearrangement." Suppose, though, that my opponent, still visibly losing, suddenly takes out a long stiletto and puts it down next to himself on the table, then takes out a pair of surgical gloves and puts the right one on, looking at my neck speculatively all the while. I use this example, by the way, not merely because of Celan's own preference for this weapon when expressing his own aggression in real life, but also because he once published a statement about his own poetry in a volume entitled "*Mein Gedicht ist mein Messer.*"[24] When he draws his knife, he opens various new possibilities, redefines the reality of the situation, and helps to create for both of us the reciprocally dependent identities of possible murderer and possible victim. When Celan writes and publishes or recites one of his poems, and he is understood, something similar happens. Celan calls what happens an "*Atemwende*"[25]—a change in breath, something that takes your breath away, changes the very air and way you breathe. Celan gives as an example that of a madman walking through the mountains who suddenly finds that he experiences the heavens as below him, and the earth above, so that he wants to walk on his head.[26] He has experienced an individual version of the "*Atemwende*" which in some sense defines poetry, a revolution, the world turned upside down. To get the full sense of what poetry is and should be, one simply has to de-individualize that.

To clarify Celan's conception, it is perhaps useful to contrast it with some other views about poetry that have or have had a certain currency. First, to say that poetry is looking for or gives someone orientation is not to say that poetry should be edifying or a form of moral preaching—to have an orientation to a possibility or an orientation in reality is not in itself to *do* anything, and so *a fortiori* not to do anything we would call morally admirable or the reverse, nor to encourage anyone to act in any one particular way. Heidegger thought that the existential analysis he was proposing was not in itself a form of ethics—although he also admitted that it was not completely disconnected from morality—because it referred to a level of the constitution of the self that was, as it were, deeper than or prior to that of the moral self. If Celan had ever asked himself the explicit question about the relation of his poetry to ethics,

---

[24] MP 31–32.

[25] MP 52, 58. "*Atemwende*" is also the name of a collection of poems Celan published in 1967. See PC 173–214.

[26] MP 50–52. This example is taken from Büchner's short prose-narrative "Lenz." A second example Celan also cites is that of Lucilie at the very end of Büchner's drama *Dantons Tod*; see MP 41–44.

I think he would probably have come out with something similar. This deep-seated moral indifferentism[27] means that it is probably a mistake to interpret Celan's search for a possible "You" as in any sense parallel to the philosophical motifs one can find in Buber or Lévinas.

Second, Celan rejects the traditional classicist view for two reasons. He denies that a poem is an object-made. Perhaps the craftsmanlike production of a word-object is a precondition of poetry, but it is no more than that. The poem itself is better understood as a gesture—he says it is not in principle different from a handshake—an individual *datable* act; not a word-object, but an act of speaking.[28] The idea of the "date" and of something being datable, connected with a *particular*—and that means unique—date, is a constant obsession of Celan's.[29] Celan's second objection to the traditional view is to the notion of imitation. Celan wrote out for himself in a notebook a statement Heidegger makes in one of his works to the effect that we should count ourselves lucky that we have overcome and got beyond the idea that art is any kind of imitation or depiction of reality.[30] Poetry is supposed to be a projection of human possibilities, not a replication of existing objects, facts, or states of affairs.

The third conception Celan rejects is that kind of Romanticism which puts a high positive value on immediacy of perception, feeling, or expression, and on having a direct connection with Nature. Nature is a category that has no positive connotations for Celan. In one of the poems he wrote for his collection *Die Niemandsrose*, he uses as a motto a line from Marina Tzvetaeva, "All poets are Jews"; and in a prose narrative he wrote at about the same time, "Gespräch im Gebirg," which describes an imaginary walk in the mountains with the philosopher Adorno,[31] Celan

[27] See Peter Szondi, "Eden," in his *Celan-Studien* (Suhrkamp, 1972), pp. 113–25. Szondi was a personal friend of Celan's and one of the most distinguished and helpful early commentators on his work. See also Raymond Geuss, "Poetry and Knowledge," in his *Outside Ethics* (Princeton University Press, 2005) pp.184–205.

[28] *MP* 31–32. By the way, the "handshake" for Celan is *not* an expression of unity or consensus, but an acknowledgment of irreconcilable difference.

[29] See also Jacques Derrida, *Shibboleth pour Paul Celan* (Galilée, 1986).

[30] "Jene glücklich überwundene Meinung, die Kunst sei eine Nachahmung oder Abschilderung der Wirklichkeit." In Martin Heidegger, "Der Ursprung des Kunstwerks," in his *Holzwege* (M. Klostermann, 1950), p. 25 (written out in a notebook by Celan; see *Celan: La bibiothèque*, p. 368).

[31] This is clearly an imaginary walk, because Celan made an arrangement to meet Adorno in Sils-Maria in the Engadin (Switzerland), but, for unclear reasons, left the day before Adorno arrived. Many found Adorno's oleaginous manner, which became especially marked when he was trying to ingratiate himself, as he seems to have been trying to do with Celan, repellent. See "Adorno and Berg," in Raymond Geuss, *Morality, Culture, and History* (Cambridge University Press, 1999), p. 116 and p.133, fn. 2. One will, of course, never know for certain why Celan left early. The correspondence between Adorno and Celan is published in *Frankfurter Adorno-Blätter VIII*, ed. Rolf Tiedemann (edition text + kritik, 2003).

refers to the surrounding vegetation in some detail, but his interest in it is purely philological—he is interested in the names of the flowers, especially the relation between their Latin names and their common German names. He then spends a whole paragraph explaining that Jews are utterly without any sense and without any "eyes" for Nature. The orientation that poetry strives for is *not* any form of reintegration into a natural landscape or some purported natural cycle of life, and there is certainly no sense that a proper encounter with nature will refresh and regenerate the spirit. Nature is misery, nakedness, embarrassing creaturely need, and insignificance, not a source of innocence or simplicity—which in any case are not properties Celan values. No encounter with nature will increase anyone's energy, health, or integrity, or cure anyone of the "corruption" of society. What is needed is not orientation in the natural world, but in language and history, and in particular vis-à-vis *dated* human events.

The final poetic program which Celan rejects is Mallarmé's conception of an "absolute poem." A poem, Mallarmé held, is an artistic structure made with words, not ideas, and it is very definitely not directed at, or addressed to, anyone in particular. It is easy to see how a person who thought, as Celan did, that a poem is a concrete act of existentially located speaking, would also think that no poem could ever be absolute.[32] So a poem for Celan is not a description or an expression of nature or of a sense of oneness with Nature, nor a purely formal artistic construct, but it is an existential gesture that operates through speech.

Writing poetry is not the only way to orient oneself in one's life, by initiating and then participating in a collective activity in which everything is completely turned upside down. What is the specific way of attaining orientation through revolution which constitutes poetry? To answer this, we might turn to the second of the three strands in Celan's speech on receipt of the Büchner Prize, to his conception of a meridian. At the end of the speech Celan speaks of "finding" a meridian. What exactly does he mean by this?

"Meridian" refers to the vertical position of the sun at midday, that is, when it stands at its highest in the sky. In addition, "meridian" can refer to an imaginary line that would connect the different geographical places at which the sun stands at its highest point in the sky at the *same* time. So when the sun stands at its highest point in the sky in Cambridge or London, it also does so in Oran, Algeria and in Accra in Ghana (all three at 0°); when it is noon in Kiev, it is also noon in Cairo (both at about 30° east). The use of the sun as an image of the source of both illumination and meaning in our world is an old one in Western

---

[32] *MP* 57.

philosophy.[33] One sees things clearly and as they really are when one sees them at midday in the full light of the sun, when it stands at its highest point. To speak of a meridian makes sense only relative to some conception of what the relevant "sun" or source of light is.

A complex and obscure passage at the end of *"Der Meridian"*[34] gives a hint about how this "light" is to be understood. In this passage[35] Celan endorses the view that poetry is a way of concentrating attention on particular events in that, as he puts it, the poem itself remains mindful of specific dates. He then goes on to claim that the poet is looking for a place—his place of origin—and conducts this search in the light of utopia. What

[33] Plato, *Politeia* 514a–517a. See also Karl Marx, "Zur Kritik der Hegelschen Rechtsphilosophie. Einleitung," in Karl Marx and Friedrich Engels, *Werke* (Dietz, 1964) vol. 1, pp. 378–79; Friedrich Nietzsche, *Jenseits von Gut und Böse* §215, in *Kritische Studienausgabe*, ed. Colli and Montinari (de Gruyter, 1980), vol. 5, p. 152.

[34]

Die Aufmerksamkeit, die das Gedicht allem ihm Begegnenden zu widmen versucht . . . ist . . . eine aller unserer Daten eingedenk bleibende Konzentration. . . . Und was wären dann die Bilder? Das einmal, das immer wieder einmal und nur jetzt und nur hier Wahrgenommene und Wahrzunehmende. Und das Gedicht wäre somit der Ort, wo alle Tropen und Metaphern ad absurdum geführt werden wollen . . . Toposforschung? Gewiß! Aber im Lichte des zu Erforschenden: im Lichte der U-topie. . . . [I]m Lichte der Utopie unternehme ich—jetzt—Toposforschung: . . . Ich suche . . . den Ort meiner eigenen Herkunft . . . Keiner dieser Orte ist zu finden, es gibt sie nicht, aber ich weiß wo es sie, zumal jetzt, geben müßte. . . . Ich finde das Verbindende und wie das Gedicht zur Begegnung Führende. Ich finde etwas—wie die Sprache—Immaterielles, aber Irdisches, Terrestrisches, etwas Kreisförmiges, über die beiden Pole in sich selbst Zurückkehrendes und dabei—heitererweise—sogar die Tropen Durchkreuzendes—: ich finde . . . einen *Meridian*.

[The attention which the poem tries to devote to everything that encounters it is a concentration that remains mindful of all our dates. What about images then? That which is and can be perceived once, that which is and can be perceived ever again once and only now and only here. The poem would therefore be the place where all tropes and metaphors try to be taken ad absurdum. The investigation of topoi? Certainly! But in the light of that which is the aim of investigation: in the light of u-topia. In the light of utopia I now undertake the investigation of a topos . . . I'm looking for the place of my own origin, but none of these places can be found. they don't exist, but I know where they, particularly now, would have to be. . . . I find that which connects and, as it were, leads the poem to its encounter. I find something, like language, immaterial, earthly, terrestrial, something circular which comes back to itself over both poles and in doing that, amusingly enough, even crosses through the tropics [or: crosses out the tropes]—I find . . . a *meridian*.] (Paul Celan, *Der Meridian und andere Prosa*, pp. 55–62)

[35] Limitations of space prohibit giving this passage the full interpretation it deserves. One aspect that would require and reward very careful attention is the play on the various senses of two German words, both derived from Greek: (a) "Topos," meaning both "place" (in a variety of senses) and the "common place," i.e., stereotypical sayings and situations that recur in certain kinds of literature, and (b) "Tropos," meaning both "tropic" (in the geographical sense) and a literary figure ("trope").

the poet actually finds is not his place of origin, but something else—
something that connects the place in which he actually finds himself with
other places, an imaginary line, a meridian. I suggest, then, that Celan
thinks that the light relative to which the meridian is determined shines
from u-topia. This will take us to the final of the three topics.

When Celan speaks of "topoi" and "utopia," the terms have a rather
specific sense, namely that given to them in the work of one of the anarchist writers the young Celan says he most admired and studied, Gustav
Landauer.[36] In 1907 Landauer published a book entitled *Revolution* which
contains a rudimentary anarchist theory of history. In this book he distinguishes two factors in human history: Topia and Utopia. "Topia" is the
total state of a society at any given time considered under the aspect of its
givenness and *stability*. "Utopia" on the other hand designates all those
individual impulses which under certain circumstances can come together
and move in the direction of a perfectly functioning social formation that
"contains no harmful or unjust elements" (". . . Tendenz eine tadellos funk-
tionierende Topie zu gestalten, die keinerlei Schädlichkeiten oder Ungere-
chtheiten in sich schließt").[37] The state of affairs intended in these utopian
strivings will not ever be realized, and so their significance consists simply
in driving Humanity on from one Topia—from one "place"—to the next.
At any given point in time, then, Landauer maintains, the utopian impulses
actually and effectively in existence derive from two sources: specific dissatisfaction with the given topia, and remembrance of all previous utopias.

The idea then is that the poet Celan investigates "where we are," what
place we occupy, in the light of our present, active dissatisfactions with
existing arrangements and of other remembered human utopian aspirations. The form this investigation takes is the linking of a particular dated
event, which is the occasion or origin of the poem, with some other dated
events in other places. When two such events are thus conjoined they
are said to be on the same meridian. The linking takes place in such a
way as to respect the phenomenal uniqueness of each of the events. On
earth to say that two places are on the same meridian means they stand
in the same relation to the sun as measurer of time. This does not mean
that London *is* Accra or Oran, or that what happens at a given time in
London is the *same event* as what happens in Accra at that time. Being
"on the same meridian" according to the conception Celan sketches in
his Büchner Prize address means that the two events reveal themselves as
belonging together in relation to the light dispensed by human utopian
impulses, hopes, disappointments, and fears. This is the link. In this utopian light distinct events can be "one"—can belong together, especially

---

[36] See Gustav Landauer, *Revolution* (Karin Kramer Verlag, 1974), pp. 11–18.
[37] Ibid., p. 13.

when *put together* by the poet—without losing their distinctiveness; presumably that is a property of *that* light.

It is of extreme importance to keep in mind that U-topia is precisely *not* a place, but in the strictest sense a "No-Place": "οὐ" + "τόπος." Thus reference to a light that shines from the non-place of U-topia is in a sense the exact reverse of the Platonic conception of a world illuminated by a light that shines from the place-beyond-the-heavens (ὑπερουράνιος τόπος, *Phaedrus* 247c).[38] Instead of a potential ascent from perception of distinct individual virtuous acts to the idea of "virtue itself," and eventually to the sun, the unitary Idea of the Good, which is the source of all intelligibility, and which anyone who wishes to act reasonably must keep in view (*Republic* 517c), Celan's utopian light does not have unitary existence as an object of knowledge in its own right. To adopt the description Walter Benjamin gives of the "angel of history," who faces the past and has his back turned to the future,[39] the poet always has his back to the source of light. To try to turn around and look at it directly, as in Plato, is not only humanly impossible, but perhaps even an inherently meaningless project: one cannot sensibly be said to have turned one's back on a place that is *not a place at all.* The spatial images are not themselves finally supposed to make sense, but rather when they are understood, they are seen to be "absurd," and thus to cancel themselves out. All that can be said is that a unique configuration of phenomenally distinct events is illuminated, held together by poetry and human memory, which operate without reducing dated events to mere instances of any single paradigm, idea, or concept, or a set of them. One cannot ever see the utopian light except as reflected *from* the things it illuminates in this world. Although the poet is said to "find" the meridian, it is not as if it were out there in existence waiting to be found in the way in which metallic ore is "out there" in the world waiting to be found. The poet "finds" the meridian in the sense of *drawing* it, that is, creating it. This marks a radical difference between Celan and Pound, or anyone who believed that "natural affinities" or "correspondences" could lie at the basis of poetry.[40]

---

[38] In his own copy of Plato's *Phaedrus,* translated into German by L. Georgii, Celan has underlined the translation of this passage, which reads: "Den überhimmlischen Ort aber hat noch nie einer der Dichter hienieden besungen, noch wird ihn je einer nach *Würdigkeit besingen.*" See *Celan: La bibiothèque,* 39. The phrase "außer-himmlischer Ort" occurs in a poem in the collection *Fadensonnen* (in *PC* 242), and "hyperuranischer Ort" is part of the title of a posthumous poem "Zwitscher-Hymnus am hyperuranischen Ort" in *PC* 497.

[39] Walter Benjamin, "Geschichtsphilosophische Thesen: 9," in his *Zur Kritik der Gewalt und andere Aufsätze* (Suhrkamp, 1965) pp. 84–85.

[40] For pressing the importance of this point on my attention I am very greatly endebted to Professor Fred Rush (Notre Dame University) and to Professor Robert von Hallberg (University of Chicago), who made it to me independently of each other.

Lest the presence of this highly speculative metaphysical strand in Celan's thinking be thought to indicate a slide back into archaic forms of belief, such as religious beliefs, the radical atheistic credentials of this poetry are impeccable. Not only is there no personal God, there is no abstract principle of meaning or intelligibility in the universe. When Celan comes, in "Der Meridian," to give his most weighty characterization of poetry,[41] he virtually defines it as the assertion of radical atheism: Poetry states that what is infinite in the universe is not God, Nature, Life, or some principle of meaning, but rather the pointlessness of it all. Poetry says that all is "in vain, for-nothing, pointless" ("Umsonst!"—note Celan's exclamation point) forever.

The poet, then, as it were, backs away from the world to another—a new—place which he creates, and which gives him a vantage point from which to see and mark out a meridian in a light which shines from the utopia of human memories and dissatisfactions. This "new" place is *not* utopia—given that it is a "place," albeit a "new," created place, it is not a "no-place" (οὐτοπία)—but from it the poet can try to map the real world with reference to a light the source of which he can never see directly.

In 1962 Celan wrote a poem entitled "In Eins" (see the appendix to this essay) which illustrates in a particularly clear way some of the characteristic features of his poetic practice. Although the poem is distributed typographically on the page in three strophes with something that looks like a coda, each strophe has a different number of lines and each line has a different length (i.e., number of syllables). The whole poem has no rhyme, no discernible metrical structure, no smooth musicality of sound ("*keine Wortmusik*," as Celan says approvingly of Mandelstamm's poetry[42]). This is poetry as concrete gesture, certainly not poetry-as-song.

Second, the punctuation and typography seem to play a more constitutive role in the poem than we are perhaps used to. Note the use of italics, of uppercase (especially "Peuple de Paris"), and also of cola (*two of them*) and of the dash. In a sense it is easier to read the poem on the page than to follow it with complete comprehension when it is read aloud.

The poem also exhibits a series of striking stylistic peculiarities. It begins in the first strophe with a paratactic accumulation of word-atoms and ends with a strophe that is still basically paratactic, but operates with larger units that are internally more highly convoluted. The remaining

---

[41] "Die Dichtung, meine Damen und Herren—: diese Unendlichsprechung von lauter Sterblichtkeit und Umsonst!" ("Poetry, ladies and gentlemen—: this assertion that mere mortality and pointlessness are infinite!"). Paul Celan, *Der Meridian und andere Prosa*, p. 59.

[42] Paul Celan, *Der Meridian: Tübinger Ausgabe*, ed. Bernhard Böschenstein et al. (Suhrkamp, 1999), p. 215. Hereafter this work is cited *MT*.

drafts show that this final form of the poem mirrors the way it arose. Celan used a kind of mosaic technique. This is in stark contrast to the practice of (Romantic) poets like Hölderlin whose extant drafts show that they started from the very beginning with the skeletons of complete sentences and then filled in some of the details as they went on.

Finally note that the level of annotation of specific references which the poem admits is very high. Celan never denied that his poetry was dark and difficult, and he made no apology for this, thinking that it was part of the task of poetry to violate habitual expectations, to short-circuit common associations, change existential attitudes and orientations, and to create new ones.[43] He did insist, however, that it was not hermetic. If one read enough of it again and again the images would begin to make sense without the need for any esoteric knowledge, or strictly private experience. Whether or not this is in general the case, I would merely point out that the references in this poem that need to be annotated are *not*, with one rather unimportant exception, *private* or biographical. They are, rather, public, human, literary, or political events. If you want to know what the 13th of February was in Paris in 1962, all you need to do is consult the archive of *Le Monde* or *Le Figaro* for that day.

The thirteenth of February 1962 happens to be the day on which the funeral was held for a large number of Parisians who had been killed by the police in a demonstration against the OAS, the right-wing military organization which was trying to prevent the French government from withdrawing from Algeria. This date was a kind of shibboleth for Celan. He had previously written a poem entitled "Schibboleth"[44] which is pretty clearly about the Spanish Civil War in which he makes reference to a "twin-February in Vienna and Madrid." The 12/13 of February 1934 was the high point of the workers' uprising against the Dollfuss regime in Vienna, during which Dollfuss called out the army and had various workers' tenements shelled. (This dual reference to Vienna and Madrid also expresses itself in the use of the Austrian form "*Feber*" instead of "*Februar*," and the Spanish Republican slogan "*No pasarán*.") This whole complex of dated events is then connected to the Old Testament story of the proto-civil war between the Gileadites and Ephraimites. The Ephraimites could not pronounce the Hebrew word "shibboleth" correctly, and so the Gileadites held the fords of the Jordan and asked anyone who tried to cross to pronounce that word, killing those who could not. So a "shibboleth" is a verbal item in itself perhaps insignificant but which allows you to identify yourself, and also to tell friend from foe,

---

[43] *MP* 51.
[44] See *PC* 83.

and the correctly production of which can mean the difference between life and death.[45] (See Appendix, line 2.)

The second strophe concerns the exiled shepherd from Huesca, continuing the theme of the Spanish Civil War (see 3, 5, 6). The shepherd gives them a word they need: presumably that is a "shibboleth," the word you need to get across the river without being killed by your enemies. It would be tempting to identify this with "*No pasarán*" because in Celan's previously mentioned poem entitled "Schibboleth" that is what the password is. There is perhaps a bit of a shift here from the situation in the first strophe: Celan names the shepherd "Abadias," who seems to represent a kind of movement *away* from the situation of civil war, because the Old Testament prophet Abadias (= Obadiah) seems consciously to reject the ethos which found its expression in the slaughter of the Ephraimites at the fords of the Jordan. (Abadias, then, is "eine Wolke/menschlichen Adels.")

The final strophe seems to be about the content of the word which the shepherd Abadias gives us, and it falls roughly into two interconnected parts: first an image of the October Revolution—the cruiser "Aurora" and the fraternal waving of people liberated—then a very condensed and complex set of references to the life and work of the poet Osip Mandelstamm, to whose memory Celan dedicated the volume of poems in which "In Eins" appears.[46] The word spoken by the shepherd must be understood in the light of these two phenomena: the Revolution, and the history of Mandelstamm, including of his changing attitude toward the revolution and its consequences. The two parts of this last strophe are held together by the reference to "Petropolis." Mandelstamm lived though a period in which the city changed its name twice: (Saint) Petersburg-Petrograd-Leningrad; describing the city as "Petropolis," often with tacit reference to its specifically cultural pretensions, was an old Russian literary conceit which Mandelstamm also adopted. So the city figures in his poems under a total of four different names, and there is good reason to think that which particular name he used in a given context was highly significant, although the actual significance of using "Petropolis" in any particular poem is an extremely complicated matter. In this case, it seems that Celan is using "Petropolis" to refer to a kind of idealized perfect realization of the aspirations of the October Revolution. A further reference to Mandelstamm is contained in the use of the

---

[45] On "shibboleth," see Derrida, *Schibboleth*.

[46] We know, too, from existing drafts of this poem that Celan originally wanted to use a line from one of Mandelstamm's poems about Petersburg (В Петербурге мы сойдемся снова) from his collection *Tristia* as a motto for this poem. The Russian original and Celan's own translation of this poem into German can be found in Paul Celan, *Werke* (Suhrkamp, 1983), vol. 4, pp. 158–59.

word *"toskanisch."* In 1933 Mandelstamm wrote a highly unflattering short poem about Stalin,[47] and as a result was sent into internal exile to Voronezh (1935–37). In January 1937 he wrote a poem entitled "He сравнивай" ("Do Not Compare").[48] Mandelstamm loved Italy, and in the poem he speaks of his longing ("тоска," pronounced *"toska"*) to see in front of him the hills of Tuscany, instead of those of Voronezh. However, he admits his "toska" alone will not get him to Tosca-ny. In fact, shortly after finishing this poem Mandelstamm was rearrested, sentenced to five years at hard labor, and died, probably of heart failure, while being transported to eastern Siberia. This strophe, then, is an extraordinarily compressed formulation of a dense knot of utopian aspirations, of hope, its disappointment, and its persistence, of the kind which constitutes the absolute center of most of Celan's poetry. (See Appendix, lines 15, 17.) The poem ends with citation of the eirenic half of the slogan that opens Büchner's revolutionary tract *Der hessische Landbote* (line 18).

The title of the poem is a condensed gloss on what a meridian does. It puts apparently different places and events together, not by subsuming them under a single concept: it does not claim that α, β, γ, and δ are—by virtue of the preexisting essential properties they all share—all instances of the same concept. There is no single "essence of revolution" which the Spanish Civil War, the Paris Commune, and the October Revolution are assumed to share. Nor is the kind of poem Celan has in mind "metaphorical," by which I take him to mean either based on "metaphors" or "similes" and claims that Φ is *"like"* Ψ. A metaphor on this view would be nothing more than a pale form of conceptualization: the appeal to "likeness" or similarity deprives the entities involved of their uniqueness just as subsumption under a concept would. Celan was as insistent as he could possibly have been in rejecting the claim that poetry was in any sense "metaphorical." As he writes, *"das Gedicht hat, glaube ich, noch da wo es am bildhaftesten ist, einen antimetaphorischen Charakter."*[49] The experiences/events Celan has in mind and the words he uses are not *"übertragbar,"*[50] and so it is not appropriate to think of them in terms of any kind of comparison. Rather the poet, through an existential gesture, conjoins them, *puts things together,* makes them "one" while admitting they are (still) uniquely individual, just as an event in London is not in any interesting sense "like" an event in Accra simply by virtue of being on the same meridian. If a poet is a maker, it is not a word-structure he

[47] Осип Мандельштам, *Сочений* (Художественная Литература, 1990), vol. 1, p. 197; see also p. 528.
[48] Ibid., vol. 1, p. 232.
[49] MT 74; see also 125, 156–60.
[50] MT 78, 158–59.

"makes," but this concrete conjunction, and so it is better to think of him as someone who *acts* in a certain way rather than as someone who makes. Doing this creates new possibilities, a new situation, and gives orientation.

This poem itself is a reaction to the events of the 13th of February 1962, but equally to encountering the shepherd from Huesca, or indeed to "encountering" Mandelstamm by virtue of reading his poetry. Celan has conjoined them—put them "together" (*"in eins"*)—on a single meridian. His doing this can serve to orient those who read his poem with understanding by allowing them to see these events, in their individuality, clearly and as they really are, in the light of human satisfied and unsatisfied, experienced, and remembered aspirations. In doing this Celan presumably hopes to embed them in the utopian memory of humanity. Given that a poem is an existential project of the kind that has been discussed, it should be obvious that "embedding events in the utopian memory of humanity" does not mean simply activating a belief about some past event but implies a much more drastic change in the mode of life of humanity. A poem is supposed to create a new human reality, to change a human world, not merely to reinforce or modify beliefs.

One difficulty in speaking about literature and philosophy is a series of assumptions that one might be inclined to make: first, that we know what philosophy, or for that matter what literature, is; second, that we can assume they are distinct; and third, that it is possible and cognitively useful to try to get a single, relatively abstract overall theory about the relation between the two of them. Certainly the final of these three assumptions would get no support from Celan. In his prose writings he was always careful to deny that he had or thought it useful to give a general theory of literature. In the interests of simplicity of presentation I have spoken in this paper as if one could find in Celan assertions about "poetry" *tout court,* but this is actually grossly incorrect, in that Celan always denied that he could speak about poetry in general or "modern" poetry in general, distinguishing between the situation facing French-language and German-language poets.[51] What he speaks of is the (German) poem—*today*—i.e., at whatever time he happened to be speaking.[52] This emphasis on the concrete, I have tried to suggest, is not an accident.

At the end of this long discussion, one might think that the question still remains of what distinguishes poetry from other forms of existential orientation, other ways of creating new encounters, new possibilities,

---

[51] *MP* 21.

[52] "Gewiß, das Gedicht—das Gedicht heute—zeigt, usw." (*MP* 21). One of the drafts for the Büchner Prize speech contains the statement: "Ich spreche . . . nicht von 'moderner Lyrik,' ich spreche vom Gedicht *heute.* . . ." *MT* 151; see also 72, 73.

new communities such as political acts. Celan was deeply suspicion of "art" that is of concern with formalism, harmonious appearance, symmetry, with the cult of beautiful words, of elegant proportions, with any kind of construction, or artifice, etc.[53] "Art," he seems to have thought, was in some sense the very opposite of poetry. Poetry is "really" "*kunst-los*" and "*kunst-frei.*"[54] He recognized, however, that, *except in very exceptional circumstances*, if poetry was to succeed in its utopian task—if it was to be an existential gesture that *worked* for an audience—it would have to go down a path that led through its opposite, and embody itself in structured, if not perhaps fully "artful," words. In poetry the existential ostension of the meridian must take place through (structured) speech.

We human beings are constituted by our capacity to remember, and the memory of previous utopian moments can help to keep our human aspirations alive. Celan's poetry in the1960s was an invitation to remember the Viennese workers rising against the clerico-fascist regime of Dollfuss in 1934, the cruiser *Aurora* firing her salvo over the Winter Palace in 1918, the demonstrations against the OAS in Paris in 1962, the defense of Madrid by the International Brigades in 1936, and Osip Mandelstamm looking at the hills around Voronezh in 1937 and wishing he was in Tuscany. We do not, of course, know what Celan would have thought about the tasks of poetry today, but to write today the kind of poem he would have found significant would require one to discover through investigation dated experiences that deserve to enter into our utopian memory, for better or for worse, and to locate them on their meridian.

[53] MP 48.
[54] MP 52.

Appendix

In Eins	In One
Dreizehnter Feber. Im Herzmund	Thirteenth of February. Shibboleth
erwachtes Schibboleth. Mit dir,	roused in the heart's mouth. With you,
Peuple	peuple
de Paris. *No pasarán.*	de Paris. *No pasarán.*
Schäfchen zur Linken: er, Abadias,	Little sheep to the left: he, Abadias,
der Greis aus Huesca, kam mit den	the old man from Huesca, came with
Hunden	his dogs
über das Feld, im Exil	over the field, in exile
stand weiß eine Wolke	white hung a cloud
menschlichen Adels, er sprach	of human nobility, into our hands
uns das Wort in die Hand, das wir	he spoke the word that we needed,
brauchten, es war	it was
Hirten-Spanisch, darin,	shepherd-Spanish, and in it
im Eislicht des Kreuzers »Aurora«:	in icelight of the cruiser "Aurora."
die Bruderhand, winkend mit der	the brotherly hand, waving with
von den wortgroßen Augen	the blindfold removed from
genommenen Binde—Petropolis, der	his word-wide eyes—Petropolis, the
Unvergessenen Wanderstadt lag	roving city of those unforgotten,
auch dir toskanisch zu Herzen.	was Tuscanly close to your heart also.
Friede den Hütten!	*Peace to the cottages!*

[Translation by Michael Hamburger, in *Paul Celan: Selected Poems* (Penguin, 1996), p. 211]

Celan, "In Eins"

Written May 1962; first appeared in 1963 in the volume Die Niemandsrose *(Fischer, 1963), which is dedicated to the memory of the Russian poet Ossip Mandelstamm.*

l.1   "*Dreizehnter Feber*":   on 13 February 1962 Parisians killed in a demonstration against the OAS (Organisation de l'armée secrète) were buried. Also the day of a workers' uprising in Vienna against the clerico-fascist regime of Dollfuss in 1934 (to which Celan also refers in an early poem; see *PC* 83).

1.2 "*Schibboleth*": Chapter 12 of the Book of Judges (Old Testament) tells of a conflict between two Israelite tribes, Gilead and Ephraim. Ephraimites could not pronounce the Hebrew word "*shibboleth*" (meaning, apparently, "ear of corn" [LXX: στάχυς] or "flood, torrent") correctly, but said "*sibboleth.*" Gileadites holding the fords of the river Jordan asked everyone wishing to cross to pronounce "*shibboleth*"; they killed all who could not pronounce it correctly. So a "*shibboleth*" is a verbal item in itself semantically insignificant, but the correct or incorrect production or use of which allows you to tell friend from enemy (and can mean the difference between life and death).

1.3 "*No pasarán*" ["They shall not pass"]: Slogan associated in the Spanish Civil War with the Republican defense of Madrid against Nationalists (General Franco).

1.5 "*Abadias*": Minor Old Testament prophet (English "Obadiah") who encouraged Israelites not to "gloat over your brother on the day of his misfortune" (verse 12) and particularly not "to wait at the crossroads to cut off his fugitives" (verse 14). In drafts Celan writes "*Abdias*" rather than "*Abadias*," which suggests to me possible reference to the story by Adalbert Stifter "*Abdias*" (1842/47) about a Jewish trading colony, hidden in the ruins of a Roman city in the desert of North Africa, which was safe as long as no one knew it was there (see lines 15–16: "*der Unvergessenen Wanderstadt*").

1.6 "*Huesca*": In a letter (23 June 1962) Celan reports that on holiday he met an old shepherd from Huesca, a former partisan of the Republican cause in the Spanish Civil War, still exiled in Normandy.

1.12 "*im Eislicht des Kreuzers «Aurora»*: The cruiser *Aurora* anchored in the Neva fired a salvo on the evening of 7 November 1917, which was the signal for the storming of the Winter Palace by the Bolsheviks, thus initiating the October Revolution—so-called, although it took place in what we call November, because Russia then still used the pre-Gregorian calendar. "Eislicht": the Neva was iced up.

1.15 "*Petropolis*": The play with the various versions of the name of the city founded by Peter the Great—the teutonic "Petersburg" (Петербург), the Slavic equivalent "Petrograd" (Петроград), and the classicizing "Petropolis" (Петрополь)—is an old topos in Russian literature, used, for instance, in one of the most famous poems in the language, Pushkin's "Медный Всадник" (1833) ("*The Bronze Horseman*"): "Petersburg" in the subtitle; "Petrograd" in line 97; "Petropolis" in line 188. (A useful edition of this work for those

whose knowledge Russian is not advanced, with introduction, vocabulary, and notes in English, is published by Bristol Classical Press
and edited by Michael Basker [Duckworth, 2000].) During World
War I the name of the city was officially changed to "Petrograd,"
and then in the 1920s to "Leningrad." Recently it has reverted to
"Peterburg." Mandelstamm (1891–1938) lived through the period
in which the city was changing names most frequently, and wrote
a number of poems about the city under its various names. Celan
translated one of Mandelstamm's poems about "Petropolis" ("В
Петрополе прозрачном мы умрем"/"*PETROPOLIS, DIAPHAN:
hier gehen wir zugrunde*"; see Осип Мандельштам, Сочинения
[Художественная Литература, 1990], vol. 1, p. 112, and Paul Celan,
Übersetzungen aus dem Russischen [Fischer, 1986], p. 57). Drafts
show that at one point Celan wanted to use a quotation from a Mandelstamm poem about "Petersburg" (which he had also translated)
as motto of what became this poem: "В Петербурге мы сойдемся
снова" ("In Petersburg we will [one day] assemble once again").
The Russian original of this poem and Celan's translation into German can be found in Paul Celan, *Werke* (Suhrkamp, 1983), vol. 4,
pp. 158–61.

l.17 "*toskanisch*":   A conflation of (a) Tuscan, and (b) тоска [= "yearn-
ing [for], nostalgia"]. In two of the Russian books in his library
Celan underlined the work "тоска" and glossed it in the margins as
"*angoisse*" and "*anxiété*." See *Celan: La bibliothèque*, p. 695. This
is a reference to a poem that Mandelstamm wrote while in internal exile in Voronezh ("Не сравнивай" ["Don't compare"]: Осип
Мандельштам, Сочинения [Художественная Литература, 1990],
vol. 1, p. 232), which ends

Где больше неба мне—там я бродить готов,	Where I shall have bigger sky—to that place I am ready to wander,
И ясная <u>тоска</u> меня не отпускает	but my bright <u>desire</u> will not let me go
От молодых еше воронежских холмов	from the still-young hills of Voronezh
К всечеловеческим, яснеющим в	to the humane, sunny hills of
<u>Тоскане</u>	<u>Tuscany</u>.
	[My translation and emphasis]

l.18 "*Friede den Hütten*":   Büchner's revolutionary tract *Der hessische
Landbote* (1834) begins with the words "*Friede den Hütten! Krieg
den Pallästen!*" ["Peace to the huts! War to the palaces!"]. See
Georg Büchner, *Werke und Briefe*, ed. Karl Pörnbacher, Gerhard
Schaub, Hans-Joachim Sim, and Edda Ziegler (Deutscher Taschenbuch Verlag, 1988), p. 39. "*Guerre aux châteaux! Paix aux chau-
mières!*" was in common use during the French Revolution.

Scholarship on "*In Eins*"

Sources I have used in constructing the above notes include:

Paul Celan, *Die Niemandsrose: Vorstufen-Textgenese-Endfassung, Tübinger Ausgabe*, edited by H. Schmull and M. Schwarzkopf (Suhrkamp, 1996)

Kommentar zu Paul Celans "Die Niemandsrose," edited by Jürgen Lehmann (Universitätsverlag Winter, 2003)

Paul Celan, *Die Gedichte: Kommentierte Gesamtausgabe*, edited by Barbara Weidemann (Suhrkamp, 2003).

IX

Heidegger and His Brother

THE SMALL TOWN OF Meßkirch lies in the extreme south of the present state of Baden-Württemberg, Germany, roughly halfway between Lake Constance and the Swabian Alps. During the first half of the twentieth century, this region was still overwhelmingly rural and Catholic. Politically Meßkirch and its surrounding villages were a bastion of the (Catholic) Center Party, which, together with the SPD, formed one of the central components of the continuing coalition of parties that kept the Weimar Republic in operation during the 1920s. In the elections of 1932 the Center Party received an absolute majority of the votes cast in Meßkirch, and in the final election before the war (March 1933) it was still the largest single party (45% of the vote; the National Socialists received 35%; other parties the rest) (pp. 48–49).[1] In the small towns of this poor and isolated area various traditional practices were retained into the 1960s that had elsewhere disappeared. Thus, Carnival (*Fastnacht*) was elaborately celebrated as a "Week of Fools" during which people dressed in outlandish costumes, told jokes, and enjoyed some relaxation of the usual rules of moderation, decorum, and social docility. The high point of the week was a banquet at which officially recognized Town Fools gave public speeches from a raised dais in front of the town hall. The speech of a Town Fool was expected to be a virtuoso linguistic display in the local dialect, full of puns, humorous metaphors, and witty juxtapositions of incongruous items. In this ultra-Catholic region, where the Counter-Reformation—and the Baroque aesthetic with which it was often associated—had struck extremely deep roots, the Carnival speeches were directed as if to a particularly crude peasant audience, and they were often informed by a religiously based gallows humor. Why worry about taxes, social advancement, or the harvest when in a quarter of an hour you could all be dead and gone to eternal judgment, and probable damnation, anyway? As in Athenian Old Comedy, the Town Fools' speeches were also expected to be full of references to local people and

---

[1] This essay originated as a review of Hans Dieter Zimmermann's *Martin und Fritz Heidegger: Philosophie und Fastnacht* (Beck, 2005). Otherwise unspecified page references are to this book.

events, and frequently had a distinctly satirical edge that could easily veer in the direction of a kind of primitive political dissidence, although the exact nature of the dissent being registered was often hard to discern.

During the 1930s, '40s, and '50s Meßkirch had an especially brilliant Town Fool, Fritz Heidegger, who was known far and wide for his quick wit, his verbal dexterity, and his sharp sense of satire. Oddly enough, he was—as it were "in civilian life"—both the head teller at the local bank and a serious stutterer. Heidegger's father was a man of extremely limited means—he had a small workshop making buckets and barrels, and was sexton of the local Catholic church—and so there had been no question of his being able to provide the necessary financial support for any form of further education for his children (pp. 14–15). In early adolescence, however, the highly gifted Fritz Heidegger obtained a scholarship from the Church authorities and went off to the archiepiscopal boarding school in Constance with the intention of studying theology and entering the priesthood. In the boarding school, though, something seems to have happened to him: he developed the speech defect which would prevent him from ever being employable as a parish priest. So he was sent home, thereby losing his chance to go to university. He eventually took a job in the local bank. Heidegger stuttered for the rest of his life—*except* when he stood up on the dais in front of the Rathaus to give his Carnival speech. Then the words and phrases poured out of him in quick, scintillating succession, fully and correctly articulated and seamlessly ordered without hesitation or interruption (p. 27).

People in Meßkirch were proud of their local celebrity. One day a visitor who had come from another village to hear Fritz asked a local: "Who is that guy standing next to Heidegger who looks so much like him?" The reply came: "Oh, that's his brother; he is a philosopher in Freiburg." The visitor paused for a moment: "Philosopher? You mean 'alcoholic'?" ("*einer der vil sooft*,"—or in High German, "*viel säuft*"— one who drinks too much). Fritz Heidegger, the Meßkirch Town Fool, liked this anecdote so much, he appropriated it for his own use: "My brother is the thinker; I'm the drinker" ("*Mein Bruder ist der Philosoph; ich bin der viel sooft*") (pp. 23–24). Fritz obviously could not resist a joke, even at his own expense, but this joke was certainly not the whole truth. Several of Fritz Heidegger's Carnival speeches have survived in manuscript, although they have never been published. During his lifetime Fritz published one or two texts on topics of local interest in Meßkirch, including a history of the local bank that placed its origin and development in the context of the wider economic situation in Germany. These clearly show him to have been a thoughtful man of high native intelligence and a reflective disposition, whose deeply pessimistic attitude toward the world, his fellow human beings, and himself expressed itself in sometimes melancholic, sometimes caustic observations. In addition to these published works, Fritz Heidegger apparently left behind after his death in 1980 a very large body of writings, essays, sketches, and aphorisms, mostly of a meditative or religious character, which he produced simply for his own use (p. 97). Zimmermann cites a certain amount of this material, and seems sometimes to suggest that it is worth reading on its own merits. He explains that he undertook to write this book because he was fascinated by the history of the "so-called little people" who for one reason or another never make it into the eye of later history (p. 156). It is, of course, a great mistake to take public reputation as one's exclusive measure of the quality of a body of writing or as implying an automatic judgment on a whole human life. Martin Heidegger is by far the most extensively discussed philosopher of the twentieth century, but that does not in itself settle the issue of the value of his work or his life. It is, however, equally a mistake to romanticize the "little man." Despite his wide reading, the obvious seriousness of his attempts to understand human life, and his copious writing, Fritz Heidegger was not, to judge from the accounts Zimmermann gives of his writings, a great philosopher or religious thinker, and, from all we know about his modest and self-ironic character, it seems clear that it never would have occurred to him to think he was any such thing. One mustn't confuse human admiration for a person who has made the most of restricted opportunities with a judgment on the final significance of what he was able to achieve. Fritz was a man who had been prevented by factors beyond his control from developing certain talents we can very clearly see him to have had, but we simply do not know what he "would have become" if he had not developed that stutter, and his writings do not seem to be of more than limited and documentary value.

The central section of Zimmermann's book is devoted to a comparison of the speeches Martin Heidegger gave as the first National Socialist Rector of the University of Freiburg in 1933 with two of Fritz Heidegger's surviving Carnival speeches, that of 1934 and that of 1937. Martin's inaugural address as rector was published at the time under the title "Die Selbstbehauptung der deutschen Universität," and has been subjected to decades of close scrutiny ever since; transcripts and reports of other speeches he gave while he was rector have been available in Guido Schneeberger's *Nachlese zu Heidegger* (Bern) since 1962. Whatever Martin's private reservations might have been in 1933—and we have no record of any reservations in 1933—his speeches, taken collectively as public performances, were certainly firm and explicit endorsements of the National Socialist regime. Fritz, on the other hand, seems, from the evidence, at the very least to have lacked his brother Martin's enthusiasm from the very beginning. To be sure, he did not

directly and unequivocally attack National Socialism in any of his Carnival speeches—if he had, he would at the very least have immediately
been taken into "protective custody" by the police (ostensibly to protect
him from "the righteous indignation of the populace") as had happened
to several prominent local Catholics in 1933, and he might well have
been taken off to Heuberg, the local concentration camp near Stetten
(pp. 48–51). Nevertheless, it is clear that at some level Fritz's speeches, if
one were to peel away the jokes, fill in the indirect allusions, disperse the
smokescreens, and think seriously about what the speaker was saying,
were at least mildly "oppositional." At this distance it is very difficult
to determine actually how subversive they were intended to be, even if
one gives Fritz the benefit of the doubt, that is, if one attributes to him
an intention that, within the limits of what a strict construction of the
actual words of his text will bear, is as close as possible to the one most
right-thinking people today think he ought to have had in 1933, namely
categorically anti-National Socialist.[2] In addition, in politics intention is
not everything, and it is also hard to know what kind of real effect these
speeches had or could have been expected to have. One ought, that is,
not to exaggerate how *effectively* subversive they could actually have
been even if Fritz had had the distinct intention to make them as subversive as possible. There are a number of reasons for this.

First, the Carnival speech was supposed to be full of obfuscation, rapid
shifts of register, associative patter, indirectness, ambiguity, and hidden
barbs and surprises.[3] For the Town Fool who wanted to use his speech
as a vehicle for political criticism, then, there would always be the risk
that his point would be so deeply concealed it would pass unperceived, or
that the message would be one that could be decoded only by those who
were already looking for it or already potentially responsive to it. It is not
nothing to preach to the already converted, or to send hidden messages
of support that can be deciphered only by those already on the lookout
for any kind of hope they can garner, but this might still be thought to
fall short of effective political mobilization. Real subversion, one might
think, would consist not in further edifying those who already have the
right beliefs and attitudes, and the mental agility to see and hear what has
escaped the censor's notice, but in changing the minds and attitudes of
people who are not antecedently predisposed. Perhaps, or rather surely,
it is too much to aspire to change the minds of those with a massively

---

[2] Exempting Slavoj Žižek from the unwelcome status of "right-thinking." See *In Defence of Lost Causes* (Verso, 2008).

[3] On the whole issue of Carnival, see Mikhail Bakhtin, *Rabelais and His World*, trans-
lated by Hélène Iswosky (University of Indiana Press, 1984), and also Lucien Febvre, *Le problème de l'incroyance au XVIe siècle: La religion de Rabelais* (Michel, 1947).

vested (political, economic, or psychological) interest in the status quo (or the New Order), but then in most situations of political conflict there are not merely supporters and opponents of any given course or program, but a great mass of "neutrals" who, at the beginning at any rate, do not firmly belong to either party. What are they to make of something they might not correctly comprehend?

There is an in fact rather optimistic view, associated with some members of the Frankfurt School, which holds that it is a characteristic of the "authoritarian personality" to be unable and unwilling to tolerate any kind of vagueness, indeterminacy, straddling or crossing of fixed boundaries, mixing of categories, disappointment of stereotypical expectations, or ambiguity.[4] Thus *any* pleasure taken in ambiguity could be looked upon as a good sign of openness to a relaxation of rigidities. This would be an effect, as it were, of the form of the Carnival performance, not of the specific content. The mere public presentation of ambiguity would have a potentially liberating effect.

Many will find this implausible, or at any rate politically insignificant, and a powerful traditional line of argument emphasizes another aspect of Carnival. The Fool's speech was a *different* kind of public performance from the speech by the rector of a university. The Rector of the University is the voice of Reason, sober reflection, and Science. The Fool's Speech at Carnival was a *licensed* deviation, or more exactly, an instance of the *tolerated* enjoyment of a strictly limited deviation. Successive generations of ecclesiastical and secular authorities had tried over the course of the centuries to repress the (relative) "freedom" the Town Fool enjoyed during Carnival, but they had failed. Still, when something is officially tolerated or even encouraged *as* a momentary licensed deviation from common sense, good manners, and decency, it may be thought inherently to lose its critical potential. What the Fool says is publicly stamped as Folly. What status does something have when it is *accepted as* a limited violation of all that is good, sensible, and decorous? One traditional view is that a well-defined, distinctly delimited area with sharply controlled boundaries within which humorous deviation is officially permitted *in fact* serves as a kind of safety valve for popular sentiments that might otherwise take a more directly subversive form. *Licensed* folly, then, is more properly understood as part of the apparatus of repression than as a form of resistance. This interpretation has a kind of initial plausibility. One promising way of defanging criticism is by associating it firmly in the people's minds with the remarks of someone who is clearly stigmatized as

[4] T. W. Adorno, Else Frenkel-Brunswik, Daniel Levinson, and Nevitt Sanford, *The Authoritarian Personality* (Harper & Row, 1950). See my *Morality, Culture, and History* (Cambridge University Press, 1999) pp. 101–2.

a fool. To say that permitting licensed folly is a comprehensible strategy for a repressive regime is not, of course, to say that doing so will always have the real effect the regime intends. Just as the intentions of the Fool are not the only thing that counts, because those intentions may not be realized in a way anyone else can recognize, and may not in any case have the effect intended, so similarly the intentions of the authorities who permit, or at any rate acquiesce in, the Carnival, do not count as the final word. Populations can be highly inventive in subverting institutions intended to control them. One cannot get a full understanding of what happened in the Carnival in any given year by focusing exclusively on the intentions of the Fool in making his speech, or on the intentions of the authorities in permitting or trying to suppress the festivities, or on the real effects of the particular performance in question, or even on the conventional, structural, or functional features of the institution itself. These are all important enough, but no one element in isolation tells the whole story. Drawing on the thought of Nietzsche and Foucault, some have begun to speak of institutions and practices like Carnival as "sites," i.e., as places that are there to be appropriated, won, lost, and fought over. Only "real" history can tell one what happened at this particular site at a particular time in the 1930s or 1940s.

Although the texts of Fritz's speeches have never been published, and one is therefore dependent on the summaries and excerpts Zimmermann gives in this book, it does seem that there is something more problematic about the substance of Fritz's speeches than Zimmermann admits. Thus, in 1934 he reportedly ends his Carnival speech by warning the audience that a "second World War, worse than the first" was to be expected. However, when the airplanes drop their poison bombs on Meßkirch, the pious inhabitants would not need to worry; their purgatorial suffering would not last long, *provided* they had "practiced and trained themselves every hour and every day from now on in striving most sincerely only to be what they really already were: From A to Z, piles of shit." This is certainly no expression of any great enthusiasm for National Socialism, but it also does not seem to leave much room for any focused form of dissidence. The social distance which irony and satire both presuppose and partly generate is a tricky phenomenon to manage. Laughter at the expense of a particular individual person or policy is under normal circumstances no real threat to the social order as a whole. Naturally enough the individual satirized might not see it that way, but that is a separate issue. Significant social criticism requires one to have available (or, in certain extraordinary circumstances, to invent and develop) an appropriate vocabulary and the ability to adopt an appropriate distance from the social structure as a whole. You need some level of analysis *between* that of individuals and that of metaphysics. Criticism of personalities will leave the basic structure untouched, but so will hyper-distanced religious or metaphysical criticism.

Admittedly, too, the Third Reich was not an instance of what anyone would be likely to call "normal circumstances," so what under other circumstances might have been thought hyperbole was perhaps not inappropriate. On the other hand, when satire takes the form of a "metaphysischer Kahlschlag"—a scorched earth policy which leads to a complete devaluation of all distinctions in the human world in the face of the brute fact of potential universal imminent annihilation—as it seems to do at the end of Fritz's 1934 speech, it is also no particular threat to any specific social and political order. Or rather, the actual beneficiaries of this sort of attitude are likely to be whatever "agencies that promise to provide salvation" ("*Heilsanstalten*" as Max Weber calls them) happen to be in existence at the given time and place, and are able to take advantage of the natural human reaction against the radical destruction of all secular meaning. For believers, the Church would be one such "agency of salvation." Martin Heidegger's philosophy, which shares the radically pessimistic vision of the human situation which one finds at the end of Fritz's speech, seemed to suggest that this view of human life simply had to be embraced actively without taking refuge in traditional religious conceptions, but then in 1933 Martin ended up a Nazi.

By 1938 Martin had moved away from National Socialism, thought he was under surveillance by the authorities, and was also beginning to expect a new war to break out. We know from independent sources that his lectures were eventually monitored for ideological and political deviance by National Socialist spies, including ostensible "students" in his lectures, although the evidence for this refers to a slightly later period (the early 1940s). Thus, Heidegger had always been notoriously unsound on the specifically "racialist" aspects of National Socialism and tried provocatively in his lectures during the war to demonstrate that Nietzsche, who along with Kant was one of the constant points of reference for National Socialist ideologists, was *not* a racist. By the 1940s Heidegger was described in the secret reports passed on to the authorities by their spies as having "retreated" into a "private" idiosyncratic National Socialism all his own. In 1938, however, he was particularly concerned lest his philosophic manuscripts be destroyed or lost in the coming military action, or confiscated by the authorities. He thus moved two crates of his handwritten texts to his brother's house in Meßkirch. Fritz agreed to type these manuscripts up for him; they amounted eventually to about 50,000 pages. Fritz did not have a typewriter at home, so he went into his bank after hours to use their machine (p. 143). He typed four carbon copies of each original, then at the end corrected what he had typed, entering Greek expressions where necessary by hand. Fritz may not have gone to university, but his old-style secondary-school education was sufficient to allow him to be able to transcribe individual Greek words correctly.

It seems incontrovertible that Fritz from the very start construed this work for his brother as collaborative rather than simply subaltern. He made marginal notes on the texts he typed, subdivided sentences that he thought had become too long, and made suggestions for improvement. He discussed Martin's work with him continuously, proposing alternatives, raising objections, and pressing him for further clarification of what he meant. This went on for over twenty years. Fritz didn't "write Martin's books for him" (p. 23) as many of the residents of Meßkirch supposed; this was no more than a town myth. It is clear, however, that Fritz was something more than the keyboard under Martin's fingers.

Although Zimmermann's joint biography does not intend to be a treatment of (Martin) Heidegger's philosophy, there is in fact one philosophical point that emerges with some clarity, and that is the continuing influence which certain forms of medieval Catholic mysticism, particularly the work of Meister Eckhart, had on both Fritz's and Martin's thinking (pp. 146–50). Eckhart thought that if what humans called "God' was really the "supreme Being," then there must be something *beyond* God. The reason for this is that there would always be conditions which were necessary for *any* entity, thus also the purported Supreme Being, to exist. These conditions would in some sense be "prior to" or "beyond" the entity in question. This "thing beyond" God should be the true object of human devotion. Eckhart calls it "divinity" ("*Gottheit*"). Given that it is not itself a being, even a "supreme" being, nothing can be *said* about "divinity," but it might still be at least partially accessible to humans in various exalted moments or in indirect ways. This is exactly the structure of what Heidegger calls "Being" (*das Sein*): an inexpressible "something" which is not a "thing" in any sense, but a condition for the existence of anything at all. It is perhaps not too far-fetched to see in this distinction between God as a "thing" and "divinity" a gesturing at what Heidegger would later call the "ontological difference." Heidegger devoted his life to trying to find some way of speaking nonconceptually about this peculiar "no-thing" ("divinity") that was the origin and precondition of everything that is without reducing it to the status of a thing or to any set of general properties of things.

Heidegger (Martin) himself always claimed that he was not really a "philosopher" but a religious thinker who was trying to destroy the pretensions of human reason in order to open a space for a more primordial form of human existence. In his early period this was a form of religious existence based on Christian faith, and what needed to be undermined was traditional theology; later the conception of what needed to be destroyed became increasingly extensive, and the conception of what was to replace it more and more elusive, but the structure remained the same. Martin also never tired of repeating that one can never get away from one's origin, but would be increasingly drawn back to it. In his case this was Meßkirch-Catholicism.

Fritz Heidegger remained a devout member of the Church until his death. Martin, born in 1889 and thus five years older than Fritz, had also intended to become a priest, and had passed through the same archiepiscopal boarding school in Constance, and begun to study theology at the University of Freiburg. His mental and physical health held out longer than Fritz's had. In 1911, however, he had a kind of breakdown that was diagnosed as "heart trouble," and when he had recovered, he shifted from study in the Faculty of Theology, which in Germany in1911 automatically meant preparation for a career as a Catholic priest, to the Faculty of Philosophy. In the 1920s Martin Heidegger left the Catholic Church with great fanfare, converting publicly to Protestantism. He said that what he objected to was the "*system* of Catholicism," meaning presumably the philosophical straitjacket of Thomism, the hierarchical organization of the Church, and traditional forms of ecclesiastical discipline. Before he died, however, Martin arranged to have himself buried according to the rites of the Catholic Church in the graveyard of the church in Meßkirch in which he and his brother had served as altar boys in their youth. Fritz Heidegger's son Heinrich, who had realized the ambition which each of the two brothers had originally had for himself and was a parish priest in the Black Forest village of St. Blasien, conducted the service (p. 151).

The milieu in which the Heideggers lived was both highly provincial and surprisingly cosmopolitan, and Martin himself did his best to cultivate the intertwining of these two features. This combination is summed up for me in the image of Martin in March 1945, sitting with what remained of the University of Freiburg—ten aged professors, too old or too disabled to fight even in the "Landsturm," and thirty young women, who had been evacuated to a castle, Burg Wildenstein, overlooking the Danube. Here Heidegger gave lectures on the poem by Hölderlin entitled "*Der Ister*" ("*Ister*" is the Greek name for the Danube); from the castle one could look down into the valley in which Martin and Fritz's grandfather had been born "in the sheepfold" ("*natus in ovile*" as the baptismal register had it) in 1803 (p. 101). A few kilometers down the Danube, at Sigmaringen, what remained of the Vichy government (Pétain, Laval, and others, including the novelist Louis-Ferdinand Céline, whose novel *D'un chateau à l'autre* gives a memorable portrait of this period) was fighting over its corpse, or trying to find ways to escape the inevitable and quickly approaching day of reckoning (pp. 105–10). Easter fell on 1 April in 1945, so Ash Wednesday, the day on which Carnival ended and Lent began, was 14 February.

X

Richard Rorty at Princeton

Personal Recollections

WHEN I ARRIVED IN PRINCETON during the 1970s my addiction to tea was already long standing and very well entrenched, but I was so concerned about the quality of the water in town, that I used to buy large containers of allegedly "pure" water at Davidson's—the local supermarket, which seems now to have gone out of business. I didn't, of course, have a car, and given the amount of tea I consumed, the transport of adequate supplies of water was a highly labor-intense and inconvenient matter. Dick and Mary Rorty must have noticed me lugging canisters of water home, because, with characteristic generosity, they developed the habit of calling around at my rooms in 120 Prospect, often on Sunday mornings, offering to take me by car to fill my water bottles at a hugely primitive and highly suspicious looking outdoor water tap on the side of a pumphouse that was operated by the Elizabethtown Water Company on a piece of waste land near the Institute Woods. This pumphouse with its copiously dripping tap was like something out of Tarkovsky's film about Russia after a nuclear accident, *Stalker*, and the surrounding area was a place so sinister one half expected to be attacked by packs of dogs in the final stages of radiation sickness or by troops of feral children who had been left by their parents to fend for themselves while the parents went off to the library to finish their dissertations. On one of those Sunday mornings in that insalubrious, but somehow appropriate, landscape Dick happened to mention that he had just finished reading Gadamer's *Truth and Method*. My heart sank at this news because the way he reported it seemed to me to indicate, correctly as it turned out, that he had been positively impressed by this book. I had a premonition, which also turned out to be correct, that it would not be possible for me to disabuse him of his admiration for the work of a man whom I knew rather well as a former colleague at Heidelberg and whom I held to be a reactionary, distended windbag. Over the years I did my best to set Dick right about Gadamer, even resorting to the rather low blow of describing to him the talk Gadamer had given at the German Embassy in occupied Paris in 1942, in which Gadamer discussed the positive role Herder could play

in sweeping away the remnants of such corrupt and degenerate phenomena as individualism, liberalism, and democracy from the New Europe
arising under National Socialism. All this had no effect on Dick. His
response to this story was that Gadamer had probably wanted to finance
a trip to Paris—a perfectly understandable, indeed self-evidently laudable
aspiration—and, under the circumstances, getting himself invited to the
German Embassy was the only way to do this. As I persisted in pointing
out that this in itself might "under the circumstances" not exactly constitute an exculpation, I came up against that familiar shrug of the shoul-
ders which could look as if it meant that Dick had turned his receiving
apparatus off. In this case, the shrug also made me feel that I was being
hysterically aggressive in pursuing a harmless old gent for what was, after
all, no more than a youthful indiscretion. In retrospect, I am not sure but
that I don't now think Dick was right about this last point, but that was
not my reaction at the time.

What Dick found interesting in Gadamer was the idea that philosophy
was a "conversation." The immediate source Gadamer cites for this idea
is one of the preliminary drafts of a hymn by the early nineteenth-century
German poet Hölderlin, entitled *Friedensfeier*:

Viel hat erfahren der Mensch. Der	[Man has learnt much. Has named
Himmlischen viele genannt.	many heavenly beings
Seit ein Gespräch wir sind	since we have become a conversation
Und hören können voneinander.	and can hear from each other.]

When Hölderlin writes that we "have become a conversation" this is obviously a very different kind of claim from the traditional one that speech
is part of the essence of man. Dick would not have been able to accept a
view that attributed to man an essence, especially a timeless essence, so
it is important that Hölderlin does not speak of man as being essentially
conversational (at all times and places) but as humans as having *become*
"a conversation" at a particular time ("*seit*"). Second, to speak of a
"conversation" is to be very explicit about the inherently social nature of
what makes us human, and finally the informality of the use of the word
"conversation" (a connotation which is perhaps stronger in the German
"*Gespräch*") directs attention away from trying to understand this activity as the activation of pre-given formal rules, or as aspiring to satisfy
some antecedently given canons of cogency, relevance, or accuracy. If to
be human ("now" at any rate) is to take part in a, or this, conversation,
then it seems but a short step from that to the claim that philosophy is
important because it is a way in which the conversation maintains itself.

Despite this, it was by no means a foregone conclusion that someone as
deeply influenced by pragmatism as Dick would find this idea congenial.
If pragmatism means not only that actions speak louder than words—

and one doesn't have to be a pragmatist to think that—but that they are finally the only thing that counts, the pragmatist might be expected to prefer to Hölderlin's "definition" of humanity as "conversation" the counterclaim by Faust when he refuses to translate the first sentence of the Gospel according to St John as "*In the beginning was the Word*" and insists on translating it "*In the beginning was the deed*":

> Ich kann das Wort so hoch unmöglich schätzen . . .
> Im Anfang war die Tat.

It is, of course, possible to construe "conversation" as an etiolated form of action, and Gadamer holds that anything that can be understood can be construed as "language." "Sein das verstanden werden kann, ist Sprache." It is hard to imagine a philosophy not embodied in language, despite Rabelais's fantasy (II.19) about a philosophical disputation conducted exclusively through gestures.[1] Still, I wonder in general whether there is not in Rorty a kind of overvaluation of the word, and a consequent undervaluation of such forms of human endeavor as politics, music, design and the visual arts, and various forms of physical discipline. Serious music, for instance, doesn't figure very visibly in Rorty's work, perhaps because he was himself completely unmusical. His ideal is the "bookish intellectual," not, for instance, the Hellenic youth trained in γυμναστική and μουσική, the man or woman who aspires to come closer to the Divine by prayer and fasting, the Goethean or Humboldtian life devoted to voracious consumption of *all* the different kinds of human experience, or the political activist whose life is inextricable from his or her contribution to social change. As Dick was well aware, there is an elective affinity between his ideal and the possible life prospects of a comfortable member of the bourgeoisie in a wealthy, powerful, and depoliticized country. Against Gadamer's view of the primacy of "conversation" one can also cite the *final (printed)* version of the very poem by Hölderlin which served to introduce this notion:

Viel hat von Morgen an,	[Starting from the morning
Seit ein Gespräch wir sind und	when we became a conversation,
hören voneinander,	and hear from each other
erfahren der Mensch, bald sind	much have we experienced,
wir aber Gesang	but soon we shall be song.]

Of course, one could try to remain unimpressed here by insisting that this is, after all, just poetic hyperbole. The idea that song could replace conversation is a Romantic conceit, not something to be taken too seriously. If one is going to take this tack at such a late point in the discussion

---

[1] *Pantagruel*, ed. P. Michel (Gallimard, 1964), ch. 19, pp. 269–81.

of what it was to be human, though, why start by appealing to poetry in the first place?

That there is no philosophy without language might not mean that the only thing, or even the most important thing, one had to understand in the history of philosophy was its language. Song is not speech, and political action, even if it "can be understood," can take place *without a word being spoken.* Think of Frans de Waal's observations about political action among nonhuman primates, or recall that one of the most interesting aspects of the events of the 11th of September 2001 was that the actions were carried out wordlessly as far as the international media were concerned. There was no reading out of a set of demands in front of television cameras, no explanations, no public political announcements of any kind, no group immediately fell all over itself to try to lay claim to these actions. The leadership of Al- Qaeda did not disclaim the responsibility, but also made no special attempt to issue any particular discursive statement explaining them. These actions spoke for themselves, and through them the perpetrators expressed a rather clear political judgment. But is flying an airplane into a building best understood as a contribution to a conversation? If students lynch their lecturer because of his heretical opinions, as seems occasionally to have happened in the Middle Ages, is that a contribution to the conversation of humanity?

On another one of our visits to the Elizabethtown Water Company Dick described to me a new undergraduate course he wanted to give. It was to be called "An Alternative History of Modern Philosophy" and would sketch a continuous conversation from the end of the Middle Ages to the beginning of the twentieth century without once naming any of the standard canonical figures. This would be a history of philosophy without any reference to Descartes, Locke, Leibniz, Hume, or J. S. Mill. I don't recall in all detail how the alternative story was to run, but I do remember very vividly that it was to start from Petrus Ramus. Dick had an extremely low opinion of Descartes as a philosopher, thinking of him as no more than a minor disciple of Petrus Ramus. I also remember that some of the high points were to be Paracelsus, the Cambridge Platonists, Thomas Reid, Fichte, and Hegel. I think the course was to end with Dewey, although I may be making that up. I thought this was a wonderful suggestion, for reasons, to be sure, that were probably rather different from those that motivated Dick, but there was one aspect of his prospective course that slightly bothered me, although I don't think I would at that time have been able to formulate my disquiet at all clearly. There was, as I would now formulate it, a slight unclarity in the conception of the course in that it conjoined two different views of the history of philosophy that Dick had not yet fully dissociated. On the one hand, there was a kind of debunking view of the canon as an unwarranted form of hero worship, singling out some *one* philosopher, often for highly adventitious reasons, and inappropriately attributing to him certain ideas, theses, arguments, or methods as his unique, original contribution, when these were actually invented by someone else, were minor variations of well known motifs, or were ideas that weren't in fact invented by anyone because they were "in the air" at the time. Descartes didn't "invent" the idea that the analytic method was the key to philosophy; Petrus Ramus did that (or perhaps: "no individual did that, because the idea was 'in the air'"). So why read Descartes rather than Ramus? This view still seems to assume that we know what the key questions and the major developments in philosophy are, that it is unquestionably important to understand and assimilate these questions and issues in themselves and in their genesis if one wanted to understand philosophy at all. The only question is to whom these major developments were correctly to be attributed.

The other idea is that at certain times in the past people called a certain kind of thinking and a resulting body of written work "philosophy" which from the point of view of the present seems highly eccentric in subject matter or method. There is no such thing as a universal set of philosophical questions or issues; Paracelsus wasn't remotely interested in asking or answering questions like those we find "philosophical," still lots of people at the time thought his work a paradigm of what a philosopher should be doing. The assumption here would be that the longer and more deeply one reflected on this fact, the more one would see that "philosophy" at different times and places referred to different clusters of intellectual activities, none of which formed a natural kind and none of which had any "inherent" claim to a monopoly on the "proper" use of the term "philosophy." Doing a history in which Paracelsus figured centrally but not Descartes, could be seen as a part of trying to give a history, not so much of philosophy, as of historically differing conceptions of what philosophy was. Dick did not confuse these two things, and in fact I learned how to distinguish them clearly only from his 1984 paper "The Historiography of Philosophy" (in *Philosophy in History*, Cambridge University Press, 1984). Rather he was consciously relaxed about doing both as part of the same project, whether a book or a course of lectures.

Actually there was, I think, also a *third* and slightly different strand also present in Dick's "Alternative History," which is the idea that philosophy is just a form of literature. The first reading is quasi-Marxist, i.e., philosophy is construed as a matter of large-scale social movements of thought which were integrated into a history of the way the species dealt with its natural environment, and then also with the social environment it itself created. In this story individuals play a subordinate role, so you can just as well study Fichte as an instance of idealism as Kant. The second reading is pragmatist (of a sort): philosophers, like everyone else, try to solve problems, and what problems there are changes over time, so the history of philosophy is radically discontinuous in the longer term although it might seem to be unitary in the short term. If, however, per the third reading, the history of philosophy is best seen as a collection of texts like a collection of, say, eighteenth- and nineteenth-century novels, of course one can make a noncanonical selection of those texts. A novel, though, is not self-evidently best understood as a part of a unitary attempt by humanity as a whole to deal with the world, nor is it very obviously a form of problem-solving. Dick had great admiration for Vladimir Nabokov ("He was *born* writing like *that*") and, despite his well-canvassed views about the potential role of literature in generating sympathy for the oppressed, he was also at the very least strongly drawn to Nabokov's purist aesthetic and rejection of any social relevance for literature; novels should not have any truck with what he called "topical trash." In philosophy, too, one might assume, the texts chosen would be ones that appealed to a refined and highly self-reflective, and also social disengaged, aesthetic sense, and structured so as to constitute a satisfying narrative.

Dick had two different worries about his planned new course. The first was that if the Committee on Instruction knew what he was up to, "They" would never permit it. Dick spoke of the Committee on Instruction as if it was a kind of academic Thought Police. One must, as it were, he said, consider the University as a complex machine with two interlocking parts, a Generator that was devoted to producing excellence in relatively abstract areas of research, primarily scientific research, and then a Transformer which turned the prestige acquired through this excellence into a force of repression, directed at legitimizing the deepest possible cultural and political conservatism. The combination of excellence and a strictly enforced backward-looking cultural ethos made the University an almost irresistible magnet for the extensive funding from the alumni, large corporations, and the government that fueled the Generator. The Committee on Instruction was the transmission belt between the two parts of the machine. "That is the way a great university protects itself from change," Dick would say to me, as a kind of refrain during the late 1970s, meaning by "change," I presume, in the first instance, cultural change. I naïvely objected that Dick's description couldn't possibly be correct because such a structure couldn't possibly maintain itself: it was like a confidence trick or a perpetual motion machine; reality would eventually break through at some point. Dick, however, was, at that time, significantly more disillusioned, or perhaps more realistic, than I was. I never was able to determine whether he thought I was right in tacitly assuming that there *were*, on the one hand, *some* universities that were serious enterprises, as it were "all the way down," and that operated according to the principles of merit and scholarship; then there were the cunning but deceptive ones, who diverted their acquired prestige to dodgy ends. Unfortunately, the dodgy ones could be successful for any extended period of time, as long as they could keep their motors running. Perhaps Dick thought that this whole distinction between the serious and the dubious couldn't be made—after all, in some sense the excellence was genuine;—or perhaps he thought that it was unimportant: how such a machine originally came into being and how it started to operate was a complicated question, but once the apparatus was fully working, as long as Princeton had enough power—in the first instance real power in the form of money, property, and other real entitlements, but also the associated forms of "symbolic capital," control of patronage, access to influential people, etc.—barring unforeseen catastrophes, it could keep the system going indefinitely. It had worked for a hundred years, Dick said, why not—if the money and power held out—for two hundred more?

Dick's second worry about this planned course was that he did not quite see how he could tell his story without mentioning Kant at all, and even to mention Kant would be to violate the rationale of the course. Since I had at least as negative an opinion of Kant as Dick had of Descartes, I encouraged him to move directly from Jacobi to Fichte, bypassing Kant altogether. He didn't seem very taken with this idea, although it was not clear to me why not. I suppose anyone who knew Dick knew his sometimes uncanny capacity simply to allow a train of thought that was moving in a direction he found uncongenial to peter out without it ever being completely clear why no further step in the conversation was made. This was not merely a gift or skill he had, but a personality trait that was integral to an aspect of Dick's philosophical makeup which I have already mention: his deeply rooted anti-Cartesianism. Once one has set the origin of a system of Cartesian coordinates, and specified the axes, one can continue to count off in any direction *ad libitum.* In Descartes this thought is presented in a rather optimistic way—we can always go on and will, as it were, never run out of space which we can measure. It is possible to take roughly the same thought in a pessimistic way, as in Beckett. Descartes remained a recurring obsession with Beckett; it is probably no accident that one of his earliest published works is a long poem on Descartes ("Whoroscope"). The narrator in Beckett's *L'innommable* talks incessantly, describing the contents of the visual field, recalling things he saw in the past, speculating about the identity of the objects apparently moving past him and laws of their motion, but the need to do this is experienced as a kind of horrible compulsion. The work ends with the unnameable narrator addressing himself and articulating this compulsion: "You must go on; I can't go on; I'll go on." Dick's reply to Descartes and to Beckett would be: *Why* exactly *"must"* you go on?

What particular questions you ask; where you need to keep asking questions; what is in the center of attention, what on the periphery, and what in the darkness outside; in what circumstances and to what exact extent clarity and explicitness are good things, and in what circumstances mere approximation—or *silence*—will do just as well; none of any of this was written in stone, inherently in the human breast, in the starry heavens, or in Plato's ὑπερουράνιος τόπος. Still in the end there seemed to me to be an unclarity about whether this was finally a pragmatist or an aestheticist position. Was philosophy a response to questions, which, although they arose contingently and were constantly changing, were questions to which we *needed* a response (which philosophy, or even, "only philosophy," could give)? Or was it a free aesthetic activity? I suspect Dick would have tried to deny that this was the alternative with which we were faced. Don't we in some sense "need" to be freely active as much as we "need" to solve the practical problems that arise in dealing with our natural and social world? This would move Dick back in the direction of the Young Hegelianism which inspired the young Dewey (and the Critical Theory which interested me). Whether this way of trying to unify the two strands is a genuine resolution of a real difficulty, an evasion, or a misapprehension on my part is a question I have never been able to answer to my own satisfaction.

Dick was deeply tolerant and amazingly generous both in action and in spirit. When I was appointed at Princeton, he had, I think, some hopes of acquiring a colleague with whom he could discuss the more metaphysical parts of the German philosophical tradition that were near the center of his attention at that time. It must have been at least a mild disappointment to him that I had little interest in any kind of metaphysics and spent my time studying philosophers like Adorno who were of no interest to him and thinking about "social theory"—at that time a purported academic discipline that has now disappeared as completely as Davidson's. Characteristically, Dick used to say to people that my first book, *The Idea of a Critical Theory,* showed the uselessness of the concept of "ideology," whereas I thought it showed the reverse. We could also find no common ground in aesthetics because of my own obsession with the philosophy of music. Dick seemed not only, as I have mentioned, like Freud, to be deeply unmusical, but he sometimes seemed even slightly irritated by the very existence of music and certainly by the thought that someone could take it sufficiently seriously to try to think about it in a sustained and systematic way. Finally, I think it puzzled him that I systematically avoided ever giving any instruction in the university on Heidegger. None of this in the least diminished the unstinting intellectual and academic support he gave me in the most diverse contexts over decades, which went far beyond anything I can have been thought to deserve.

As the years went by, and we both left Princeton, I am afraid the incipient intellectual and emotional gulf between us got wider, especially after
what I saw as Dick's turn toward ultra-nationalism with the publication
of *Constructing Our Country*. Dick had always been and remained to the
end of his life a "liberal" (in the American sense, i.e., a "Social Demo-
crat"): a defender of civil liberties and of the extension of a full set of
civic rights to all, a vocal supporter of the labor unions and of programs
to improve the conditions of the poor, an enemy of racism, cruelty, arbitrary authority, and social exclusion. On the other hand, I found that
he also enjoyed a spot of jokey leftist-baiting when he thought I was
adopting knee-jerk positions which he held to be ill-founded. That was
all fair enough. I tried not to rise to the bait, and usually succeeded, but
this did not contribute to making our relation easier or more comfortable for me. The high (or low, depending on one's perspective) point of
this sort of thing occurred sometime in the 1980s when Dick sent me a
postcard from Israel telling me he had just been talking with the Israeli
official responsible for organizing targeted assassinations of Arab mayors
on the West Bank. He closed by saying he thought this was just what the
situation required. I often wondered whether in acting in this provocative
way he was treating me as he would have liked to have treated his father,
a well-known poet and man of the (relatively) hard Left, who eventually,
as Dick put it, "became prey to *very powerful* fantasies on which he was
perfectly willing to act"; Dick had to have him institutionalized after
some potentially murderous outbreak. Probably by wondering about this
I was trying to convince myself that I had an importance in Dick's imagination that I surely did not have.

Constructing Our Country, though, represented a step too far for me.
The very idea that the United States was "special" has always seemed
to me patently absurd, and the idea that in its present, any of its past,
or any of its likely future configurations it was in any way exemplary, a
form of gross narcissistic self-deception which was not transformed into
something laudable by virtue of being embedded in a highly sophisticated
theory which purported to show that ethnocentrism was in a philosophically deep sense unavoidable. I remain very grateful to my Catholic up-
bringing and education for giving me relative immunity to nationalism.
In the 1950s the nuns who taught me from age five to twelve were virtually all Irish or Irish-American, with sentimental attachment to certain
elements of Celtic folklore, but they made sure to inculcate into us that
the only *serious* human society was the Church, which was an explicitly international organization. The mass, in the international language,
Latin, was the same everywhere; the religious orders were international.
This absence of national limitation was something very much to be cher-
ished. "*Catholica*" in the phrase "*[credo in] unam, sanctam, catholicam,*

et apostolicam ecclesiam" should, we were told, be written with a lower-case, not an uppercase, initial because it was not in the first instance part of the proper name of the church, but an adjective meaning "universal," and this universality was one of the most important "marks of the true Church." The Head of the Church, to be sure, and Vicar of Christ on earth, was in fact (at that time) always an Italian, but that was for contingent and insignificant reasons. The reason most commonly cited by these nuns was that, as Bishop of Rome, the Pope had to live in the "Eternal City," but only an Italian could stand to live in Rome: It was hot, noisy, and overcrowded, and the people there ate spaghetti for dinner everyday rather than proper food, i.e., potatoes, so it would be too great a sacrifice to expect someone who had not grown up in Italy to tolerate life there. I clearly remember being unconvinced by this argument, thinking it set inappropriately low standards of self-sacrifice for the higher clergy; a genuinely saintly character should be able to put up even with pasta for lunch and dinner every day. I have since myself adopted this diet for long periods of time without thinking it gave me any claim on the Papacy. In any case, it was obvious even to a child of six or seven that none of these sisters had ever been within a thousand kilometers of Rome.

Similarly, the (mostly) Hungarian priests who taught me from age twelve in a boarding school near Philadelphia had some residual Hapsburg loyalties—Grillparzer and Nestroy played a larger part in the curriculum than they would have in some other schools—but they were all very distinctly tri- or quadrilingual men of the world, who knew very well that it was the accidents of history—specifically the closure of their schools by the Hungarian Communist regime in the late 1940s, and the failure of the uprising of 1956—that had brought them to a culturally insignificant place they would in the normal course of events never have chosen even to visit. They were not in any doubt but that the United States (in the 1950s and early 1960s) was an empire which engaged in continuous displays of exaggerated self-praise, as all such empires had always done, showed its soft side when that was politically expedient, but was as capable of impatient, insouciant, or fully intended brutality as any other empire. These points were driven home pretty sharply in between discussions of the syntax, lexis, and meter of Vergil's *Aeneid*. "*His ego nec metas rerum nec tempora pono/imperium sine fine dedi*" (I.277–78); that's what they all think (in their prime), the "*rerum domini et gentes togatae*"; it didn't usually last. The two Spanish priests on the staff had had some experience in Central America and did not refrain from enlightening anyone interested about the operations of the United Fruit Company (and the CIA) there and about some of the uses to which the U.S. Marines were put. All the priests made the assumption which was all the more effective for not usually even ever being explicitly articulated, that American power, influence, and prosperity, and the relatively relaxed and tolerant regulation of the nonpolitical aspects of everyday life which such prosperity permitted, were highly contingent and transitory, a result of a geographical and historical conjunction that would not last or recur. McCarthy had recently shown how thin and fragile the veneer of tolerance was. We were all encouraged to get on with our lives as quickly as possible: the prosperity and relative freedom might last twenty, even thirty or forty years, but that would be it, and the bubble *could* unexpectedly burst even more quickly than that, so it was best to make the most of the resources on offer at the moment. Philadelphia in 1960 was a pale shadow of Vienna in 1830: City Hall was a second-rate imitation of Vienna's *Rathaus*, the Lyric Opera a poor provincial cousin of the *Volksoper*, and the orchestra, like virtually all the other major American orchestras in the era of Szell and Solti, was directed by a Hungarian (Eugene Ormandy). The recently departed John Foster Dulles was a kind of latter-day Metternich, and NATO was the Holy Alliance. One might in the final analysis prefer the Holy Alliance to its opponents, but that was no reason to idealize it.

Looking back from the present (2007), one can see that the *imperium* in fact lasted longer than expected, fifty or sixty years from 1945 rather than twenty or thirty, and everyone else, amazingly enough, seemed to realize it *was* an *imperium* only as its star was discernibly beginning to wane about the turn of the twenty-first century. Perhaps Hegel was right about the owl of Minerva. Even more oddly, they seemed to mistake the dusk of an empire gradually coming to an end with the early dawn of a *new* imperial period. A miscalculation by thirty or forty years may be very significant in the biography of an individual, but historically it changes little. The priests who taught me were capable of taking both the long and the short view. Their attitude to the then-present (1960) was already proleptically elegiac, summed up by the plaintive song I can still recall hearing played repeatedly on some kind of primitive gramophone: "So war's anno '30 in Wien, / und die Zeit, sie kommt nimmer zurück" ["That's the way it was in 1830 in Vienna, / and that time will never return"]. "Vienna" survived even the revolutionary year 1848, and lingered on until 1918, albeit much diminished. Similarly, after two or three decades—or, if it came to it, five or six decades—of affluence, the United States would gradually settle back into a kind of shabby obscurity, like one of the Latin American places in Conrad or that would later be described in the novels of Gabriel Garcia Marquez. For these nuns and priests believing that the United States was "a City upon a Hill" would have been simply a bit of risible Protestant nonsense, palpably contrary to religion, historical experience, and common sense, like believing in banshees or vampires.

Originally I took Dick's forays into the world of "patriotism" as one of his little ironic jokes, as when he would offer to run me home in his car instead of letting me walk because "We have to burn the oil while we have it." When I realized he was actually *serious*, I was first perplexed, and then appalled. Perhaps it will be thought that I overreacted to this, for two reasons. First of all, this sort of nationalism is a very common phenomenon in many places, and many of these expressions of national sentiment are perfectly harmless, if not very edifying, like the obsession with pseudo-Celtic knickknackery among the Irish-Americans of my mother's generation. In particular, it is also the case that many people in the United States, given the geography and history of the country, the constriction of what the mass communications network offers, and the political agenda of those in charge, really have no way of overcoming their provincial view of the world. One must try to muster as much understanding of this phenomenon as possible, and see that it is not the fault of many of the individuals involved, who really could not be expected, especially in the increasingly difficult economic conditions, to make the great effort that would be required to break out of the world according to CNN or the *New York Times*. Still, Dick's case seemed to me different first of all because he had relative economic security, leisure for reflection, access to information, and ample intelligence and good will. He ought, I felt, to have known better. The second reason Dick's lapse seemed to me serious was that although nowadays (although not, perhaps, in 1920) decorating the house with pictures of shamrocks is innocuous, preaching nationalism of any kind to a country armed to the teeth with every possible weapon, hyperaggressive, resentful in the face of its incipient economic and political decline, and prone to paranoia is very dangerous indeed.

Hegel says at some point that a great man causes others to write commentaries about him and his work. I have probably spent more time thinking about Dick than about anyone else outside my narrow circle of intimates. His philosophical position contains much of great interest and importance, along with, as one would expect, some things I cannot bring myself to agree with, but that position is clearly and plausibly put, and elaborated and defended with great ingenuity. As a person, however, he remained a complete mystery to me. I rarely had the sense I really understood why he did anything he did. There seemed to be a deep streak of weirdness in his personality and beliefs. I experienced this as being very odd because I don't find most people that unfathomable, although it must also be said that generally I don't care that much about why most of the people I know act as they do. Perhaps it is simply that I *cared* enough in his case to want genuinely to understand him, because I admired him, more than I cared about understanding other people, and so was not satisfied in his case with the superficial "explanations" of people's behavior which we normally accept.

As a person Dick was thoroughly lovable, and as a philosopher both extraordinarily perceptive and, at times, intensely irritating. The one thing he was not—*not ever*—was predictable or boring. I won't see his like again in my lifetime. I hope he would have been pleased to know that he would be remembered as this kind of person and this kind of philosopher.

XI

Melody as Death

HUMAN MEMORY IS A tricky phenomenon. We remember so easily what we take pleasure in recalling, and also what we most definitely do *not* wish to recall. Sometimes if one is quick and nimble enough, one can even catch the process of "reconstructing" one's past in memory on the hop, that is, one can recall the original impression and also the gradual way in which it began to fade, shift, and be transformed. Very occasionally, the original experience is so vivid, one cannot help thinking it is preserved in the mind in a form that excludes serious error or uncertainty about it. I have had two dozen or so moments like that in my life, and one of them was connected to Wagner.

My father was a steelworker in the Fairless Works of U.S. Steel in Fairless Hills, Pennsylvania. Access to music in a working-class household during the early 1950s was limited. There was the local (AM) radio, my grandmother had a primitive gramophone, and some people had "45" record players which spouted a few moments of pop or rock music; that was about it. My father had a pleasant, but of course completely untrained, light tenor voice, and he sang in the U.S. Steelworkers' Chorus, a group of a dozen or so men who put on dark blazers—provided by U.S. Steel in an attempt to gain public good will—six or eight times a year, and performed Christmas carols, Broadway show tunes, and perhaps the odd light classical piece.

When I was about eleven or twelve, I had a school friend from a slightly more affluent background than mine who invited me over one afternoon and played an LP record on the new hi-fi system his parents had just purchased. The recording was of the beginning of act 3 of *Walküre*, the "Ride of the Valkyries." I distinctly recall two impressions I had in quick succession that are among the most vivid I have ever received. The first was simply that of being overwhelmed by the richness and complexity of the sound, and the electricity of those crisply executed initial upward-reaching flourishes (in B minor, as I now have learned to call it) in the first four bars. More indescribable flourishes on the horns and bassoons followed, and then the alternation of the ascending motif with descending slurred quintuplets in the violins.

The second impression I recall is my disappointment, in fact complete and utter dejection, when the horns and the bass trumpet entered *forte* at bar 13, and an easily discernible motif emerged very clearly as an individual theme from the general whirl of sound. I remember thinking: "Oh, no. There is a tune in this after all." Obviously what I had especially liked about the beginning was that *there was no discernible melody*, and it disturbed me that the entrance of the horns and bass trumpet retrospectively turned what I had previously heard as a mere pattern of dotted eighth notes (starting in the horns and bassoons in bar 5) into the precursor of a "tune." What did I have against tunes? I knew only music with clear "tunes"; what I had liked about this music was that it seemed to be articulated sound *without* a distinct melodic line. This was something utterly outside my previous experience. To hear for the first time music that was structured but not standardly individuated was exalting; it was a liberation, for which I have never ceased to be grateful.

The experience of liberation, genuine as it was, was not the whole story, though. There was also the sense of being let down when there did turn out to be a melody after all. I would not have been able to express it clearly at the time, but I believe that my reaction to this initial encounter with Wagner had its power partly because it reactivated a memory of another event in the then recent past involving music and my father, which had called forth in me intense but deeply ambiguous feelings. Wagner himself was well aware, as I discovered much later when I read his theoretical works, that the well-defined thought, sentence, image, or musical theme is not as good a vehicle for ambiguities as a wash or ocean of sound is.

My father suffered from Crohn's disease, a severe, and in his case recurrent, ulceration of the small intestine, for which, at the time of its onset in 1948, there was no treatment except surgery, so in a series of operations he gradually had most of his small intestine removed. During my childhood I was always told to be ready for him to die at any moment—this is what the doctors were said to be predicting—and the loss of most of his intestine seriously impaired his ability to absorb nutriments, so, no matter how much he ate, he looked like a skeleton. In between bouts of the disease, and recovery from surgery, however, he continued to work in the mill, and to sing in the Steel Workers' Chorus.

One Christmas they gave a concert, the high point of which was the carol "O Holy Night." The end of this had an *ossia* section, with the top variant ending on a long-sustained high note, I believe a high C with fermata. Most of the men could not sing the upper variant at all; my father could (just barely), although he had a tendency to run out of breath and cut off the fermata slightly before the director wanted. I watched and listened at the rehearsals as my father tried again and again to sustain the note to full value, and again and again failed. The evening of the performance was tense. At the crucial point, I could hear my father's voice soar out, alone, in the upper *ossia*, loud and clear above the dull sound of the rest of the Chorus, like the sharply defined theme in the "Ride of the Valkyries." He hit the final note, held it firmly for its full value—this seemed to go on forever—and collapsed on stage. Individuation, of course, is tantamount to death, in that only that which steps out of the amorphous state of undifferentiated mere existence, and takes on a distinct shape of its own, comes to live at all—and perhaps sing its own *ossia*—but then must die. My father was not dead, but had, it turned out, merely hyperventilated.

Wagner's Valkyries were predatory scavengers, picking up corpses from the battlefield, slinging them over their saddles, and making off with them. When I listened for the first time to my friend's LP of the beginning of act 3 of *Walküre* in 1958, the appearance of an individuated "tune" meant, I assumed, that "they" were coming for "him"; he would have to be warned (or not). It was, however, as I well knew, already too late. My father already looked like a walking corpse, and, sadly enough, the Valkyries had long since got him. This was a terrifying, but also oddly attractive, and deeply depressing train of thought. Wagner, as we all know, prided himself on having access to hidden depths in the human soul, areas that human society—what he called "the State"—had declared taboo: the inextricable mixture of love for, fear and hatred of, pride in, and disappointment with one's father is one of these. How could fifteen bars of mere orchestral music open that abyss? I have no idea, but I know it happened. One could not, perhaps, ever close it, but one could try to turn away. The price for doing that would be an impoverishment of one's life, and this is a price which I have done my best not to pay. Wagner's music has remained an integral part of my life ever since.

XII

On Bourgeois Philosophy and the Concept of "Criticism"

AT SOME POINT IN 1931 Ludwig Wittgenstein wrote a note about his colleague Frank Ramsey, who had died the previous year at the age of 27. This note reads:

> Ramsey war ein bürgerlicher Denker. D.h. seine Gedanken hatten den Zweck, die Dinge in einer gegebenen Gemeinde zu ordnen. Er dachte nicht über das Wesen des Staates nach—oder doch nicht gern—sondern darüber wie man *diesen* Staat vernünftig einrichten könne. Der Gedanke, daß dieser Staat nicht der einzig mögliche sei, beunruhigte ihn teils, teils langweilte er ihn. Er wollte so geschwind als möglich dahin kommen, über die Grundlagen—*dieses* Staates—nachzudenken. Hier lag seine Fähigkeit und sein eigentliches Interesse; während die eigentlich philosophische Überlegung ihn beunruhigte, bis er ihr Resultat (wenn sie eins hatte) als trivial zur Seite schob.[1]

> [Ramsey was a bourgeois thinker. That is to say, his thoughts had as their goal the ordering of the things in a given community. He did not reflect about the essence of the state—or at any rate he did not like doing this— rather he thought merely how one could arrange *this* state in a rational way. The thought that this state might not be the only possible one partly disturbed him and partly bored him. He wanted to come as quickly as possible to reflection about the foundation of *this* state. Here is where his ability and his real interest lay; whereas genuine philosophical reflection disturbed him, until he pushed its results (if it had any) aside as trivial. (RG)]

I am very grateful to my colleagues in the "Cambridger Philosophisches Forschungskolloquium," Manuel Dries, Fabian Freyenhagen, Richard Raatzsch, Jörg Schaub, and Christian Skirke, for extensive discussion of an earlier version of this essay, although I have in the end ignored their well-intentioned and well-argued advice that I withhold this paper from publication pending further revision.

[1] Ludwig Wittgenstein, *Vermischte Bemerkungen* (Suhrkamp, 1977), p. 40. I am particularly endebted to Richard Raatzsch for numerous conversations about the philosophy of Wittgenstein from which I have learned much.

This note is extremely interesting for a number of reasons, not least for the use of the term "bourgeois" to describe the basic philosophical stance of Ramsey. To call Ramsey a "bourgeois" thinker seems to mean for Wittgenstein, among other things, that Ramsey is not at all interested in—perhaps is even actively hostile to—the very idea of *radical* criticism of our state, and presumably our society, as it is now constituted. Ramsey in fact thought that "history and politics are not suited for discussion except by experts. Others are simply in the position of requiring more information; and till they have acquired all available information cannot do anything but accept on authority the opinions of those better qualified."[2] This was congruent with Ramsey's general view that "Essentially philosophy is a system of definitions."[3] "In Philosophy we take the propositions we make in science and everyday life and exhibit them in a logical system with primitive terms, definitions, etc."[4] Beyond exchange of information and the ordering of that information there is no significant cognitive task; discussion of "the old general questions become[s] either technical or ridiculous."[5]

One might wonder, as against Ramsey, whether it was not possible to think that the acquisition of correct information and well-supported general theories was of the utmost importance for the study of politics and human society, *and yet refrain* from drawing the conclusion that the only task was to *order* what we have into a coherent system. If, with Ramsey, one does reject, whether from boredom or anxiety, the very idea that there could be some (fundamentally) *other* kind of state, then surely any attempt to criticize our state and society "radically," i.e., down to its very roots, must seem pointless: the only task left for the thinker would be one of discovering cognitively the order which really existing social institutions and practices in fact exhibit, and perhaps proposing to rearrange them in minor ways *within* a basic social framework that is unquestioned and remains presupposed as invariant. The principle of such a rearrangement would be people's "feelings";[6] indeed within a closed universe like the one envisaged here, to what else could one appeal? Whether or not Wittgenstein was correct in his historical analysis of the structure and motivation of Ramsey's thinking, one might still wonder whether this kind of philosophizing was most appropriately described as "bourgeois."

[2] Frank P. Ramsey, *The Foundations of Mathematics* (Routledge, 1960), pp. 287–88.
[3] Ibid., p. 263.
[4] Ibid., p. 263.
[5] Ibid., p. 290.
[6] Ibid., p. 291.

Perhaps the best way to pursue this thought is by reflecting on the terms with which "bourgeois" is often notionally contrasted. There are at least three of these that have special philosophical importance.[7] First, "bourgeois" as opposed to "aristocratic" or "feudal; second, "bourgeois" as opposed to "bohemian" (or: "artistic");[8] and third, "bourgeois" as opposed to "radical" (or: "revolutionary"). What for our purposes is the bedrock sense which underlies all three usages is one that derives from a historical analysis of the realities and the ideologies of the *ancien regime*. During the period before the French Revolution the "bourgeoisie" was a particular legal, political, and social group, an Estate or Order, which was distinguished from two other Orders: the feudal aristocracy and the clergy.[9] "Bourgeois" then would refer to those characteristic properties of the members of that Third Estate that were *not* thought to be shared by aristocracy and clergy.[10] The basic intuition behind the contrast of "feudal" and "bourgeois" was that a feudal aristocracy derived a certain legitimation of their status from the traditional standing of their dynastic lineage, and they led lives devoted to the pursuit of "honor," particularly military honor, as a special kind of socially based, nonutilitarian virtue. The clergy, too, had a privileged social position which was justified by reference to a nonutilitarian form of consciousness, that of religious faith. Such faith gave access to "truths" that were understood as potentially going beyond or even violating all the usual canons of quotidian rationality. Forms of interaction in our everyday social world were construed, in accordance with Christian doctrine, as inherently unstable and in some sense not real, so it made no sense to devote anything more than the absolutely minimally required amount of energy to dealing with them; anyone seeking fundamental existential satisfaction in them was deeply deluded. The right attitude was to turn away from this world in self-abnegation and prayer.[11]

---

[7] Of course, there are at least two further distinctions, "bourgeois/peasant" and "bourgeois"/"proletarian," which play an important role in philosophy influenced by Lenin's *Materialism and Empiro-Criticism*, but I will not explore these distinctions in this paper.

[8] See esp. Thomas Mann, "Tonio Kröger."

[9] Needless to say, the historical claims in this section of the paper are true only, at best, as crude first approximations. So, for instance, during the later periods of the *ancien regime* the aristocracy contained both members of the old, landowning, military feudal caste, *and* the holders of certain royal offices (*noblesse de robe*).

[10] It is important to keep in mind that what is at issue here is the meaning of a concept, *not* a proper account of the reality to which that concept refers. Thus, it does not matter whether or not the clergy or the feudal aristocracy was *in fact* more or less "soberly calculating" than the bourgeoisie; for the history of the *concept* what is important is what were widely *thought* to be the characteristics of each Estate.

[11] The best model of this is Augustine. See his *Confessiones*, ed. Martinus Skutella (Teubner, 1996).

In contrast to both of the two other Estates, the bourgeoisie was functionally the Estate not of military-political power or of religion, but of mundane, everyday life, of manufacture and commerce. Characteristically, members of the bourgeoisie might be interested in their "credit(-rating)" and perhaps in a certain kind of general reputation for respectability, but not in their "honor" in the sense in which the aristocracy used this term. Or rather, whether or not they, as individuals, were interested in something *they* called their "honor," there was no socially effective mechanism by which members of this Order could pursue this interest in the way the nobles did. Members of the bourgeoisie were, after all, *"nicht satisfaktionsfähig,"* they could not, that is, fight duels with feudal aristocrats because the aristocrats would not condescend to fight with them, and thus excluded them from the existing system of "honor." Similarly, the bourgeoisie were not characteristically keen on miracles, the active castigation of the flesh, or the devaluation of the satisfactions to be obtained in this world. As Max Weber pointed out,[12] an Order like the bourgeoisie, which is devoted to peaceful, systematically organized commerce, requires a world that is stable, "disenchanted," secure, unchanging in its basic structure, surveyable and analyzable, and about which it is possible to make reliable predictions. In contrast to the mercurial temperament of the aristocrat who wagers all on the outcome of a single battle or a throw of the dice, and to the otherworldly faith of the clergy, the bourgeois is sober, orderly, moderate, calculating, utilitarian, but has a characteristically distorted temporal horizon, being oriented toward the acquisition of objects of solid value in the short- and medium-term future, but relatively unconcerned with the distant past, the fleeting moment, or an eschatological world-to-come. In strong contrast to the official ideology of the clerical establishment, the bourgeois is actively and intensely engaged in this-worldly transactions in a manner which in practice *at the very least* shows no fundamental disgust at these activities, taking them as if participation in them did not require special justification. The characteristically bourgeois attitude toward this world and its objects is deeply *affirmative.*

The world of the bourgeoisie is not, to be sure, one of complete Eleatic immobility, or Laplacean predictability: without change, no commerce, but the change in question must be moderate and regulated within a surveyable framework. If the whole economy really were to be totally regulated by a Gosplan, the function of the bourgeoisie would be replaced by that of various functionaries, whose tasks would be those of mere

---

[12] *Wirtschaft und Gesellschaft* (Mohr, 1972) pp. 502–3. The *locus classicus* is *"Die protestantische Ethik und der Geist des Kapitalismus,"* in *Gesammelte Aufsätze zur Religionssoziologie* (Mohr, 1963), vol. 1, pp. 1–236.

routinized administration. *"Bürger"/"Beamter,"* of course, is another possible contrast. On the other hand, the bourgeois world cannot survive if there is too much unpredictable change: if hyperinflation renders assets worthless overnight, sudden depletion of resources makes certain whole branches of trade nonviable, the stock market is abolished by political events, or if religious prophecies of an eschatological kind are realized and people give away all their worldly goods, etc., few of the characteristic beliefs, habits, and convictions of the bourgeoisie will retain their relevance.

In the first contrast (bourgeois, clerical, feudal) we start with the notion of a functionally and then legally specified group with distinct duties, obligations, and rights, which is clearly contrasted with other well-defined social groups, then we move to a certain form of life, a certain set of characteristic attitudes, interests, and beliefs, and finally we discover a style of thinking. In general usage the second contrast—between "bourgeois" and "bohemian"—refers less immediately and clearly to a specific social configuration or legal Order and more to a style of living and thinking. "Bohemia" refers to a sector of society that is outside the main armature of predictable commerce, and devoted to art, knowledge, entertainment, leisure, and other nonproductive forms of social activity. In the late eighteenth and nineteenth centuries this group would have included actors, prostitutes, traveling musicians, and déclassé intellectuals like proto-journalists; in the twentieth century, beatniks, hippies, certain kinds of artists, denizens of certain *"alternative Szenen,"* and the trust-fund-supported children of the wealthy who infest certain fashionable urban areas and the penumbra of certain universities. However, this is not as well-defined a social, legal, or economic group as "the clergy" or "the aristocracy" was. The primary emphasis is on the attitudes or psychological traits, individual ways of living, not on the formal legal or real economic status of an actual social group. A "bohemian" is someone who does not have a utilitarian orientation toward solid values and the middle-term future, but who seems more deeply devoted to display or appearance, aesthetic properties, or immediate gratification. This usually accompanies a failure to appreciate the "respectability" which resides in conformity to the details of prevailing style, fashion, and morality, and which forms the backbone of the ethos of the bourgeoisie, who have good reason to be constantly concerned about their credit-worthiness.[13] The bohemian belongs with those types of character whom Baudelaire describes in *Peintre de la vie*

---

[13] Max Weber, *Die protestantische Ethik und der Geist des Kapitalismus,* in *Gesammelte Aufsätze zur Religionssoziologie* (Mohr, 1963), vol. 1, pp. 1–236.

moderne[14] as the archetypical "modern" (and urban) men: the *flaneurs* and dandies. Despite some appearances to the contrary, the Kingdom of Bohemia is often thought not to be a realm from which any form of serious social criticism can be originated, because it is parasitic on the "real" operations of society. The bohemian artist can turn up his nose at the bourgeois because he can rely on the fact that the bourgeois actually organizes the provision of food and other commodities and services without which the bohemian could not really exist.

The third use of "bourgeois" identifies it with one term of the opposition: "reformist"/"radical." As the etymology of the term suggests, a "radical" account of some phenomenon would be one that goes to the "root" of the phenomenon in question, and "radical criticism" is a call for a fundamental transformation of the status quo. "Reformist" in contrast relates to changes in the superficial form that problems or difficulties take. To shift to a medical metaphor, we might say that reformist proposals treat symptoms rather than causes. Thus "radical" can be used as a term of *contrast* to "bourgeois"—other uses are, of course, possible—because the bourgeois is interested not in the "roots" of social phenomena, but merely, for instance, in procedures through which existing structures can be modified in minor ways to increase profit or decrease visible instances of particularly gross and egregious injustice or forms of entrenched immorality that are thought to be especially excessive or otherwise scandalous. As suggested above, the bourgeois requires stability of the framework, and is generally characterized by a deeply affirmative attitude toward the world-as-we-know-it. Philosophically this expresses itself in a predisposition to assume that a conceptual vindication of the rationality and positive value of the world as we know it can be given.

The commitment of the bourgeoisie to fixity of the basic social and economic framework does not imply immobilism, and the affirmative nature of bourgeois thinking does not imply a complete lack of criticism. Bourgeois philosophy starts from the claim that the world is *basically* or *fundamentally* in order. However, this does not mean that every detail is as it should be; one needn't be naïve or simpleminded in developing the bourgeois project. The world is full of *individual* problems, "issues" (as people now say), pain, hard choices, and these cannot be simply denied or treated as if they did not exist. Not even the most self-satisfied member of the traditional bourgeoisie that was depicted by Balzac was *that* foolish. To say that the world is basically in order is not to exclude the possibility of the need for local criticism and reform. As Hegel thought, Prussia, as a "modern" Protestant (potentially) constitutional monarchy,

---

[14] In *Écrits sur l'art* (Gallimard, 1971), vol. 2, pp. 133ff.

was "basically" rationally acceptable; however, it needed some minor reforms: a constitution, universal trial by jury, and a few further institutional bits and bobs which Hegel could specify. The criticism, to be sure, must be reformist, not revolutionary, that is, it had to accept the basic structure of the society as given and even in some sense endorse it, but suggest that certain subordinate features or structures must—for one reason or another—be modified. A further assumption of "reformist" criticism is that such a modification of a subordinate feature is possible within the existing global structure. The primordially "bourgeois" attitude is that expressed by Tancredi in Lampedusa's novel *The Leopard*: "If we want things to stay as they are, things will have to change."[15] So the reforms must be ones that allow everything basically to stay the same. Hegel's logic is partly an attempt to describe how the "same" basic structure can maintain itself through reformist change (but also, although it is unclear to what extent this is intended, under what circumstances the basic structure will not be able to maintain itself).[16]

To put it a slightly different way: the whole idea of putting "critique" or "criticism" of a restricted kind into the center of human attention was itself an integral part of the bourgeois project. A feudal lord or a high cleric did not "criticize": the lord originally used his fist or sword, or, later, appealed to "tradition" or to the inborn tact and judgment of the gentleman, who knew what was required in every situation without necessarily being able even to say beforehand what that was; the cleric appealed to faith, the consensus of the Church Fathers, or the decision of the Pope. Commitment to "criticism" (of a further undefined sort) was therefore not *in itself* in any sense a commitment to leave the comfortable world which the bourgeoisie had made for itself. "Criticism," after all, was the watchword and main tool of that arch-bourgeois figure, the Encyclopedist.

"Bourgeois philosophy" refers in the first instance to a particular historical complex, like Christianity, liberalism, or feudalism, in which over the course of time various different elements emerge successively

[15]Tomasi di Lampedusa, *The Leopard*, trans. Archibald Colquhoun (Vintage, 2007), p. 19. This is a complicated example because Tancredi is a member of the Sicilian nobility, and he makes this statement in the context of explaining why he is going off to join a rebellion against the king. As he puts it himself in this same passage, "Unless we ourselves [i.e., members of the nobility] take a hand now, they'll foist a republic on us." However, the point here is that Tancredi has a new bourgeois attitude which his uncle, the Prince, a genuine representative of the older feudal aristocracy, does not comprehend.

[16]The distinction between "reformist" and "revolutionary" criticism is not the same as the distinction between "internal" and "external" criticism. "Internal/external" refers, as it were, to the structure of the criticism and perhaps the *source* of the critical energy; "reform/revolution" refers to the extent of change required to obviate criticism.

as differentially prominent and important. For phenomena like this it would be inappropriate to expect to be able to find a formal definition which would cover all and only forms of philosophizing which we are inclined to call "bourgeois."[17] One might be tempted to say that to call a kind of philosophizing "bourgeois" is to refer to a *holistic* property of it, and certainly not to any individual property or collection of individual properties that could be ticked off in a list. Within the generally "bourgeois" approach, however, there are historically more deeply embedded elements, and less deeply embedded elements. Two of the most deeply embedded elements are a set of views about the nature of knowledge, and a particular kind of theoretical and practical optimism. An archetypically "bourgeois" form of philosophy, that is, is constituted by:

I. a commitment to the existence of a clear, well-grounded, secure or certain, instrumentally useful kind of knowledge which is our fundamental mode of making sense of our world and which I can reliably use to help me get around in and deal with the really existing natural (and social) environment. This knowledge is assumed to be of great importance to human life, and it is further tacitly assumed that we ought to cultivate it assiduously, and extend its domain and scope as much as possible.

and

II. a basic commitment to a positive solution to the problem of "theodicy" in something like the expansive sense in which Hegel uses that term, i.e., commitment to the view that it is possible to demonstrate discursively that the world as a whole is rational, good, and basically conformable to human interests, needs, and aspirations, so that we should "warmly embrace" and affirm it.[18]

To put one ideal-typical conjunction of these two components in a slightly more analyzed form, the basically instrumental/theodicic structure of bourgeois philosophy might be represented as follows:

---

[17] See Nietzsche, *Zur Genealogie der Moral*, in *Kritische Studienausgabe*, ed. Colli and Montinari (de Gruyter, 1976), vol. 5. I have discussed the methodological issues of this kind of inquiry before in print, and so do not propose to repeat this discussion here. Anyone interested in this can consult R. Geuss, *History and Illusion in Politics* (Cambridge University Press, 2001), pp. 6–10, 51–52, 69–73; *Public Goods, Private Goods* (Princeton University Press, 2001), pp. vii–xxiii; *Glück und Politik* (Berliner Wissenschaftsverlag, 2004), pp. 106–21.

[18] I have discussed these issues previously in my "Art and Theodicy" (in *Morality Culture, and History* (Cambridge University Press, 1999, pp. 78ff) and "Outside Ethics," in *Outside Ethics* (Princeton University Press, 2001), pp. 40ff.

1. The world as we encounter it *really is* in order;
2. I can thus "make sense" of what I encounter in the world,
3. and I can make sense of the world by use of clear forms of surveyable knowledge which will
   a. be instrumentally useful and
   b. be capable of being "justified";
4. I ought to embrace/endorse the world warmly.

The result is a purportedly theoretically grounded optimism.

Just to reiterate a point already made, "bourgeois" designates a historically changing constellation of various specific items. In fact you can see various "bourgeois" philosophies as taking one or the other of the items listed above as basic or particularly important:

> rationalism with fixity of framework (priority of 1, 2, 4: Leibniz)
> clarity (special concern with 3: contemporary analytic philosophy)
> certainty (priority of 3b: Descartes)
> usefulness (priority of 3a: the various forms of pragmatism, utilitarianism)
> radical affirmation despite tragic division (2 and 4: Hegel)

The fact that the holistic context is so important in determining what counts as "bourgeois" means that the constituent items, *if considered in isolation or in a different context,* might have a different significance. That is to say, philosophers' concern with a certain kind of clarity goes back at least to the Sophists in antiquity, and so the presence of *that* component in itself—a special concern with conceptual clarity—is not sufficient to make the philosophical position as a whole bourgeois. This also means that in a possible post-bourgeois era some of these elements might well survive, albeit in a slightly modified form and in a different context. Marx, for instance, was very clear about the way in which certain developments of human powers may have a "bourgeois" form which can be stripped away to reveal an underlying universal human significance, and something similar might well be true about methods of conceptualization and forms of theory-building:

> So erscheint die alte Anschauung, wo der Mensch in welcher bornierten nationalen, religiösen, politischen Bestimmung auch immer als Zweck der Produktion erscheint, sehr erhaben zu sein gegen die moderne Welt, wo die Produktion als Zweck des Menschen und der Reichtum als Zweck der Produktion erscheint. In fact aber, wenn die bornierte bürgerliche Form abgestreift ist, was ist der Reichtum anders, als die im universellen Austausch erzeugte Universalität der Bedürfnisse, Fähigkeiten, Genüsse, Produktivkräfte etc. der Individuen? Die volle Entwicklung der menschlichen Herrschaft über die Naturkräfte, die der sogenannten Natur sowohl, wie seiner

Natur? Das absolute Herausarbeiten seiner schöpferischen Anlagen, ohne andre Voraussetzung als die vorhergegangene historische Entwicklung, die diese Totalität der Entwicklung, d.h. der Entwicklung aller menschlichen Kräfte als solcher, nicht gemessen an einem *vorgegebenen* Maßstab, zum Selbstzwecke macht?[19]

[The ancient conception according to which man in whatever narrow national, religious, or political ideal form appears as the goal of production, seems to be very sublime compared with the modern world, where production appears as the goal of man and wealth the goal of production. In fact, however, when the narrow bourgeois form is stripped away, what is wealth other than the universality of the needs, abilities, productive powers, etc. of the individuals generated in universal exchange? The full development of human domination over natural powers, both of so-called nature and of man's own nature? [What is wealth other than] the absolute elaboration of his creative capacities without any further presupposition that the previous historical development which makes this totality of development, that is the development of all human power as such, not measured by any *pregiven* yardstick, into an end in itself? (RG)]

Some difficulties for the above bourgeois synthesis immediately arise. Some of the central members of the Frankfurt School, for instance, insisted that there was a basic inconsistency between the unbounded development of instrumental knowledge (I above) and the theodicic goal (II above) of "bourgeois" philosophy, and analyzed the historical working out of this contradiction as part of a "Dialectic of Enlightenment." "Useful knowledge" as it has developed historically can by its very nature never succeed in showing us that the world is fundamentally good and to be endorsed. There are several reasons for this. First, there are strict limits to the kind of claim that appeals to "instrumental" forms of cognition can possibly justify. There is no legitimatory path from any form of "useful knowledge" to the conclusion that the world is good and deserves to be affirmed by us. To make any such claim would be to fall prey to a paralogism. In addition, the more the acquisition, testing, and application of instrumental knowledge is seen as the model of all rationality, the less humans have a grasp on the kind of thinking that would be necessary for them to develop a true theodicy. Finally, the actual development and deployment of forms of instrumental knowledge have in fact made the world in some sense *less* deserving of being warmly and positively embraced than it once was—if as a result of scientific progress we *could* now

---

[19] Karl Marx, *Grundrisse zur Kritik der politischen Ökonomie* (Dietz, 1953), p. 387.

solve the problem of hunger in Africa (but fail to do so), our "world" is one that is *less* deserving of being positively and warmly endorsed than the world of one hundred years ago, in which this possibility was not even in principle available.

Putting aside for the moment the part of the bourgeois project that deals with the analysis and cultivation of (useful) knowledge, and concentrating on the issue of theodicy, one can distinguish a number of different views, but the main line of development seems to be one that goes at least as far back as Aristotle and reaches its culmination with Hegel. There is a visibly intelligible order in our world, and all one needs to do is reveal it. Endorsing it once you have discovered it is a virtually automatic process; after all, what alternative would one have? Aristotle and Hegel, to be sure, represent slight variants of this general approach. The former assumes that we can make sense of the appearances of the world-we-live-in more or less as it is; the latter holds that with some minor reforms (such as the introduction of trial-by-jury in Prussia) which are in any case already prefigured in the existing social institutions, the latent intelligible structure of the world will be clearly and unmistakably revealed.

In view of what was said earlier in this essay about "bourgeois" as a term referring to a *context*, not an isolated item or set of items, it wouldn't be correct to call Aristotle a "bourgeois" thinker. He seems, after all, to have been the dandified friend of petty tyrants (e.g., Hermeias of Atarneus) and the ingratiatingly grinning lackey of the bloodthirsty Macedonian regime that put a definitive end to Hellenic experiments in self-rule. It is hard to see that context as "bourgeois" in any interesting sense.[20] Still, Aristotle is an important precursor of one characteristic feature of bourgeois philosophy to the extent to which he formulates and tries to comply with the injunction σώζειν τὰ φαινόμενα (or perhaps: τιθέναι τὰ ἔνδοξα).[21] So to suggest, as Aristotle does, that the task of philosopher is to start from commonly held opinions and then go on to try to "save the phenomena" implies that the phenomena, i.e., what we see around us, the world as it appears, *admits* of being put into intelligible order. In addition, it seems to assume that the most expedient way to discover that order is by starting out from the "commonly accepted" views and arguing from them.

Hegel has what is perhaps a slightly more sophisticated take on what it is to be "intelligible." One can see him as distinguishing between:

[20] Perhaps it is better to see him as a kind of Expert or Special Advisor, a Biology Man with the clattering apparatus of rudimentary scientific inquiry (lobster pots, etc.) and a handy "category" for every occasion.

[21] Aristotle, *Ethica Nicomachea* 1145a15–1145b7.

a. I can't make sense of some first-order phenomenon, X.

and

b. I can (or: can't) make sense of why I can't make sense of X.

Particularly interesting are cases in which I *can't* make sense of X, but *can* make sense of (= understand) *why* I can't make sense of X. If I can't make sense of X (for instance, because it is contradictory), but can give a coherent account, albeit perhaps a complex one, of why that particular failure of "reasonableness" or "intelligibility" exists, then I can be thought to have made significant philosophical progress. I will call this "(rational) regression." The image is that when I find X unintelligible, I "step back" or "move to the higher ground" or "rise to a higher level" and there, on that "higher level," come to understand why I can't make sense of X.[22]

There is a well-entrenched Hegelian thesis which gives special importance to the process of "rational regression." Hegel assumes that such regression can in principle successfully continue indefinitely. There is no point at which intelligibility simply breaks off or ends. To say that some phenomenon is philosophically "intelligible" or "meaningful" is not best understood as the ascription of some static property. Rather, to be intelligible is to be the object of an appropriate process or "movement" of appropriating the phenomenon in question philosophically. Nevertheless, it is possible for a philosopher eventually to have acquired a final grasp of things that will permit him to render everything he encounters intelligible (including the process of attaining that final view of things). The abstract structural description of why rational regression is possible is that for Spirit to realize itself is for it to realize its own rationality and freedom, but it can do that only through *a*-rational particulars. That is, I can't make sense of why James marries Jill (rather than Mildred), but I can make sense of why "marriage" has to be an institution in which what are in some sense contingent individual partners join together "a-rationally." An important part of Hegel's theory is that he thinks that in general when I "regress" or rise to a higher level, my idea of what it is to "make sense" of something itself changes; i.e., when I can't make sense of X, but can make sense of why I can't make sense of X, "make sense" is being used in two slightly different senses (a first-order sense and a second-order sense). Since this process can be iterated, one gets a nested hierarchy of different ways in which things can "make sense." For Hegel, this process of regression does not terminate, but an agent who has gone

---

[22] This structure is analyzed very clearly in Dieter Henrich's "Hegels Theorie über den Zufall." See his *Hegel im Kontext* (Suhrkamp, 1971), pp. 157ff.

through it fully and appropriately will be able to make sense of the process as a whole, although, again, what is meant by saying he will be able to "make sense" of the whole is something that is so different from what we usually mean by "making sense of" that its meaning will not be clear to any outsider (that is, to anyone who has not gone through the process itself and properly assimilated it), and, Hegel thinks, *could not* be made clear to any such outsider.

In the modern, post-metaphysical world, we might expect the component of the program of theodicy that required demonstration that the world *really* was in order would drop out completely. This is what Kant believes: We don't and couldn't know whether the world as a whole is "really" in order or not, so the whole project of trying to *ground* our subjective attitude toward it—one way or the other, that is optimistically or pessimistically—in a set of justifiable beliefs doesn't make sense.[23] Or, to be more exact, the difficulty is not, according to Kant, primarily one about the *reality* of the world in some metaphysical sense, but about our inability to make a grounded theoretical judgment about the world-of-appearances *as a whole*. Those initially excited by this departure from the established bourgeois pattern are doomed to quick disappointment, because most of the relevant doctrines are maintained, or reinstated with some minor revisions: they are merely reinterpreted not as substantive claims about the reality of the world, or the way it must appear to us, but as unavoidable "postulates of pure practical reason." Crudely put, it is construed as a demand of "practical reason" that we must act as if the world were for the best.

"Bourgeois optimism" retains its power in the twentieth century, as witness two lines of argument developed respectively by the philosophers Jonathan Lear and Frank Ramsey, both of which dispense altogether with metaphysics. In his book *Love and Its Place in Nature* Jonathan Lear argues from a consideration of the nature of childhood development, as analyzed by such psychologists as Winnicott and Spitz. To the extent to which any individual human being has developed into a mature thinking person at all, this shows that the environment in which he or she grew up was "good enough" to allow that process of maturation to take place. "The environment" here means not merely the physical and biological circumstances, but also the emotional conditions. As a result, there are grounds for any person who has in fact succeeded in attaining the age of reason to have a kind of contingent, nonmetaphysical optimism about his

[23] Immanuel Kant, "Über das Mißlingen aller philosophischen Versuche in der Theodizee," in Kant, *Werk-Ausgabe* (Suhrkamp, 1977), vol. 11, *Schriften zur Anthropologie, Geschichtsphilosophie, Politik, und Pädagogik*, vol. 1, ed. W. Weischedel, pp. 105ff.

or her surroundings; if they had been *too* bad, he would not be in a position to recognize that.[24]

In the 1930s Ramsey argued that if there is no way the world can be said to be, then no sense can be given to the idea that one set of "feelings" is more appropriate to reality than any other.[25] Nevertheless, he thought, there is an obvious way to discriminate between different sets of feelings toward the world. Our feelings themselves give us this criterion. It is "pleasanter" (and "better for all one's activities")[26] to have a set of feelings that allows one to be "thrilled" by the world than to have a set that causes one to be "depressed" by it. From this he seems to draw the conclusion that there is at any rate nothing irrational in my adopting an optimistic attitude toward the world as a whole.[27]

Lear's ingenious and illuminating argument provides an explanation only for the natural inclination to be optimistic, which might be a characteristic of those humans who reach normal maturity, but we might ask, as the Spartan did when shown the many statues dedicated to the god Asclepius by those whom he had cured: "Where are the statues of those who died?" The argument also leaves it an open question whether we can and should struggle against this natural inclination. Perhaps we have a reason to think our world *was*, if not the best of all possible worlds, at least "good-enough" for us, as Winnicott used to put it. However, understanding why that is the case—children have parents, or others, who took care of them—also allows us to see that we have no particular reason, although perhaps a strong inclination, to assume that it will continue to be good-enough, and that was the question that actually interested us. To demonstrate anything more than this would require an argument which demonstrated at the minimum that if we had good-enough parents that means that the world will ensure that other people will now continue to be "good-enough" to us. No such argument is known to me.

Those interested in politics and society may find that Ramsey's approach starts from an inadequate conception of the problem, and represents a kind of throwback to the antediluvian views of Leibniz.[28] "The world" for Ramsey seems to mean the object of astronomy,[29] and if that is what is at issue, then it might seem perfectly reasonable to consider the issue of the appropriate human attitude toward the world in terms merely of some given individual and his or her set of "feelings"—of what "I find

[24] Jonathan Lear, *Love and Its Place in Nature* (Harper-Collins, 1990).

[25] Frank P. Ramsey, *The Foundations of Mathematics* (Routledge, 1960), pp. 290–91.

[26] Ibid., p. 292.

[27] Ibid., pp. 287–92.

[28] See G.W.F. Hegel, *Vorlesungen über die Geschichte der Philosophie III*, in *Hegel: Werke in zwanzig Bänden*, ed. Moldenhauer and Michel (Suhrkamp, 1971), vol. 20, pp. 247–55.

[29] Ramsey, *The Foundations of Mathematics*, p. 291.

pleasant and exciting."[30] My feelings and attitudes, after all, do not influence in any significant way the realities of the objects of astronomy. It is not so obvious that this is the case with the social and political world. Adopting an optimistic, critical, or neutral attitude toward the social world is partly constituting that world to be a world of a certain kind. Depending on the circumstances, adopting an attitude toward my world that was based *simply* on "what I find pleasant and exciting" might involve me in deep complicity with social evils. It is arguably more pleasant and exciting to wear cheap, elegant, and well-cut clothes than expensive but lumpish garments. This, however, might not be the last word, if the well-cut clothes are produced by child or slave labor in the Third World. Conceivably I might be able to break out of that complicity only by failing to be blithely optimistic at least in some respects. Whatever one might finally think about the ultimate plausibility of this position, which is, I take it, the one Adorno holds, it is certainly a prima facie possible position, but one that is arbitrarily excluded from consideration by Ramsey's way of setting up the problem.

There have been several different distinct ways in which philosophers have tried to deviate from the straight-and-narrow "military highway" (Kant's "*Heerstraße*") of bourgeois optimism. Lukács, or more exactly, the Lukács of *Geschichte und Klassenbewußtsein*, tries to adopt a strategy of *fuite en avant*: One cannot fully make human sense of this world as it is, because it is dominated by the capitalist mode of production and, as such, it is riven by *real* conflicts and contradictions that no amount of sophisticated intellectual maneuvering will resolve. However, we could change our social and economic system radically by abolishing capitalism—this, Lukács thought, was a genuine practicable possibility—and the resulting world would lack the irresolvable contradictions we now encounter and become transparent, coherent, and surveyable. This new world would "make sense," but to bring it about requires a radical political decision. Here a combination of Marxist and Kierkegaardian elements come into their own. Adorno represents a kind of *attentiste* version of this Lukácsian motif: Only a radically changed world could fully make sense, but one cannot, for deep-seated reasons, see how a transformation of the appropriate kind could be executed (because instrumental reason is subject to the Dialectic of Enlightenment), so all one can do is wait and hope.

Finally, there is the deviation from bourgeois rectitude exhibited by Nietzsche and (the late) Wittgenstein, who both (in different ways) could be seen as taking their cue from the Kantian view of rejecting the project of a cognitively grounded theodicy altogether, but do not lose their nerve as he did by finding another way back, via the "postulates of practical

[30] Ibid., p. 291.

reason," to orthodox optimism. Neither Nietzsche nor Wittgenstein think that one can "make sense" of everything, nor that one can always make sense of why one cannot make sense of something. At a certain point inquiry into the relevant context of human thought and action simply stops, and this does not mean (as with Hegel) that it terminates in a "moving" but comprehensive, circular, self-grounded, self-transparent system of reason. Rather it means that one at some point will simply encounter *facta bruta*, either expressions of human volition (will), natural phenomena, or human practices embedded in historically contingent institutions. These may be registered as facts, but they are not thereby rationalized. There may be no *determinate* point at which inquiry stops: it may peter out, gradually lose focus and determinateness, the total life-span of the human species may turn out to be inadequate to continue, etc., but still it ends. One may perhaps think of this on the model of the way in which something by being moved further and further to my right eventually exits from my visual field without it being the case that there is a clear, predetermined, specifiable point at which that happens.

Even if one could assume that history had allowed us to see through the claims of bourgeois optimism, two very serious questions would still remain unanswered. First, what would a contemporary non-bourgeois form of philosophizing look like? Second, what results would the abandonment of the bourgeois philosophical project have for the possibilities of radical social criticism?

I have no answers to either of these two questions, but there is one kind of suggestion of a way forward which has begun to appear with surprising frequency recently, but which seems to me seriously misguided. This is the suggestion that one can rehabilitate the Christian concept of "evil" and use it as the central concept in the attempt to find a post-bourgeois way of grounding, or at any rate structuring, a form of radical criticism.

Paradoxically enough, I am suggesting that fascination with "evil," which nowadays generally presents itself with all the pomp of special profundity, is usually a cheap way to assume that one's own moral intuitions are basically in order. Almost obsessive discourse about "evil" can be a way in which a certain kind of bourgeois optimism expresses itself, a way to evade the necessity of using one's imagination to face reality, and a way in which bourgeois subjects make themselves feel at home in the world. The contemporary usage I am criticizing distinguishes very sharply between "bad" and "evil." Something, some act, habit, practice, institution, or decision, is not just bad but "evil" (a) if it is incomprehensible, meaning both that it does not easily fit into the explanatory categories I have at my disposal, and also that I in some sense do not want it to fit; I wish to turn my attention away from it; (b) if it can be seen as an individual deviation for which some specified subject can be held responsible; and (c) if it causes a special kind of resentment, outrage, and fear which goes beyond the usual aversion we feel for that which is bad, harmful, disadvantageous, etc. The second of these three properties (b) is connected with the tendency to personalize evil, and the first and third (a and c) are connected with the tendency toward blind or misguided and excessive action which the use of the category "evil" seems to foster.

Recent history has given us a very striking example of the way in which appeal to the claim "That is simply evil" is both a way of trying, inappropriately, to "personalize" politics, and a way of refusing to try to understand it. In November 2002 a group of academic experts on the Near East tried to make Tony Blair aware of the complexity of the actual situation British troops would encounter on the ground after the invasion of Iraq:

> [The six academic experts who were invited to Downing Street] were not asked to produce written memos. Before the meeting they decided not to risk antagonising Blair [!!! RG] by saying an invasion was unwise, they thought they would have more impact by concentrating on the nature of the consequences.
>
> [An expert Arabist named] Joffe recalled that "We all pretty much said the same thing: Iraq is a complicated country, there are tremendous intercommunal resentments, and don't imagine you'll [i.e., British troops] be welcomed." . . . Blair reacted [by looking at Joffe and saying:] "But the man's uniquely evil, isn't he?" "I [Joffe] was a bit nonplussed. It didn't seem to be very relevant." Recovering, Joffe went on to argue that Saddam was constrained by various factors, to which Blair merely repeated his first point: "He can make choices, can't he?" As Joffe puts it "He meant he can choose to be good or evil, I suppose."
>
> The six men left Downing Street after an hour and a half . . . Joffe got the impression of "someone with a very shallow mind, who's not interested in issues other than the personalities of the top people, no interest in social forces, political trends, etc.[31]

Here, appeal to the concept of evil is pretty clearly a defensive strategy aimed at preventing a cognitive engagement that would potentially upset a comfortable worldview, and interfere with a decision already taken on other grounds, while at the same time mobilizing and focusing self-righteous energy. Deploying the concept of "evil" in this kind of highly moralizing "criticism" does seem, in the wider scheme of things, to be more appropriately understood as a way of reinforcing the status quo than as any kind of contribution to radical change.

[31] Jonathan Steele, *Defeat: Why They Lost Iraq* (Tauris, 2008), pp. 18–19.

Trying to free ourselves of the hold which the concept of "evil" has over our thinking about the world also means trying to comprehend that which is deeply unpleasant and alien. This understanding is potentially reflective: we can see how we could have come to experience what evil people value as "good," too. Ironically enough, the proudly self-confessed, although internally divided, *Bürger* Thomas Mann[32] gives a model of one way of trying to do this in his essay "Bruder Hitler."[33] There is no special method for attaining this. We proceed by a combination of history, experience, empathy, imagination, and reason. What other choice do we have? This essay also has the merit of reminding us, if reminder we needed, that there is more than one way to be anti-bourgeois, and that not all of such ways are equally good.

One important strand of thinking about human society that developed in Europe during the nineteenth and early twentieth centuries had the property that it was directed at developing a form of criticism that would *both* be radical *and* also eschew appeal to the stale leftovers of archaic religion, such as concepts like "evil." At the moment, in the first decade of the twenty-first century, calls for such radicalism have lost much of their attractive potency. There seem to be two reasons for this. First, the short-term improvement in the material life conditions of European populations has dulled some of the sharp urgency previously felt by large segments of the population. Second, the failure of Soviet-style regimes has led to a wholesale devaluation of a whole series of positive social ideals that were associated with these regimes, even some to which they paid only lip-service. Both of these two factors have had the effect of making people less willing to consider proposals for drastic change in the socioeconomic system.

To be sure, this situation seems unlikely to last. Realistically speaking, the comfortable bourgeois world of Western Europe seems in any case about to collapse, not, to be sure, as the result of any form of criticism, but under the weight of events beyond any Western parliament's control: increased world population, irreversible environmental degradation, the continuing division of humanity into economically and politically competing blocks, and the military conflicts over scarcity of resources of which the Gulf Wars were the opening prelude, and which can be expected to become more severe until the collapse of the economic system makes any organization of large groups of people and machines, even for the purposes of war, impossible.

---

[32] See his "Bürgerlichkeit," in *Betrachtungen eines Unpolitischen*, but Mann was notoriously split.

[33] *Schriften zur Politik* (Suhrkamp, 1970). Mann's essay appeared in 1939.

"Criticism," especially "radical criticism," was itself a daughter of the bourgeois age, and is unlikely to outlive that age. Various forms of what used to be called (usually derogatorily) in the eighteenth century "enthusiasm" might survive—religious doctrines, emotionally inflamed forms of ethnic identification, fundamentalist attachment to various traditional customs, institutions, or bits of archaic lore—and these might well remain capable of giving some direction to human life, but then these were precisely the sorts of things "criticism" was originally intended to dissolve. Criticism had its moment, as Hegel realized, when there were pressing problems to solve and confusion about how to proceed, but there was *also* leisure enough to reflect, and some sense that systematic ratiocination could be effective in dealing with systemic difficulties. In circumstances of acute urgency and the need for immediate action—among groups of desperate people struggling to find enough water to survive—it has no place. The outlook for radical social criticism, then, is poor. It is a very expensive luxury good.[34] What is more, it is a luxury good that has showed itself to be in practice almost completely ineffective. What theory-guided revolution of the nineteenth or twentieth century can count as a success? Any attempt to rehabilitate the critical tradition must start by engaging in a sober reflection on these facts.

[34] Bertold Brecht, *Flüchtlingsgespräche* (Suhrkamp, 1961), p. 83.

Eine halbwegs komplette Kenntnis des Marxismus kostet heut, wie mir ein Kollege versichert hat, zwanzigtausend bis fünfzigtausend Goldmark und das ist dann ohne die Schikanen. Drunter kriegen Sie nichts Richtiges, höchstens so einen minderwertigen Marxismus ohne Hegel oder einen, wo der Ricardo fehlt, usw. Mein Kollege rechnet übrigens nur die Kosten für die Bücher, die Hochschulgebühren und die Arbeitsstunden und nicht was Ihnen entgeht durch Schwierigkeiten in Ihrer Karriere oder gelegentliche Inhaftierung, und er läßt weg, daß die Leistungen in den bürgerlichen Berufen bedenklich sinken nach einer gründlichen Marxlektüre; in bestimmten Fächern wie Geschichte oder Philosophie werdens nie wieder wirklich gut sein, wenns durch den Marx hindurchgegangen sind.

Bibliography _____

Texts in Greek and Latin cited according to the most recent OCT, except as otherwise noted.

Adorno, T. W. *Minima Moralia* (Suhrkamp, 1951)
———. *Dissonanzen* (Vandenhoek and Ruprecht, 1956)
———. *Philosophie der neuen Musik* (Europäische Verlagsanstalt, 1958)
———. *Ästhetische Theorie* (Suhrkamp, 1970)
Adorno, T. W. (ed.). Der Positivismusstreit in der deutschen Soziologie (Luchterhand, 1969)
Adorno, T. W., Else Frenkel-Brunswik, Daniel Levinson, and Nevitt Sanford, et al. *The Authoritarian Personality* (Harper & Row, 1950)
Anderson, Benedict. *Imagined Communities* (Verso, 1983)
Attali, Jacques. *Une brève histoire de l'avenir* (Fayard, 2007)
Auerbach, Erich. *Mimesis* (Franke, 1971)
Augustini, S. Aureli. *Confessiones*, ed. Martinus Skutella (Teubner, 1996)
Badiou, B., and E. Celan (eds.). *Paul Celan und Gisèle Celan-Lestrange: Briefwechsel*, with commentary by Barbara Weideman (Suhrkamp, 2001)
Bakhtin, Mikhail. *Rabelais and His World,* trans. Hélène Iswolsky (Indiana University Press, 1984)
Ball, T., et al. (eds.). *Political Innovation and Conceptual Change* (Cambridge University Press, 1989)
Baudelaire, Charles. *Écrits sur l'art* (Gallimard, 1971)
Benedict, Saint. *The Rule of Saint Benedict*, ed. Justin McCann (Burns Oates, 1952)
Benjamin, Walter. *Illuminationen: Ausgewählte Schriften* (Suhrkamp, 1977)
Berlin, Isaiah. *Four Essays on Liberty* (Oxford University Press, 1969)
Bourdieu, Pierre, *La distinction* (Minuit, 1929)
Brecht, Bertold. *Flüchtlingsgespräche* (Suhrkamp, 1961)
———. *Schriften zur Politik und Gesellschaft 1919–1956* (Suhrkamp, 1973)
———. *Die Gedichte* (Suhrkamp, 1981)
Büchner, Georg. *Werke und Briefe*, ed. Karl Pörnbacher, Gerhard Schaub, Hans-Joachim Sim, and Edda Ziegler (Deutscher Taschenbuch Verlag, 1988)
Canavaggio, Jean. *Don Quichotte, du livre au mythe* (Fayard, 2005)
Canguilhem, Georges. *Le Normal et le pathologique* (PUF, 1966)
Carbonell, Bettina (ed.). *Museum Studies* (Blackwell, 2004)
Celan, Paul. *Die Niemandsrose* (Fischer, 1963)
———. *Werke* (Suhrkamp, 1983)
———. *Übersetzungen aus dem Russischen* (Fischer, 1986)
———. *Der Meridian und andere Prosa* (Suhrkamp, 1988)
———. *Die Niemandsrose: Vorstufen, Textgenese, Endfassung*, ed. Heino Schmull, Michael Schwarzkopf, and Jürgen Wertheimer (Suhrkamp, 1996)

Celan, Paul. *Paul Celan: Selected Poems*, trans. Michael Hamburger (Penguin, 1996)
―――. *Der Meridian: Tübinger Ausgabe*, ed. Bernhard Böschenstein et al. (Suhrkamp, 1999)
―――. *Die Gedichte*, ed. Barbara Weidemann (Suhrkamp, 2003)
Cervantes, Miguel de. *The Ingenious Hidalgio Don Quixote de la Mancha*, trans. John Rutherfort (Penguin, 2000)
Chollet, Mona. *Rêves de droite* (Zones, 2008)
Constant, Benjamin. *De la liberté chez les modernes*, ed. Marcel Gauchet (Gallimard 1980)
Coombes, Annie. *Reinventing Africa* (Yale University Press, 1994),
Cuno, James (ed.). *Whose Muse?* (Princeton University Press, 2004)
Dante. *Dantis Alagherii Epistolae* (Oxford University Press, 1920)
Derrida, Jacques. *Shibboleth pour Paul Celan* (Galilée, 1986)
Dewey, John. *Human Nature and Conduct* (New York: Random House, 1930)
―――. *John Dewey: The Late Works, 1925–1953*, ed. Jo An Boydston (Southern Illinois University Press, 1988)
Diels, Hermann, and Walther Kranz. *Fragmente der Vorsokratiker* (Weidman, 1951)
Dunn, John. *Setting the People Free* (Grove Atlantic, 2005)
Durkheim, Emile. *De la division du travail social* (PUF, 1986)
Elster, Jan. *Sour Grapes* (Cambridge University Press, 1983)
Febvre, Lucien. *Le problème de l'incroyance au XVIe siècle: La religion de Rabelais* (Michel, 1947)
Foucault, Michel. *La naissance de la clinique* (PUF, 1963)
―――. *Les mots et les choses* (Gallimard, 1966)
―――. *L'usage des plaisirs* (Gallimard, 1984)
―――. *Dits et écrits* (Gallimard, 1994), 4 vols.
France-Lanord, Hadrien. *Paul Celan et Martin Heidegger: Le sens d'un dialogue* (Paris: Fayard, 2004).
Freud, Sigmund. *Studienausgabe* (Fischer, 1974)
Gaius. *The Institutes of Gaius*, translated with an introduction by W. M. Gordon and O. F. Robinson, with the Latin text of E. Seckel and K. Kuebler (Duckworth, 1988)
Gambetta, Diego (ed.). *Making Sense of Suicide Missions* (Oxford University Press, 2005)
Geuss, Raymond. *The Idea of a Critical Theory* (Cambridge University Press, 1981)
―――. *Morality, Culture, and History* (Cambridge University Press, 1999)
―――. *History and Illusion in Politics* (Cambridge University Press, 2001)
―――. *Public Goods, Private Goods* (Princeton University Press, 2001)
―――. *Glück und Politik* (Berliner Wissenschaftsverlag, 2004)
―――. *Outside Ethics* (Princeton University Press, 2005)
Glare, P.G.W. (ed.). *Oxford Latin Dictionary* (Oxford University Press, 1982)
Goethe, Johann von. *Faust*, ed. Erich Trunz (Wegner, 1963)
Grotius, Hugo. *De jure belli et pacis*, 2nd ed. (Guilielmum Blaeuw, 1631)
Halper, Stefan, and Jonathan Clarke. *America Alone* (Cambridge University Press, 2004)

Hampshire, Stuart. *Thought and Action* (Chatto and Windus, 1959)

Hegel, G.W.F. *Werke in zwanzig Bänden,* ed. Eva Moldenhauer and Karl Markus Michel (Suhrkamp, 1970)

Heidegger, Martin. *Holzwege* (Klostermann, 1950)

——. *Seit und Zeit* (Niemeyer, 1963)

——. *Erläuterungen zu Hölderlins Dichtung* (Klostermann, 1963)

Henrich, Dieter. "Hegels Theorie über den Zufall." In his *Hegel im Kontext* (Suhrkamp, 1971)

Henrich, Dieter (ed.). *Über Theorie und Praxis* (Suhrkamp, 1967)

Hinske, Norbert. "Kant über Lesen und Bücher." In *Inselalmanach auf das Jahr 1964*

Hobbes, Thomas. *Leviathan,* ed. Richard Tuck (Cambridge University Press, 1999)

Johnson, Carroll. *Cervantes and the Material World* (University of Illinois Press, 2000)

Kant, Immanuel. *Werk-Ausgabe* (Suhrkamp, 1977)

Khosrokhavar, Farhad. *Quand Al-Qaïda parle* (Grasset, 2006)

Kundera, Milan. *Die Kunst des Romans* (Hanser, 1987)

Lampedusa, Tomasi di. *The Leopard,* trans. Archibald Colquhoun (Vintage, 2007)

Landauer, Gustave. *Revolution* (Karin Kramer Verlag, 1974)

Lawrence, Bruce (ed.). *Messages to the World: The Statements of Osama bin Laden* (Verso, 2005)

Lear, Jonathan. *Love and Its Place in Nature* (Harper-Collins, 1990)

Lehmann, Jürgen (ed.). *Kommentar zu Paul Celans "Die Niemandsrose"* (Universitätsverlag Winter, 2003)

Lenin, V. I. *Materialism and Empiro-Criticism* (Foreign Languages Press, 1972)

Lukács, Georg. *Theorie des Romans* (Lucherhand, 1963)

Luschan, Felix von. *Die Altertümer von Benin* (Vereinigung Wissenschaftliche Verleger, 1919)

Mann, James. *The Rise of the Vulcans* (Viking Penguin, 2004)

Mann, Thomas. *Betrachtungen eines Unpolitischen* (Fischer, 1929)

——. *Leiden und Größe der Meister* (Fischer, 1935)

——. *Sämtliche Erzählungen* (Fischer, 1963)

——. *Schriften zur Politik* (Suhrkamp, 1970)

Мандельштам, Осип. (Mandelstamm, Ossip.) *Сочений* (Художественная Литература, 1990)

Marlin, Robert O. IV (ed.). *What Does Al-Qaeda Want?* (North Atlantic Books, 2004)

Marlowe, Christopher. *The Complete Plays*, ed. Frank Romany and Robert Lindsay (Penguin, 2003)

Marx, Karl. *Grundrisse zur Kritik der politischen Ökonomie* (Dietz, 1953)

Marx, Karl, and Friedrich Engels. *Marx-Engels Werke* (Dietz, 1962)

Meyer, Christopher. *DC Confidential* (Weidenfeld and Nichols, 2005)

Miles, Margaret. *Art as Plunder* (Cambridge University Press, 2008)

Monbiot, George. *Bring on the Apocalypse* (Grove Atlantic, 2008)

Montaigne, Michel. *Essais* ed. A. Micha (Flammarion, 1969)

Nabokov, Vladimir. *Lectures on Don Quijote* (Harcourt, Brace, Jovanovich, 1983)

Nietzsche, Friedrich. *Kritische Studienausgabe (KSA)*, ed. Giorgio Colli and Mazzino Montinari (de Gruyter, 1967)

———. *Kritische Gesamtausgabe*, ed. Giorgio Colli and Mazzino Montinari (de Gruyter, 1967)

Pauly, August, Georg Wissowa, Wilhelm Kroll, Kurt Witte, et al. (eds.), *Paulys Realencyclopädie der classischen Altertumswissenschaften: Neue Bearbeitung* (Metzler, 1894–1980), 83 vols. plus supplements

Pushkin, Alexander. *The Bronze Horseman*, ed. Michael Basker (Duckworth, 2000)

Rabelais, François. *Oeuvres complètes*, ed. Guy Demerson (Gallimard, 1973)

Ramsey, Frank. *The Foundations of Mathematics* (Routledge, 1960)

Reichel, Peter. *Der schöne Schein des Dritten Reichs* (Fischer, 1993)

Richter, Alexander, et al. (eds). *Paul Celan: La bibiothèque philosophique* (Editions Rue d'Ulm, 2004)

Richter, Raoul (ed.). *Aussprüche von Kant* (Insel, 1923)

Rorty, Richard. *Philosophy and the Mirror of Nature* (Princeton University Press, 1979)

———. *Truth and Progress* (Cambridge University Press, 1998)

Roth, H. Ling. *Great Benin: Its Customs, Art and Horrors* (Routledge, Kegan Paul, 1968; originally published 1903)

Rousseau, Jean-Jacques. *Oeuvres* (Pleiade, 1995)

Ryder, A.F.C. *Benin and the Europeans 1485–1897* (Longmans, 1969)

Schiller, Friedrich. *Werke* (Hanser, 1967)

Schlegel, Friedrich. *Kritische Ausgabe*, ed. Hans Eichner (Paderborn, 1961)

Schneeberger, Guido. *Nachlese zu Heidegger* (Bern, 1962)

Spotts, Frederick. *Hitler and the Power of Aesthetics* (Hutchison, 2002)

Steele, Jonathan. *Defeat: Why They Lost Iraq* (Tauris, 2008)

Steinberg, Leo. *Other Criteria* (University of Chicago Press, 2007)

Stifter, Adalbert. *Abdias* (DTV, 2005)

Sulzer, Dieter et al. (eds.). *Der Georg-Büchner-Preis 1951–1987: Eine Dokumentation* (Piper, 1987)

Suskind, Ron. "Faith, Certainty, and the Presidency of George W. Bush," *New York Times Magazine,* 17 October 2004

Szondi, Peter. *Celan-Studien* (Suhrkamp, 1972)

Taplin, Oliver (ed.). *Literature in the Roman World* (Oxford University Press, 2001)

Tuck, Richard. "Grotius, Carneades, and Hobbes," *Grotiana* News Series, vol. 4 (1981)

Urmson, J. O. "On Grading," *Mind,* vol. 59 (1950)

Valéry, Paul. *Pièces sur l'art* (Gallimard, 1934)

Védrine, Hubert. *Face à l'hyperpuissance: Textes et discours 1995–2003* (Fayard, 2003)

Vigo, Peter (ed.). *The New Museology* (Reaktion Books, 1989)

Weber, Max. *Gesammelte Aufsätze zur Religionssoziologie* (Mohr, 1963)

———. *Wirtschaft und Gesellschaft* (Mohr, 1972)

————. *Politik als Beruf* (Duncker und Humblot, 1977)

Weinrich, Harald. *Lethe* (Beck, 2000)

Williams, Bernard. *Ethics and the Limits of Philosophy* (Harvard University Press, 1985)

————. *Truth and Truthfulness* (Princeton University Press, 2002)

Wittgenstein, Ludwig. *Philosophische Untersuchungen* (Suhrkamp, 1971)

————. *Vermischte Bemerkungen* (Suhrkamp, 1977)

Zimmermann, Hans Dieter. *Martin and Fritz Heidegger: Philosophie und Fastnacht* (Beck, 2005)

Žižek, Slavoj. *In Defense of Lost Causes* (Verso, 2008)

Index